STANLEY KRAMER

FILM MAKER

STANLEY KRAMER FILM MAKER

Donald Spoto

SAMUEL FRENCH
HOLLYWOOD · NEW YORK · LONDON · TORONTO

for
Irene Mahoney, O.S.U.
and
Michael S. Engl

"We are advertis'd by our living friends."
Shakespeare, *King Henry VI, Part III*

First Samuel French Edition, 1990

Library of Congress Cataloging-in-Publication Data

Spoto, Donald, 1941-
Stanley Kramer, film maker/by Donald Spoto
p. cm.
Reprint. Originally published: New York: Putnam, c1978.
Filmography: p.
1. Kramer, Stanley. 2. Motion picture producers and
directors—United States—Biography. I. Title.
PN1998.3.K73S6 1990   791.43'023'092—dc20 [B]   90-3190

ISBN: 0-573-60609-9

Cover design by Heidi Frieder

Printed and bound in the United States of America

Published and distributed by
Samuel French Trade
7623 Sunset Blvd.
Hollywood, CA 90046

Acknowledgments

I am in the debt of very many good people who provided various assistances during the course of the project.

David Thuesen opened to me the hospitality of his home in Los Angeles on the several occasions my work took me there. He and Jerry Murra sustained with patience and affection a writer's odd hours and persnickety habits, and I am hugely grateful for their generosity and friendship.

At the film archives of the University of California at Los Angeles, I was greatly helped by the cooperation of Charles Hopkins, Robert Gitt, Graham Dent and Robert Epstein. Patrick Sheehan and his staff at the Motion Picture Division of the Library of Congress provided additional necessary screenings. In the research department of the Museum of Modern Art, New York, Emily Sieger provided access to important material, and in the film stills archive there, Mary Corliss and Carol Carey helped me find important photos.

Edward Dmytryk, Princess Grace of Monaco, Sidney Poitier, Teresa Wright and Fred Zinnemann were most gracious in recalling their experiences with Stanley Kramer, and Katharine Hepburn demonstrated kind interest in the book, too.

For other help, information and suggestions I am grateful to

Don Carle Gillette, Roy Frumkes, Leonard Maltin, Robert McLaggar, James Paris and Richard Plant.

Stanley Kramer was always very helpful and friendly, willing to answer hard questions and devote time to me and my tape recorder when he was engaged in other tasks. He and his assistant, Edith Robinson, made my visits to the offices of Stanley Kramer Productions, Inc., most enjoyable.

Dean Allen Austill is first among many at The New School for Social Research, New York, who, along with my students in the cinema department, continue to give me collegial support and encouragement. Since this book went into galleys, Charles Winecoff has been at the ready with quiet devotion: he, too, deserves a large measure of joyful thanks.

And at G. P. Putnam's Sons, William Targ—no mean writer himself—was the kind of editor every author hopes to have. My agent Bertha Klausner first suggested this book, and her acuity and affectionate guidance saw it to a happy conclusion.

DONALD SPOTO
Christmas 1977

Contents

Stanley Kramer

FILM MAKER

Stanley Kramer in Hollywood, 1948.

Kramer on Kramer

You have to be very alert when you're listening to Stanley Kramer, and very quick when you ask or answer questions.

His interests are varied and lively, and his words, as one of Enid Bagnold's characters says in *The Chalk Garden,* leap and change color in the mouth like fishes. In one sentence he can shift from pointed critical remarks about his work to an anecdote about the Hollywood Ten in the early 1950s, then to a neglected Kramer picture, and conclude with vehement remarks about Hollywood or the national "establishment" or himself. He's an enigmatic, intelligent, opinionated, sensitive, friendly gentleman, and is probably the director who has been the subject of more outrage and controversy among critics and public than any other American in Hollywood. A riveting conversationalist, he chats as if you'd been a friend for years. He stands on no ceremony and is enormously likable.

Labeled at various times a Red and a Red baiter and a churner of "quota quickies" in the 1950s, he's become the representative of the so-called "liberal school of message movies." That's a designation more redolent of damnation than praise, and therefore his merits, as a man who's worked within and against the system of Hollywood as an independent producer for over thirty years, are obscured by the anger and smirks of the sophisticates who have refused to consider his work seriously.

But it's impossible not to take seriously a man who was the first to make a film in which some very nasty racial epithets were heard onscreen, and this with grave purpose. And a man who made films about interracial marriage at a time when Hollywood wouldn't touch the subject, long forbidden by the formidable Production Code. And a man who brought to the screen Marlon Brando. And who, in interviews and his frequent seminars with students, discusses his failures freely—in fact with greater interest than his successes.

Called "the boy wonder of Hollywood"—in the tradition of Irving G. Thalberg—Kramer has grown into what he calls "a discarded liberal." He's critical but not ashamed of his work, and he enjoys discussing its relation to the times in which each film was produced. It was this element of the relationship of his films to Hollywood culture in particular and to American culture in general that first attracted me to the man and his work. This book, therefore, is not a critical biography of Stanley Kramer— it's not a biography at all, since he promises his own "explosive" memoirs at some distant date. What is offered here is a consideration of a man's life in terms of his work, and his work in terms of the vagaries of his own inner life such as he's willing to discuss. His career, which spans from just after World War II to the present, has been waffled with argument and controversy. (As recently as 1961—the same year that his colleagues in the Academy of Motion Picture Arts and Sciences bestowed on him the Irving G. Thalberg Award "for distinguished contributions to the American film industry"—various religious splinter groups in America were calling him "the anti-Christ.")

Film scholars may not rank him as a creative genius in the history of the medium, and some movie buffs may become churlish over what they consider his frequently perverse casting. But no one who knows much about American film in the last thirty years can say that his work may be ignored. *Champion* and *High Noon* and *The Wild One* and *On the Beach* and *Judgment at Nuremberg* and *Guess Who's Coming to Dinner* are simply too well known, too hotly debated, to be swept under the critical carpet.

The reasons for their production deserve scrutiny, as do the ideas of the man who insisted—usually quite alone—that they be made.

Should Stanley Kramer be called a cinema *auteur,* an artistic author of films which have consistent and recurrent qualities of technique and vision? I think not, but not because *he* rejects the designation. "I want to make it clear that I don't believe in the *auteur* theory," he told me at the start of our first conversation. "Nor do I believe, although I am a member of the board of the Directors Guild, that film is a director's medium. Film is a concert effort, it involves the work of a lot of people. The director just doesn't have that sort of overriding control, and he has to depend on the creative collaboration of writers, technicians, cameramen, actors—everybody connected with the picture."

And yet he sees this as a double-edged enterprise which frequently destroys his "dream." And at this point the *auteur manqué* in Stanley Kramer may be discerned. "It's frustrating when you buy a story and then the number of people involved in making it into a film grows to be so numerous. You try to get the best collaborators, but then you have to give them their own range, since they're also artists in their own right. The amazing part is that you have the annoying responsibility of curtailing their impulses and even standing against them sometimes as you try to achieve the 'painting' you want. It's frustrating because it never turns out the way you've foreseen. Sometimes it can be better, but it's never exactly what you visualized.

"Working with Spencer Tracy is a good example. I knew he didn't like to experiment, he didn't care for surprises. He was comfortable acting only when all the details were laid out carefully before him and he knew precisely what he was supposed to do. Gene Hackman, on the other hand, wants to have plenty of freedom to work out an improvisation. So as a director, it would be a mistake for me to give too much freedom to a Tracy or to be overly restrictive with a Hackman. I always come to the set totally prepared to give an actor the range he requires. If an actor needs a friend, I'll even be his friend"—an attitude, by the way, which calmed a troubled and anxious

Montgomery Clift, nearing the end of his career with his performance in *Judgment at Nuremberg.*

"At other times, a cameraman doesn't get the idea of what you want. You may ask for a certain distortion in the image, and you either get a distortion so pronounced that the image isn't clear, or you get no distortion at all! Or the composer puts in four violins too many in the final scoring. That's when it's frustrating. I suppose the thumbprint of the director is on films today, but in the days when I just produced films"—from 1948 to 1954—"it was the producers who were the *auteurs* of the day. Even before my time, there were Selznick, Thalberg, Mayer, Goldwyn: they called all the shots."

Yet Kramer has always realized the creative possibilities of directing, and he has added this function to his producer's control on all of his films but three since 1955. "I always wanted to direct, and I got into the production of films by accident. When I was in the army I found that I had lost my civilian job at the studio. So when I returned from service I decided the best way to make films was to form an independent company and be the boss. That way, in due time, I could appoint myself the director. But it didn't work out quite that way: it took somewhat longer than I expected. Meantime, however, I cast every part for every film and got deeply involved in script, set design— everything."

Stanley Kramer may reject the concept of the *auteur* but he's certainly worked hard for the practice of it. And that's one of his most intriguing creative contradictions.

The overriding concern in his life and work has been the search for values, the questions, the sense of mistakes and of wonder about the path he and America take at any given time. "I'm primarily concerned with the disintegration of values in our whole society," he said at one point in our discussions. At the same time, however, "I've always been a searcher, and I'm still searching. I'm trying to determine my own sense of values, and sometimes I've done that searching in my films, which hasn't always been *good*, but it's always been *me*. I became a director to try to preserve the integrity of my dream. . . .

"My grandfather once told me that friends are the most

important thing in life, and it sounded terribly profound to me at the time. It was years before I realized that this is nonsense. Friends are okay, but what's more important is believing in something and taking a stand on it. Once I stake out my position on any issue, I automatically lose 50 percent of those who were supposed to have been my friends. I'm not speaking as a martyr, but merely reporting the experience I've had as a man who speaks his mind. I could have got along easier with others if I accepted things easily, but my nature is to ask questions."

As various chapters of this book try to show, Kramer has almost always courted social disaster in this regard. "I've questioned everything—my political and social and personal values included. Even my home life doesn't escape questioning." And there's no doubt that just as certain of his films (*The Caine Mutiny* and *On the Beach,* for example) angered some major government officials, they also angered actors, Hollywood colleagues and the public. "Sometimes the bitterness which greeted a film made it the dearer to me—you know, like a poor relative. But I have no contempt for the mass audience. That great wave of people who laugh and cheer and weep is a magnificent group to behold. They transcend reviews, awards—anything else! I like to go to theatres that show my films only if there's a crowd there to enjoy them—or even to reject them, as long as they react. As long as they're stimulated to think about something, just as making the particular picture raised questions for me."

Sometimes Kramer runs afoul of his own ideas, as when he equates a film's worth with its box-office receipts.

"There's no getting around it. If a film doesn't make money, there's something fundamentally wrong with the project. Either it cost too much in the first place or it's made at the wrong time or it's marketed poorly. Whatever the explanation, the fellow who made the thing has to take the blame. I'll accept the blame for the box-office failures of *On the Beach* and *Judgment at Nuremberg,* but I'd also like credit for aiming at quality."

In statements like this, Kramer falls victim to the common fallacy about the equation between a film's worth and its financial success. But films like *The Defiant Ones, On the Beach* and *Judgment at Nuremberg* are quite successful as film dramas—as successful as the occasional financial blockbuster he's enjoyed (*Guess Who's Coming to Dinner* is the biggest example). He's not the only director whose very best work realized comparatively little income. And history, of course, is filled with other artists and craftsmen in a variety of other fields with similar experiences.

It's refreshing to chat with a man who has worked consistently for almost half a century in the film industry, who is so disarmingly honest about his confusions. "I'm a mess of contradictions—conservative in some ways, liberal in others, occasionally cautious but most of the time a sporting type, a baseball player looking longingly at the grandstands, a reckless gambler, a crapshooter. I've always gambled with films, and I still do. The movie distributors told me no one wanted to see a film about prizefighters, but *Champion* was a big success. They told me people would ignore a film about paraplegics living in wheelchairs, but *The Men* rolled up a nice score. They told me I was crazy to try a film about racial intermarriage, but *Guess Who's Coming to Dinner* was powerful at the box office."

Naturally, Kramer has his favorites among the thirty-four films he's produced (fourteen of which he also directed): *The Defiant Ones, Judgment at Nuremberg* and *Bless the Beasts and Children.* But before he'll admit to them, he utters stern statements about his own estimation of his work.

"I've aspired to so much in my films—reflecting on the plight of the black man, the threat of nuclear war, human greed, the freedom to teach, world guilt. The canvas in each case is so big that there had to be something wrong with each picture. And there is. They all fall short. The dream I had for each was fantastic, but the realization is so much less than the dream. Many of them had high-sounding themes. But looking back, I think most were too ambitious to qualify as true art. Very often the canvas was so big that I simply fell short of what I'd hoped to achieve. Sometimes I've been like a baseball player trying for a home run when I should have been content to hit a single. Several times, for example, I've made films about the black man's struggle for justice. James Baldwin criticized me for being naïve, and he was right, because a white man can't know the depths of a black's suffering. I search for truth but it's never there for me in its totality. All I ever seem to find is part of it."

It seems to me, after studying his work, that this admission is a human manifesto of a rare and special sort. Few filmakers are quick to situate critically their own work within the specific culture that inspired and therefore limits them. And there are few who understand that insofar as the films accurately reflected their times, they reflected its liabilities as well as its assets. Kramer's films do not seem to be timeless reflections on great metaphysical realities—in the way that many of the films of Buñuel or Bergman or Hitchcock are—but they are often deeply felt and passionately produced works, never undertaken simply for reasons financial, and frequently for reasons quite personal and unpopular. Even his severest critics must allow him credit for this track record.

Although some have accused Kramer of being anti-American, since so many of his films locate social pathologies in our country, there seems no more dedicated citizen than he. "Any American film that contains criticism of the American fabric of life," he once reflected, "is accepted, both critically and by the mass audience overseas, as being something that could never have been produced in a totalitarian state. This in itself builds tremendous respect for American society among foreigners—a respect I've always wanted to encourage."

The films so accused, of course, are those which are most clearly "message films"—movies with a conscious intention of teaching a lesson, locating dangers, correcting unworthy attitudes.

"I was brought into the film world in the era of Franklin Roosevelt, an era noted for 'the liberal approach.' Now nothing is more anathema in the present day than the liberal approach—it's called the failure approach. That's the one that promised a good deal and didn't deliver it. I have been the flag-bearer of that viewpoint, and therefore somewhat viciously attacked along the way for being part of a 'do-good' era. But I never started off a film with a message. If to make a film contemporary and provocative, if to make film drama out of what is already drama, is to communicate a 'message,' then I am guilty. I think everything has a message; I don't care what it is. Some critics and theatre operators have stuck me with the label 'message filmmaker,' but in fact I see myself as a storyteller with a point of view. Maybe I'm out of step with the times, because a lot of movies are made today with no statement at all, just shock and sensation, or a motivationless kind of approach to a story, a senseless crime, a pointless love affair. That's all right for those who want to do it, but personally I don't find it particularly compelling. Like lots of kids in the 1930s, I wanted to right all the wrongs of mankind. But quite aside from the rhetoric of politics, what grabs me in cinematic terms is the idea of telling a story against a background of social or political conflict. I'm not interested in changing anyone's opinion, just in telling a story."

Looking at his films chronologically, with attention to their situation in American culture, it's possible to see the ways by which Kramer has been successful, and those by which he's gone wrong.

First, there's the problem of the stage plays which he filmed. Seven of Stanley Kramer's movies are based on plays, and one is based on a television play. (In 1974 and 1975 he also produced, directed and narrated three taped television plays. The series, all taken from actual trial transcripts, concern Julius and Ethel Rosenberg, General Tomobumi Yamashita and William Calley. Conceived for another medium than general theatrical release and considered by him as quite distinct from his motion-picture career, these teleplays are not studied in this book.) For the most part, the filmed plays are among the great disappointments of his career—unimaginatively directed, static, flat and unmoving. But there are perhaps two exceptions—*The Member of the Wedding* and the play that has been changed so drastically that it's virtually a new work, *Home of the Brave*. But Kramer is right in assessing the filmed plays in general: " I would like never again in my whole life to make an adaptation from a play. I have never been successful with any of them. The only reason I originally undertook to produce plays on film was because as a producer I wanted control of many things and I had made many commitments. I bought plays because I thought I could get them into production quickly, assign directors, and everything would turn out just fine. Well, they never did because they're from too different a medium as far as I'm concerned."

Second, there is the occasional unwise casting: Fredric March in *Death of a Salesman*, for example, who plays Arthur Miller's pathetic Willy Loman as a loony right from the start, thus short-circuiting a sense of real suffering or decline or struggle. There are also Rex Harrison and Lilli Palmer in *The Four Poster*, an altogether too urbane and sophisticated couple to be playing such middle-class folk. And Kirk Douglas in *The Juggler*, a dimple-chinned toughie who is incredible as a German refugee in Israel. And Olivia de Havilland in *Not as a Stranger*, who gives an admirable attempt at the role, but who is really almost a parody as a blond Swedish nurse. And the three leading players in *The Pride and the Passion*, since it's impossible to accept Frank Sinatra as a Spanish peasant, Cary Grant as an arid professional soldier, and Sophia Loren as an Iberian Ava Gardner. And Burt Lancaster in *Judgment at Nuremberg*, because he doesn't seem to know the difference between spiritual anguish and being in a sulk. And Judy Garland in *A Child Is Waiting*—one of the most embarrassing performances ever recorded by a woman who was suffering grievously off camera. And Yul Brynner in *Invitation to a Gunfighter*, because we simply can't accept him as a French Creole dandy. And Anthony Quinn in *RPM* as a professor of sociology, bedding down with doctoral candidate Ann-Margret and then taking over the presidency of a student-besieged university—the casting is perversely funny.

Kramer often saved money by hiring second-line and feature players for his early films. But when he started to direct, only the big names were invited. (*It's a Mad Mad Mad Mad World* and *Judgment at Nuremberg* are so star studded that it's hard to watch the characters; you're constantly recognizing a famous face!) While this usually worked for him, it often did not. One of his favorite films (and arguably one of his best) is *Bless the Beasts and Children*—it hasn't a bankable name in it.

Third, there is an egregious lack of humor in the Stanley Kramer filmography. (Between his first film, *So This Is New York*, and *It's a Mad Mad Mad Mad World*, only one vaguely amusing movie was produced, and it was faithful to the Samuel Taylor play on which it was based.) *It's a Mad Mad Mad Mad World,* has some riotously funny moments, but it has a Premingerian heaviness and very little cinematic economy. Only *Guess Who's Coming to Dinner* and *Bless the Beasts and Children* have a natural unforced comic tone.

The reason for this humorlessness is probably the insistent gravity with which Kramer has viewed the world and himself. Although he repeatedly says that he's preserved his sanity by not taking himself too seriously, this appears, after spending time with him and scrutinizing his films, to be more the wish of retrospection than the fact of history. His approach to the great social and humanitarian issues has always been direct and unsubtle—"Perhaps I should have been a social worker!" he said to me with a smile—and as becomes clear in watching the films, this usually works to further the audience's comprehension. But the directness and even the haste of many of his productions has also stifled the wit and made the tone gray and oversolemn.

Fourth (and this really leads to an appreciation of the ways in which he's succeeded), Kramer has often been too close to his material—his passionate involvment foreshortens the aesthetic distance that could have resulted in a purer and more controlled film. Feeling so strongly as he does about racial prejudice, anti-Semitism, about indifference to the possibility of nuclear war, genocide and the fine art of human exploitation, Kramer sometimes forgets that film should use *the camera* to tell a story, and he seems content to let the theme, through words, dominate. At other times, he fills the frame with actors' faces (as, for example, in *Ship of Fools*). In the first several films he directed (not especially remarkable for visual imagination), the camera is a narrative device—and not always a clarifying narrative device, either—and there is no real cinematic method of establishing mood or describing feelings. It is a danger to which the best of his features occasionally fall prey.

But it's important to realize the lasting contributions that Stanley Kramer has made to the American motion-picture industry. He was the first to make mainstream Hollywood films about pressing and often unpopular issues, and this he did, as Sidney

With the teenagers of *Bless the Beasts and Children*, 1971.

Poitier has said, without consideration of his future or of critics or of the estimation of his friends. Out of the materials of his own youth in New York City, he produced *Champion*—a film which to me seems preferable to the recent glossy and less honest *Rocky*. In 1949, distributors weren't interested in a film about corruption in the boxing world. But the critics and the public thought differently, and the film's angry delineation of human savagery is still intensely startling. *Home of the Brave*, by boldly altering the theme of Arthur Laurents' play from anti-Jewish to antiblack prejudice, was the first film to deal head-on with the black man's white-enforced feelings of inferiority. Kramer insisted that Carl Foreman's screenplay open up all the festering sores, break open the clichés and start sounding the nasty ring to the epithets of racial slurs. It's easy, after the harsh and iconoclastic films of the 1960s and 1970s, and in light of the loud and often rude rhetoric of struggle in films since *Home of the Brave*, to look at it with too much sophisticated hindsight. In 1949, it was a landmark film.

A year later (1950) colleagues again looked anxious when Kramer planned to make a film about the psychological, physical and sexual problems of paraplegics. Was it possible to be blunt, yet not indelicate, without appearing squeamish? *The Men* is all that and more. Kramer had doctors as technical advisers, he used real patients as supporting actors, and, in bringing one of the great actors of the time to the screen, introduced Marlon Brando in a film that helped change the attitudes of countless people toward disabled young war veterans.

(The plays have their moments, too: Julie Harris is now the only surviving member of the star trio from *The Member of the Wedding*; we have to be grateful that Kramer brought that delicate, fragile, mood piece by Carson McCullers to the screen, and that he had the good sense to hire Fred Zinnemann as director. It's a wonderful filmed documentation of an important American play. Similarly, we have Mildred Dunnock's luminous portrayal of Linda Loman in *Death of a Salesman*—a performance that is light years better than the material with which she worked.)

It's a sense of primacy about the social issues that Kramer has insisted on, and for this he's been pummeled by the purists. But watching *On the Beach* and *Judgment at Nuremberg* and even the drawing-room comedy of *Guess Who's Coming to Dinner* and the youthful and quite pure sentiment of *Bless the Beasts and Children*, you have the sense of a man driven mostly by his own feelings, and although this frequently gets him into trouble (because of a certain humorlessness and lack of creative reflection), it has also given him a record of considerable fearlessness in dealing with timely issues. When no studio would challenge the Production Code's taboo about interracial marriage and back a film on the subject in 1967, Kramer approached Sidney Poitier, Katharine Hepburn and Spencer Tracy. They agreed, without reading a script, to do the film that would be called *Guess Who's Coming to Dinner*.

"I have one major regret about my early life: I was shoved through Manhattan's schools, and through New York University from the age of fifteen to nineteen, so fast that I forgot my youth. . . ."

Stanley Earl Kramer was born in New York's knuckle-bruising "Hell's Kitchen" section (in the midtown West Side) on September 29, 1913. His parents separated when he was very young, and he has little recollection of his father. His mother worked in Paramount Pictures' New York office; he was cared for mostly by his grandparents. At the age of nineteen, in the spring of 1933, he received a degree in business administration from New York University, where he had written for the weekly newspaper, *The Medley*. This gave him a zest for writing, and after graduation he went at once to Hollywood, hoping to join a big studio as a scriptwriter. He settled, however, for a twenty-two-dollar-a-week job moving furniture on Twentieth Century-Fox's back lot. Soon a friend led him to MGM's research department, where he worked as an apprentice writer and did general office work. A sympathetic superior assigned him to the editing room ("The pay was low, the glory was small, but it was a good place to learn how to put a movie together"), and by 1938 he was a senior editor. In 1939 and 1940, he was a staff writer for Columbia and Republic Pictures companies. And at the same time he wrote for *Lux Radio Theatre*, *The Rudy Vallee Show* and Edward G. Robinson's radio series, *The Big Town*.

One of his stories caught the attention of a producer who

brought Kramer back to MGM in 1942, where he was executive assistant to producer David L. Loew in the making of Somerset Maugham's *The Moon and Sixpence.*

World War II interrupted his Hollywood work, but not his experience: while in the Army Signal Corps, he made training films, and when discharged in 1945 he raced back to work. His career began in earnest at this time.

(There has been a private life, of course. Kramer is married to the former Karen Sharpe, and they are the parents of two girls, Katharine and Jennifer. By his prior marriage to Anne Pearce, he is also father to Larry and daughter Casey.)

"In the army I met a man named Armand Deutsch, who was one of the Sears Roebuck heirs. He happened to be interested in theatre and film, so I lit a fire under him and encouraged him, when we were mustered out of the service, to buy a book—a big seller by Taylor Caldwell, *This Side of Innocence.* All the studios were bidding for it. I went to Annie Laurie Williams, who was agent for that book. She was a great believer in astrology and always consulted the stars before reaching a business decision. Well, she read in the stars that I was going to be a great success, so she sold *me* the book, against Fox and MGM, who also wanted it! So here we were, Deutsch and I, two nobodies. He had a little money, I had even less. But I owned this hot book! A fellow named Don Ettlinger had been a writer when I was at Fox before the war and, since he was a friend of mine, Deutsch paid him to do the screenplay for the Caldwell book. Once he completed the script, it was so hot that everyone was offering us deals. At this point Armand Deutsch got cold feet about me: I was just a kid, he realized, and he was afraid I knew nothing and couldn't handle this big project. So he insisted on bringing in Hal Horne, who was publicity man for Fox. Horne started to enlarge our little company, which made me unhappy, and then he kept on doing publicity for Caldwell's book. In fact, he got so involved in book sales that he never made a deal for the film! Enterprise Productions, which was the David Loew-Charles Ein-feld company, wanted to make it, but the deal fell through. Loew and Deutsch gave me a very small fee to break the contract, and the picture never got made."

It was 1947, and with the little bit of money he received from this abandoned and aborted project, Stanley Kramer formed his own company.

"I invited Herbert Baker and Carl Foreman, both of whom I'd known in the army, to join me in this new company. I also gave them shares in it. In addition, I hired George Glass, a publicity man who was also supposed to have worked on *This Side of Innocence,* and an attorney named Sam Zagon." (The latter two are still associated with Kramer, in fact.)

"So there we were—army buddies with a new film company! It was certainly strange. With the money from the broken Deutsch contract, I took an option on two stories by Ring Lardner that struck my fancy."

And this is where the real career of Stanley Kramer begins. . . .

Dave Willock and Henry Morgan.

CHAPTER 1

The Luckless Overture—
So This Is New York, 1948

The Ring Lardner stories chosen for production could not have been more different from each other. The first was a breezy little nothing called "The Big Town," whose title had to be changed for Hollywood since it was also the name of a popular radio show. Scenarists Carl Foreman and Herbert Baker extracted instead a line of Lardner's dialogue which emphasized the characters' wisecracking. *So This Is New York* was filmed in forty-eight days. It was an ambitious (if not an auspicious) beginning for an independent producer, and neither the critics nor the distributors nor the public cared much for it.

The story is simple. Just after Ernie Finch (Henry Morgan) completes his World War I army service, his wife, Ella (Virginia Grey), and her sister Kate Goff (Dona Drake) inherit sixty thousand dollars from a recently deceased uncle. A simple, undemanding chap with a plain and sometimes plaintive expression of strained patience, Ernie is hustled off to New York by the two women, whose sudden fortune will, they believe, buy a more sophisticated life for them all and a husband for Kate.

In the big city, however, they meet one disappointment after another—and each takes the form of an opportunistic or demented nongentleman caller for Kate. First, Francis Griffin (Jerome Cowan) slithers along, all suited up and brilliantined, his smile flashing on and off like a movie marquee. But his attentions are directed toward Ella.

Undaunted, the sisters shuffle Ernie into a luxurious New York apartment, where an elderly neighbor (Hugh Herbert) notices Kate. His apartment looks like Frank Buck's warehouse, however, and it takes a slightly wild luau and some exotic Polynesian libations to relax the nervous Kate. This tender scene, however, is interrupted by the unscheduled arrival of the man's wife. End of rugged romance number two.

New York, however, has lots more eligible male fish swimming about in its social sea, and the sisters soon meet a rich Texas rancher (Rudy Vallee), whose New York racehorses seem a sure bet for augmenting wealth and initiating romance. But a scandal develops, the rancher's jockey (Leo Gorcey) tries to woo Kate, and the girls lose a good deal of their money.

In considerably less grand circumstances now, the girls meet a monumentally dull Follies comedian (Bill Goodwin) who convinces Ella and Kate to finance a play he has written. Why, Kate can even have a part in it! Predictably, it's a disaster, and now the group is virtually penniless.

Ernie, however, is offered his former job with the Gluskoter Cigar Company of South Bend, and Kate's butcher boyfriend appears, like an awkward *puer ex machina,* proposes to Kate and takes the family back to the quiet security of Indiana.

While the cast was in a rigorous three-week rehearsal, Broadway columnists received a questionnaire from Enterprise Productions, in which they were asked to list the twenty most objectionable aspects of New York living. The poll results—cannily foreseen by Kramer and his writers—got heavy emphasis in the shooting.

Most of the film's $1,250,000 budget was allotted for the cast (Henry Morgan received $100,000). A minimum of cash was spent for sets, costumes and, it seems, for careful lighting. The quality of the images shifts abruptly from Gothic Shadowy to Operating Room Bright, and neither is apt for the tone of the

Henry Morgan and Virginia Grey, on the set.

film, which tries to be a send-up of urban life and a put-down of social climbing. Foreman and Baker kept the story chugging along at a brisk pace, but the film leaves a nasty feeling about cities, and Lardner's fundamental target—*nouveau riche* women whose unamiable gullibility takes them all the way to childish fantasies again—is very nearly overshadowed by the picture's acidulous attitude toward New York. Its most amusing sequences, in fact, derive from unsubtle diatribes against city dwellers. The taxicab driver's jargon is so incomprehensible it has to be rendered by subtitles. Waiters are incorrigibly venal. Streets are filthy. Residents are unfriendly. Flashy visitors are invariably opportunists.

Kramer worked closely with editor Walter Thompson on the

seamlessly edited series of stock shots of New York (circa 1920) in the film, and his involvement is perhaps curiously relevant. It's easy to discern a young ex-New Yorker's ambiguous feelings about the city in this picture: the flatness of the interiors and the crudeness of the rear-projection photography is compensated by the gentler, truer stock shots, and it is these that balance the picture's snappish attitude toward New York that bobs, like a perverse buoy, in the script. Produced by a man who had left New York (and felt he could never return to it as home), the film's resentment of East Coast sophistication and pretensions to the Good Life really seems too eager an attempt at sociospiritual chic. It may have been, in fact, rather more personal than ideological.

In this regard, the character of Ernie Finch provides the film's real center of interest. "Henry Morgan," Kramer remarked during production, "is not being made over to fit a character. The character that Lardner created in Ernie Finch, the lad from South Bend, happens to fit Henry Morgan. Henry is a humorist rather than a comedian. He is a funny guy but he works with his brains. That makes him primarily a satirist, and it is by using him in this way that I hope to get over Lardner's own satirical treatment of the big city and its people."

Kramer apparently thought of Morgan in terms of Will Rogers, but Morgan's air of simple wisdom was more radio bred than homespun. In its May 12, 1948, issue, *Variety* wondered how radio audiences would respond to Henry Morgan, the cinematic *arrivé* who varied wryness and nastiness. "Marquee strategy," *Variety* suggested, "will have to be based almost exclusively on Henry Morgan." That would have been a great gamble, and although it was reported that Kramer signed Morgan to a multipicture contract, this is contradicted by Kramer's refusal to sign up any actor for more than one film at a time—not even Marlon Brando, not even Spencer Tracy. In his first independent effort, Kramer was in no position to promise anyone very much. He was operating on lots of energy, but minimal experience.

In any case, it's interesting to watch an established radio personality in his screen début. "I found myself talking too

Dona Drake and Hugh Herbert.

loud," Morgan recalled. "I had to work on that voice to get it down to what seemed like a whisper to me. Then I had to learn to start talking with my hands. It was the reverse of the old gag. I had become so used to talking without my hands that when it came to this work, I didn't know what to do with them!" In addition, because the story is told within the framing device of a flashback (a conceit which writer Carl Foreman favors), Morgan is called upon to play a dual role: he is in the action as one of the characters, but he is occasionally removed from it (though still in character) to comment on the people or situation with the droll distance of hindsight. The terms and timing and texture of this withdrawal from the action were carefully supervised by Kramer during script-writing and shooting, and the successful rhythm of this in strictly cinematic terms may in fact ultimately derive from Kramer's own experimentation earlier in his career.

"We did things in the army documentary training films that would have horrified the orthodox Hollywood producer, but they turned out to be highly successful," Kramer said many years ago. "For instance, we employed narration but the words spoken offscreen did not necessarily apply to the visual scene. We found that we could hold the attention of the audience in two ways. We could explain the action while it was going on, and we could digress from the action to explain something that related to it. Far from distracting the audience, this method reinforced what we wanted to put over."

This method is never overworked in So This Is New York, but rather enlivens the comic narrative and acts like an automatic editing device which adds some sparkle to Richard Fleischer's direction. Fleischer's later films, even when they have narratives more coherent and convincing than this, are often afflicted with an overabundance of static medium shots and uneven pacing. He was able to overcome this for Disney, in 20,000 Leagues under the Sea (1954) and in the tightly terrifying film The Boston Strangler (1968). But when he tries to be consciously serious or deliberately comic (as in the studiously nauseating Mandingo, released in 1975), Fleischer loses control of his camera and seems to grow somewhat contemptuous of his audience.

Kramer's first production has dated badly—when it turns up

on television it looks like a postwar situation comedy made for that medium—and apart from the archetypal cool projected by Morgan, and the lacquered, whiny caricatures neatly turned by Virginia Grey and Dona Drake, there is little memorable in the picture, and it would have been hard to predict that, within months, one of the most important dramas of the decade would be in production under the "wunderkind." Unlike almost every other early Stanley Kramer picture, *So This Is New York* was safe in its style and posture and its injunction to simple suburban living—which was a dream of many people after the Second World War—and there's a strong reminiscence of Depression-era comedies in the film's fabric.

George S. Kaufman once remarked that satire is something that closes on Saturday night, which is just about how long Kramer's first film ran in any big town. In fact it never even got to Manhattan: distributors let it die peacefully in Brooklyn.

This was, as it turned out, good fortune, since Kramer was able to finance a second Ring Lardner story before the bad news about *So This Is New York* traveled too far.

No one could have guessed that the young independent producer of this flaccid little comedy was about to make a gritty and greater film, one which would win an Academy Award and place him firmly in the ranks of the important Hollywood producers.

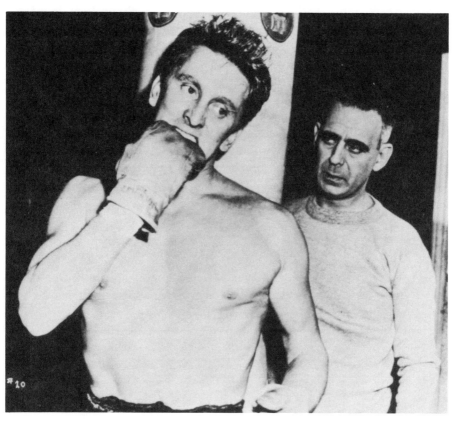

Kirk Douglas and Paul Stewart.

CHAPTER 2

Playing Footsy, for Big Stakes—
Champion, 1949

His second film, undertaken with great personal conviction, was an instant hit, and since he was an independent, Stanley Kramer became at once an object of admiration from some and bitter jealousy from others. Hollywood, after all, does not usually extend instant success. "The old American dream was," as Kramer put it, "that you go to work at MGM when you're twenty-one years old and if you're nice and keep your nose clean for twenty years you become whatever you want to become. Well, of course that's not the way it happens and it never really did." He is himself living proof to the contrary.

"The reason I made *Champion* was that I desperately hated the fight game. I grew up in the tough area of New York known as Hell's Kitchen and went to DeWitt Clinton High School, at Fifty-ninth Street and Tenth Avenue. It seemed that all the kids I went to school with turned out to be priests or hoods or prizefighters. Especially prizefighters. I came to hate that business. I've been in a lot of those underground tunnels, seen a lot of those managers and a lot of that mayhem."

Kramer doesn't like to admit it, but *Champion* is very much an

American *film noir*—an exploration of dark passions and motivations against shadowy and ominous backgrounds. At the very beginning, a prizefighter, robe-clad, walks through a darkened underground tunnel, from which he emerges into the blinding light of the boxing ring. The crowd roars. A voice-over announces solemnly: "This is the story of a boy who rose from the depths of poverty to become the champion of the world." In fact, the story is about a boy who rises so high from the depths of poverty that he ends up in the depths of cruelty and moral stagnation. The characters in the film haven't enough grandeur, and there isn't enough at stake, to relate it to the tradition of tragedy; but it certainly ranks within the development of American *film noir*.

Before *So This Is New York* had its ill-fated gallop to an early death, Kramer approached the vice-president in charge of motion-picture loans at the Bank of America. He told him he owned Ring Lardner's short story "Champion," which, as he admits, wasn't true; he simply had a very cheap, thirty-day option to buy the story, but the Lardner estate still owned the rights. He also told the bank he had signed the young New York stage actor Kirk Douglas for the lead, and that United Artists had agreed to release the film. These, too, were more hopes than facts: Douglas had not been negotiated, and United Artists hadn't even been approached.

Kramer knew he was playing what he called "an advanced game of footsy" based on what he was supposed to say or what might interest bank officials. The Bank of America hedged; however, it agreed to advance him the needed production funds only if some sort of guarantee could be offered. Eventually, therefore, *Champion* was backed by a Florida dry-goods manufacturer, an elderly retired man who'd recently married a nineteen-year-old university coed. From the very start, this production had human interest value. . . .

Champion is the dark account of Midge Kelly (Kirk Douglas), a grindingly poor country boy who makes his way to California after the war to take over his share of a roadside luncheonette. Once there, however, he discovers he's been cheated by a former partner. Midge travels with his brother Connie (Arthur Kennedy), whose partial lameness is due to a childhood accident. Connie falls in love with Emma (Ruth Roman), daughter of the owner of the luncheonette, but she is drawn to Midge's sullen, crusty virility. Promised marriage, she becomes, briefly, his mistress, until her father forces Midge to marry her—literally at the point of a gun. The sour Midge abandons her just after the ceremony. The loyal Connie follows Midge to Los Angeles. After months of rigorous training, Midge becomes a boxer under the management of Tommy Haley (Paul Stewart). "Boxing is a racket, not a sport," Haley tells him, and since only the tough and the ruthless can survive, he shows Midge how to take unfair advantage of opponents in the ring, how to get away with every dirty trick in the business while resembling a paragon of sportsmanship.

In his personal life, Midge is no fairer than he is in the ring, and in short order he has added friends, mistresses, his manager, his brother, and finally his mother to the list of those he abuses, neglects, exploits, casts aside like used tissue. In a final, vicious bout Midge sustains a brain hemorrhage and dies in his dressing room. His brother tells newsmen, "He was a champion, and he went out like a champion. He was a credit to the fight game to the very end." The words are two-edged, and if their irony is lost on the scribbling reporters, they're clear to the film's audience, who have seen that Midge Kelly has become a credit to a deadly, criminal game. The title "champion" has never been awarded more emptily.

In the Lardner story, Midge Kelly was a singularly monstrous man, physically cruel to his family. "Initially, no one was interested in backing a story like that," Kramer remembered. "They all figured, how could you film a story that starts with a guy who kicks his crippled brother down the stairs and hits his mother?!" In his screenplay, however, Carl Foreman removes just enough of the character's undiluted nastiness to make him, in fact, more human—and thus to make the whole premise of the story more credible. Kelly's inhumanity grows with a grotesque logic, like a cancer, and it's impossible to give sociology textbook reasons for the characterological deterioration. Partly through pride ("Call me Mister—not 'Hey, you!' " he demands, baring his teeth and clenching his fist) and partly through resentment of his humble beginnings ("It's hard to be happy when you're poor—cold poor, hungry poor!"), he's a prey to the hazardous dalliance with money and fame. But there's something malignant lurking in the character, and from the very start there's the look of ill-destined ugliness.

Before shooting on the film began, there were several weeks of rehearsals for cast and crew—a Kramer tradition which has been rigorously maintained over the years. In addition, director Mark Robson, writer Carl Foreman, cinematographer Frank (later Franz) Planer, and the art director, production manager and set decorator worked closely with Kramer for several months, dissecting the script, drawing story boards and plotting the action with meticulous attention to detail. In an interview with *The Christian Science Monitor* in April 1949, Kramer remarked that an initial outlay of $50,000 for such preproduction expenses would later save him more than three times that amount.

"We had no second unit crew," Kramer recalled. "I did the second unit direction myself. In fact, I directed the major fight scenes. Mark Robson didn't know very much about fighting, so I directed and edited all the exercise montages—in cadence to a musical beat I'd worked out in my head. On the set I directed the action in time to a four-count beat, so when Dimitri Tiomkin scored and we mixed sound, it came out like a little dance."

But the major concept that Kramer brought to *Champion* was the character of Midge Kelly and the men of the boxing world, and this concept Carl Foreman incarnated in his acute and powerful screenplay. The speech patterns of the tough guy and the hard staccato phrases of organized criminals contrast vividly with the languorous dullness of the manager's girlfriend and the boss's wife, and the plain, flat statements of morally inert commonfolk. The script makes Midge neither a hideous monster nor a whining victim of circumstances: he is rather a credible man of unreflective brutality, self-interested arrogance and vices which are indeed terrible but all too common.

Mark Robson directed the early sequences of the picture with particular attention to the subtle shifts in Kelly's character: as Kelly sleeps in a boxcar en route to California, there's a hint of fundamental innocence about the boy-man: he's surrounded by sheep—it's almost a manger scene—and the tone is gentle, pastoral. But there's a rapidly moving countryside in the background, and the dreary dirtiness of the hobos who share these unglorious accommodations and who are about to rob and eject Midge and Connie

Kirk Douglas undertook the leading role for Kramer against the advice of his friends and agent. Brilliantly cast here (as he was not to be in Kramer's *The Juggler*), he had supporting roles

Ruth Roman and Kirk Douglas.

until *Champion.* To prepare himself at the age of thirty-two, he trained many hours daily, six days a week for six weeks, under the demanding tutelage of "Mushy" Callahan, formerly the world's junior welterweight champion. At St. Lawrence University, Douglas had been intercollegiate wrestling champion, but that was in 1938, and the closest he'd come to boxing even at that time was jumping rope. By the time Callahan turned him over to Kramer for rehearsals, Douglas was in such fine form that the man hired to double for the fight scenes never appeared in a single shot and was sent away, salaried, but with no film experience. It's Kirk Douglas in there, punching and feinting.

There's a moment in the dialogue that in fact reveals the core of the Douglas character. Arthur Kennedy—whose loyalty finally knows its bounds and yields to the strength of his love for Midge's deserted wife—remarks, "His anger in the ring is anger toward all the people who ever hurt him." Midge replies airily, "They're cheering for *me!*" His eyes become so blank, he stares so hard that you expect to see the early signs of apoplexy. The Douglas trademark—tough earnestness, his words hissed through clenched teeth as if he were trying to distract your attention away from that amusingly boyish dimple on his chin—was totally covered with a sheet of steely bravado for most of the scenes of *Champion.*

All the subtleties of character and theme are refracted through Planer's carefully placed camera, which always highlights the dark, enclosed spaces in which boxers dress, prepare, train, and the gray, subterranean rooms, with bare bulbs hanging overhead. The boxer spends most of his time in a room that looks like a morgue—and that, of course, is just what the champion's dressing room will become for him. The camera is kept low when we're watching the fighter on his deluded climb to power, and the oppressive ceilings, which create eerie lighting effects, deepen the claustrophobia and sense of social constriction. *Champion* is, after all, about a man who finds it expedient to discard virtually every moral value and is thus beaten by his own ambition. In the dialogue with his brother and with an opponent's girlfriend (Marilyn Maxwell), the cuts from character to character are abrupt, and you have the impression of relationships ruptured and emotions exploited. The single possibility of human feeling for this fighter would have been a reaching out to Emma (Ruth Roman), and in those scenes the camera moves with graceful, longing fluidity.

But all of these cinematic gestures eventually support the film's major theme, corruption through power. "You stink with corruption," says Kennedy to Douglas. "You're worse than a murderer, you're a graverobber." The response to this is Douglas' grimace and empty gaze, his taste for power transformed to a thirst for blood. Prizefighting, the film postulates, is not only inextricably linked to the dark underworld of organized crime; it also exposes in all its horror the loss of humanity to which this most brutal of all sports must lead.

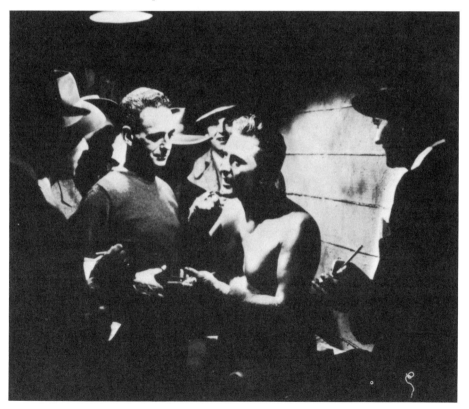

Moments before the final fight . . .

Champion's premise is diametrically opposed to that of a later and equally popular film, *Rocky* (1976). Whereas the earlier movie established the ineluctable human tragedy and the erosion of civilized responses by boxing even as it documents the fine art of exploitation, *Rocky* transfers to the boxing ring and the parlor the conventions of the fairy tale. The recent film, which describes the efforts of a lovable if slightly dimwitted hunk of fighting beefcake (Sylvester Stallone), pitches to our sympathies for the underdog, and for that part of us that struggles, tries to retain integrity, gets beaten, tries again. *Rocky* betrays a facile unconcern for any of the physical or moral issues involved and simply revives the image of the mumbling commoner of the 1950s. It shows the contemporary audience's desire for the fighter to win, to beat his enemies, get the girl, come up from life's ring bloodied but unbowed. Kramer's champion was doomed early on—not because of any cruel destiny or capricious, maleficent god, but because he squandered his own kindness and manhood by arrogant ambition, crushed the feelings of others in his grip and finally beat his own truth out of himself. It is a film in which the man's physical power is at once an equivalent and a metaphor for what eventually corrupts.

Champion's editor, Harry Gerstad, won the Academy Award that year. Watching the film's multiple rhythms (in the fight scenes), it's easy to see why. More important, the film forever changed the tradition of the boxing movie. There had been little but romanticism and a sunny glamorizing running through films like *Golden Boy* and *Body and Soul,* but the main character here becomes more and more savage and pathetic as the story progresses. The film is at once an antiboxing tract and a testimony to the possible results, in independent filmmaking, of uniting passionate conviction with determined talent.

CHAPTER 3

Filmmaking in Secrecy—
Home of the Brave, 1949

Champion premiered in American theatres early in April 1949. Weeks earlier, as postproduction details (sound mixing and dubbing, last-minute editing and print processing) were being completed and publicity prepared, Stanley Kramer was already deeply involved in a new project. On February 2, shooting began on a film which was posted in the studio logs as *High Noon*—a title that aroused only minor lunchtime discussions and shrugs of low-key speculation. Most people were unprepared for a series of surprises when the film, under another title, was finished twenty-five days later. Within seventy-two hours of the last day of shooting, at the end of February, editing was completed. The final print was sent to United Artists on April 2, and the film was distributed for screening early in May. *Champion,* meanwhile, had been gathering vast crowds and favorable reviews during April; now a new film would make it a doubly memorable springtime for Kramer and his colleagues.

The film produced so quickly and quietly was the first of a number of plays he brought to the screen, and it was the one he changed most in the transference. Just as important, the film marked several innovations in the American movie: it was the first picture to deal with the nasty problem of discrimination against the black man and, bluntly and unprettily, to detail the psychological scarring caused in both blacks and whites by hatred and prejudice. It was also the first Hollywood film to proceed from concept to release in a mere three months. And it was the first American film to be planned, written, cast and produced in absolute privacy.

"The whole film was made in secret," Kramer recalled in 1977. "All the actors received the same amount of money—$750 a week. They came in through the rear entrance of the set, had lunch there. Everything was very quiet so no one would know what we were really doing." But even though the soundstage was closed to visitors, and the cast consisted of only a handful of actors, Kramer had to extract promises of secrecy from almost six hundred crew members and technicians. Once the script had

James Edwards, Frank Lovejoy, Douglas Dick, Steve Brodie.

been completed, in fact, he avoided the actors' agents and approached his prospective cast directly. And four hundred people employed at the film laboratory where the picture was processed were also asked to pledge their confidence. "It was our intention to make an important entertainment feature in its completed form without the usual attendant publicity, so that we would be free of pressures, suggestions and advice of those not connected with its making."

But the secret got out several days before the film's premiere. Word quickly spread: the picture, based on a prize-winning play, had undergone major changes. Critics were rubbing their hands with glee over the impending furor. Distributors began to get sweaty palms, too. And audiences scoured their local newspapers to see when this controversial film would open in their neighborhoods. This was the first Hollywood product in which words like *nigger, boogie, shine, nigger-lover* were heard. They sliced out from the screen and cut into everyone's feelings. Prejudice was opened up and shown to be the festering, dangerous disease it is. The tormented soul of the black man was exposed with all its psychic scars and gaping emotional wounds. And although several other films on the same theme were to be released within months, Kramer's movie was the first, the strongest, the least compromising of all. It owed allegiance to no trend or cycle. It angered just about everyone, sometimes for very different reasons. It generally pleased the critics, it entertained millions and called forth all sorts of political and social responses from defensive Southerners and nervous Northerners.

The cause of all this furor was Stanley Kramer's *Home of the Brave,* based on Arthur Laurents' play about anti-Semitism within the ranks of soldiers during World War II. The New York Drama Critics' Circle cited the play as the best of 1946, but the public, as the saying goes, stayed away in droves. By 1949, there had already been several major movies about anti-Semitism *(Gentleman's Agreement* and *Crossfire* were probably the best), and Kramer shifted the center of concern from prejudice against Jew to prejudice against black.

The film tells the conflict surrounding the plight of a young black GI, Peter Moss (James Edwards, in his screen début), who is brought back, partially paralyzed, from a particularly dangerous reconnaissance mission to a Japanese island. Suffering also from shock and from a deeply rooted persecution complex, Moss is helped by a sympathetic doctor (Jeff Corey) who leads him back through a fog of amnesia to uncover the psychological cause of his affliction. During the mission, the years of baiting and inferior treatment reached a breaking point when the prejudice of several of his comrades blazed angrily forth. Even a former high-school friend, Finch (Lloyd Bridges), was tainted by subtle prejudices, and when he dies in Moss's arms, the black man suffers a sudden onslaught of paralysis.

Mocked by a bigoted Northerner (Steve Brodie), Moss was prevented by years of resentment and anxiety from accepting even the good will of his friends (Bridges and, as Sergeant Mingo, Frank Lovejoy)—men who are neither wholly good nor bad. They are all, like Moss himself, conditioned by background and experience. The trauma of war and death has enlarged and made clear their strengths and their weaknesses, and it is the acceptance of their common humanity which the doctor hopes Moss and his surviving comrades will learn. The film ends as Moss's hysterical paralysis is overcome by narcosynthesis, and psychological recovery is indicated as the next stage in his healing process.

Other films were about to come from Hollywood dealing with the theme of America's long tradition of racial discrimination—Louis De Rochemont's Lost Boundaries, Elia Kazan's Pinky and Clarence Brown's Intruder in the Dust followed within a few months—but Home of the Brave was the first to portray the black man as other than a menial or a buffoon. Some distributors claimed, locally, that the film would cause public rioting. Surveys were taken across the country during the film's first days, however, with special attention given to racially sensitive areas: blacks turned out in great numbers for Houston's "separate-for-blacks" midnight showings and for seats in the segregated section of Dallas' Majestic Theatre by day. (A black elevator operator in the latter city was quoted as saying that "99 percent of the people say it's educational, the other 1 percent say it's good.") The film brought in $21,000 in Dallas during the first six days—a huge revenue in those days—and San Antonio was said to have done an even brisker business. When it became clear that Americans were not likely to riot in the streets over a movie, the film critic for *The New York Times* contributed a reflective essay on the history of certain forbidden themes. "Many taboos of our screen," wrote Bosley Crowther, "have been engineered by inside bigots and not by public taste. People

Lloyd Bridges and James Edwards.

are always ready to patronize a film that will grip and entertain them, no matter what the theme. It is only when those who govern pictures make up their corporate minds that a subject is dangerous or 'unpopular' that it becomes a segregated thing." Crowther concluded that the Kramer film introduced a big, urgent subject admirably: "The only people who will scorn it are those who would segregate truth."

Kramer's interest in Laurents' play dated back to the time of its Broadway run. He was then associated with Hal Horne, and their fledgling company—Story Productions—acquired an option on the play. "Arthur Laurents was a gigantically talented young playwright," Kramer remarked years later. "So I went to New York and bought the rights for $35,000. A pittance. But I didn't tell Laurents that I wanted to make the switch from a Jewish to a black protagonist. The play had been a failure because it depended on a great deal of talk about a man feeling different. But what was so different? For the dilemma to be understood, the character had to *say* he was Jewish. But the play was certainly about the kind of prejudice we all knew when we were young in New York."

In fact, Kramer's own experience in the army during World War II closely paralleled the play. "I was in a signal corps photography company. The captain told me at once that he didn't like Jews—Hollywood Jews, particularly—and he told me to apply for a transfer. But I had been commissioned directly from civilian life, and so I couldn't be transferred out for a year. I had to stay with that man for a whole year!" It was undoubtedly this that influenced the young producer's original choice of material.

"We used the play word for word, except for the race change. And Foreman introduced flashbacks to show how the black and white men met as high-school students and how long their friendship had mattered to them. In the army, we'd all known about narcosynthesis, too"—the use of drugs in psychotherapy—"and we used that for dramatic effect. You could say this picture was really a result of the war experience of all of us. And the plight of the black man has always been very close to me.

"And since the working title for production was *High Noon*—a name we just dreamed up to cover the film we were really making—no one outside, not even Laurents himself, had the faintest idea of what was going on." (Foreman remembered this title a few years later, of course, when he adapted John W. Cunningham's story "The Tin Star" for what would be a Kramer classic.) "Actually," Kramer said at the time of the film's release, "the theme of *Home of the Brave* remained unchanged, for the basic conflict was the same."

Kramer apparently wanted to be the first producer to release a film about racial prejudice and stereotyping: he hurried this film through production for a half million dollars in twenty-five days in order to assure that. But although it was the bluntest of the lot, it was not without flaws, and even the most enthusiastic critics admitted that there were logical gaps and sacrifices of artistic integrity for the sake of the film's strong message. The film greatly pleased critic Bosley Crowther, who found it "moving, fair, honest and affecting." And Edwin F. Melvin, writing for *The Christian Science Monitor* said it was "fresh, persuasive and unforced."

But they ignored an annoying facet of the film, as the critic for *Theatre Arts* magazine indicated in the June 1949 issue. The young black soldier—loyal, mature, intelligent enough to be considered the best surveying specialist in the corps of engineers—would have been the type of man to have made, by this time, the kind of adjustment to prejudice that would prevent a hysterical paralysis deriving from mental shock at the death of his buddy. *Home of the Brave* thus pays a heavy price for depicting men as if they readily incarnated the symbols of an antiprejudice tract. And the arguments against discrimination, added *Time*, get badly mixed up with the subtleties of psychiatry. This psychiatric treatment is not very convincing in any case and depends on the grossly melodramatic, awkwardly written and woodenly acted scenes in which Corey and Edwards sweat a lot and shout "Listen to me!" and "Oh, Doc, I can't!"

The combat scenes are disappointing, too, set in an overused studio jungle which seems short on rubber tree plants. There are, however, plenty of loud insect sounds and exotic bird calls on the track.

The film's production values, therefore, suffered in Kramer's breakneck race to introduce a new kind of cinematic social statement. But in spite of the B-picture economy, it achieves a kind of raw power. Somehow the feeling of the film is always right: as the men crawl through the indoor jungle to reconnoiter the enemy's position, there's a morbid claustrophobia that affects them and the viewer. The director, Mark Robson, insists here on medium shots of the exhausted, parched, frustrated soldiers— always within minutes of being discovered and shot by the enemy. This not only caters to the film's modest sound-stage possibilities: close photography and the predominating oppressive darkness create a terrifying stasis that perfectly reflects the moral stagnation of prejudice. For a combat film, there is also a refreshing lack of the typical war-movie techniques—distant explosions, intercut with stock shots of bombs dropped from fighter planes and long shots of advancing soldiers. *Home of the Brave* sees the world situation as the logical extension of the torn relationships between individuals—and it locates the ultimate cause of international dissension within blind prejudice. In this regard, the flashback to the high-school origins of the friendship between Bridges and Edwards is the structurally critical prelude to the finally senseless nature of their misunderstanding. For all their good will, they come from a society which presumes white supremacy and black inferiority—presumptions which, brought into adulthood, finally become poisonous and quite literally crippling. The scene in which Bridges dies, cradled in Edwards' arms, is perhaps the most painful scene Carl Foreman ever wrote: there's the sense of an opportunity for reconciliation missed moments earlier, just after the prejudice sprang, unbidden, to Bridges' lips. It's only for a moment, and you have the feeling that back home the problem would have been resolved over a couple of beers. But here in the jungle there's little time for sociological self-analysis, and before dying Bridges ducks into the jungle to complete his mission. But he doesn't come back, and the bitterness of their last encounter is branded into Edwards' mind so deeply that, paralyzed by fear and dismay, his legs refuse to carry him away after his friend dies. It is this, of course, that illuminates the ironic significance of the recurrence of Eve Merriam's uninspired little poem and its key line,

"Coward, take my coward's hand." We're all cowards, indeed—made so, it seems, by feeble consciences. At this point we also see the new irony of the title, for this is really a story about a special type of moral cowardice. The movie refuses to expand the center of attention beyond this handful of men: the real enemy, the ultimate enemy, is the hatred within.

Robson's direction only occasionally fails to maintain the necessary rhythm. Since *Home of the Brave* is afflicted with severe prolixity, Robson had to prevent it from contracting a fatal indolence. The camera thus often catches the actors' faces just before they utter crucial remarks—and we see how socially juvenile they are, how badly their souls are equipped for this kind of personal trauma and for the disclosure of their own folly. The low camera and the oppressive ceilings of the doctor's office are the right visual analogues for the black man's depression and pain. And as he steps into the past, under the doctor's treatment, the flashbacks within flashbacks give the film's texture a vertiginous, dreamlike effect that never tilts over into a fraudulent surrealism.

In fact, the picture's hard realism depends on the performances. It's easier to identify with these unfamiliar men, and their acting is scarcely acting at all; it's more like documented living. James Edwards had latterly been the star of Broadway's *Deep Are the Roots,* and his artlessness was just right for this fundamentally attractive if heavily burdened young man. Steve Brodie gave an uncharacteristically convincing performance as the Northern bigot, and Lloyd Bridges, in his forty-first film, subdued his usual diffidence—he comes from the Aw Shucks School of Acting. Here, he conveys a genuine affection and a sort of misappropriated need.

Oddly, however, Frank Lovejoy gives perhaps the most inevitable performance. Elsewhere, he seemed to have his brows in perpetual frown, and his baritone voice ordinarily offered a bark more readily than a remark. Here he plays a man who's learned his wife is leaving him and yet was able to keep his humor and strength in the midst of hysteria. He has the film's key line: "I have no more use for a bad black man than for a bad white man, and I've known plenty of both."

Home of the Brave may depict its characters with strokes too

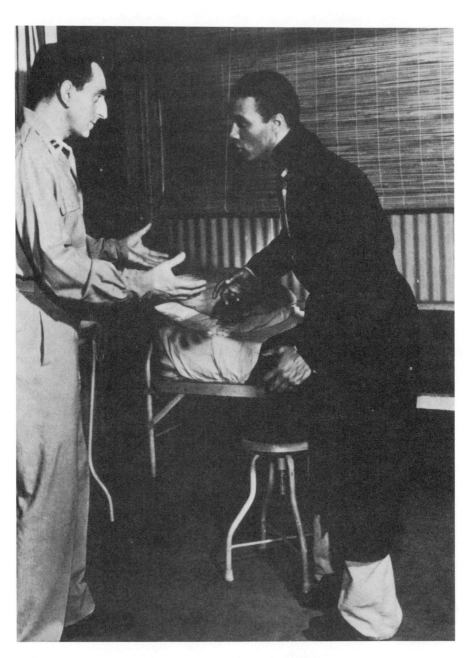

Jeff Corey and James Edwards: the healing process begins.

broad, and the emotional palette may lack certain subtle shades, but at least the film does not fall into the trap of a syrupy liberalism. The film stumbles almost fatally in the final moments of facile triumph over physical paralysis—indicating the black man's first steps toward self-respect and, equally, his acceptance as an equal by his white brothers. But the picture always wrestles with a very real problem and doesn't simply shadow-box with a contrived theme. It has an elusively awkward sincerity which is probably hard for most viewers to respect today, because the conventions of dialogue, acting and setting now seem very dated. But in 1949, *Home of the Brave* was a revolutionary exposé of a real social evil. It laughed at the clichés of black laziness and watermelon munching long before the socially alert humor of performers like Bill Cosby and Godfrey Cambridge.

The Hollywood Reporter, not usually remarkable for its political or social sensitivity, went so far as to say that "the whole future of the motion picture industry is dependent on the kind of imagination, courage and ingenuity that went into the making of *Home of the Brave*." The film has, in fact, a clumsy rightness that demands admiration. The noble sentiments do not in the final analysis arise organically from an entirely convincing dramatic situation—the events are exploited for the message they serve—but, as Andrew Sarris has written of Kramer, his approach may not often have been natural, but it is never fake. The consistent concern for the issue of the black man's place in American society was to be examined more deeply and more maturely in a trio of later Kramer works—*The Defiant Ones, Pressure Point, Guess Who's Coming to Dinner*. But the break in the wall began, for Kramer and for Hollywood and for the moviegoing public, with *Home of the Brave*, and for this reason alone it is a landmark movie.

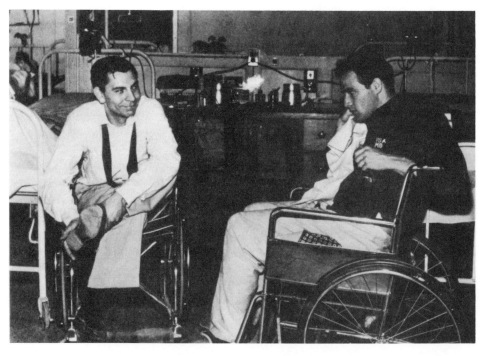

Jack Webb and Marlon Brando preparing for the day's shooting.

CHAPTER 4

Brando Wheels Himself into Movies— *The Men,* 1950

"One night shortly after *Champion* opened," Stanley Kramer recalled, "Kirk Douglas and I took it to show to the patients at the Birmingham Veterans Administration Hospital. It was then and there that I got the idea for a film about the problems these men faced." Soon afterward, Kramer and Carl Foreman and director Fred Zinnemann returned to the hospital and interviewed the patients and Dr. Ernest Bors, chief of the paraplegic section. After many weeks, they had established deeply friendly relationships with the men whose wounds had paralyzed them from the waist down and who were thus sentenced for life to wheelchairs.

"It soon became clear," according to Kramer, "that this would be a very special film and would require a very special talent. There was at that time a young agent working for MCA whose name was Jay Kanter. He was one of a small group assigned to cover the independent producers. It was Kanter who told me about the bidding that was then going on for a young New York stage actor named Marlon Brando. I had seen Brando on tour in *The Eagle Has Two Heads* with Tallulah Bankhead. I thought he was great, but odd." And it was Kramer who finally won the bid—with $50,000 and Carl Foreman's screenplay for *The Men,* which intrigued Brando.

"We brought him to California for the picture, and he was absolutely miraculous. He went and actually lived for a month with the paraplegics in the Birmingham Hospital. They adored him. He lived like them, he stayed in the wheelchair, he hooked himself up to a catheter. He went out to the local haunts at night and drank with them." It was an unusual preparation for an unusual film.

The Men is the painfully moving story of Ken (Brando) who as a result of a war wound is paralyzed below the waist. In the hospital back home, he passes through an initial period of depression with the help of a brusquely sympathetic doctor (Everett Sloane) and his faithful fiancée, Ellen (Teresa Wright).

Ken's bitter isolation is also overcome with the help of his fellow patients, especially the intelligent young cynic Norm (Jack Webb), the witty Leo (Richard Erdman) and serious young Angel (Arthur Jurado). Soon Ken throws himself into the work of rehabilitation and after a long period of physical therapy even suspects he may regain the use of his limbs. With the approval and help of the doctor, he and Ellen marry, but on their wedding night both have misgivings about the marriage: the full realization of Ellen's new responsibilities frightens her and makes her more uncertain than ever, and Ken reverts to self-pity. There is a violent argument, and he goes back to the hospital. But his blazing anger finds no sympathy from his buddies, and after a surprising conversation with the doctor, Ken realizes that he must return to his wife, with whom he must try to build his new life, in spite of all the attendant difficulties.

As Carl Foreman developed the shooting script after his prolonged visits to the hospital, it became clear that for the dialogue and situations to have any authentic resonance, they would have to be based in great part on the real-life situations he had heard about there. It was also apparent to Kramer and Zinnemann that, apart from a few leading actors, most of the cast should in fact be patients. And so, with the cooperation of Dr. Bors and of the veterans at Birmingham, forty-five paraplegics appear in *The Men.* Once this decision was made, Brando drew even closer to the patients, now fellow actors. During the weeks of preproduction and rehearsal, he continued in the ward, practicing the exercises, enduring the semimobility, learning to manipulate a wheelchair and braces.

This time was filled with memorable—and even amusing—incidents. One day Brando and some of the men from the ward were at a local bar. A religious fanatic turned from her bar stool toward them, urging them to faith, assuring them that they could walk again if only they would believe. The men said nothing, the drunken fanatic droned on. But then everyone noticed that Brando was clutching desperately at the armrests of his wheelchair, agonizingly trying to push himself up. He fell back exhausted, then tried again. Finally Brando rose on tottering legs,

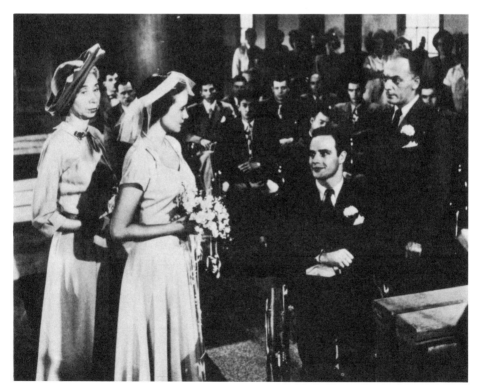

Virginia Farmer, Teresa Wright, Marlon Brando, Everett Sloane.

took a few hesitant steps and suddenly broke into a leap. Sprinting from the bar, he returned in seconds with a bundle of newspapers which he hawked wildly: "Now I can make a living again!" The men howled and applauded Brando's fine performance. "But the drunk," recalled Fred Zinnemann, "was instantly sober and very resentful at being the victim of a practical joke."

Prior to this film, there had been a proliferation of combat movies during and immediately after World War II. The worst of them had emphasized antienemy propaganda and never addressed the issues of the war itself—films like *Destination Tokyo* fall into this category. There were also films about men returning home, the best of which probed the problems of the veteran's reentry to a peacetime society. *The Best Years of Our Lives* is a fine example of this type. But *The Men* is different from both and stands in fact as a postscript to war stories. The following year, Mark Robson's *Bright Victory* tackled a similar plot and theme, substituting blindness for paraplegia.

Foreman's script manages a delicate balance between stony realism and a tasteful, honest treatment of the problems of love and marriage when one of the partners is severely crippled. It shows that, long after the surrenders have been signed and the last troops welcomed home, a war continues. The hospital and rehabilitation ward become the new battlegrounds, the combat is with oneself and even, more poignantly, with family and friends. Patients discover their deepest beliefs about life and learn to accept being dependent on others for simple needs. And relatives and friends learn that their love must not lead to a condescending pity.

The Men is remarkable for the way it does not flinch, in its opening moments, from the more unpleasant aspects of paraplegia. Based on the discussions with Dr. Bors, Foreman's dialogue between the wives and patients and the chief doctor (played by Everett Sloane) presents discreetly the sexual and alimentary problems of the paraplegics—discussions which are all the more moving when we realize that most of the young patients in the film face precisely the same problems.

But the film is actually two stories: one about rehabilitation and one about love. The camera focuses, in its second half, on the awkward relationship between Brando and Teresa Wright, and the adjustment to their marriage. But before and over this individual story is one about a ward full of crippled men who are first conditioned by the abrupt but not uncompassionate doctor to accept the futility of hoping for a cure. The fight for Brando and his buddies is not one to regain a temporary loss, but to develop a new life from the shards of a former one. And there is a certain alienation between the crippled and the physically whole, too, and the script confronts this. "Normal

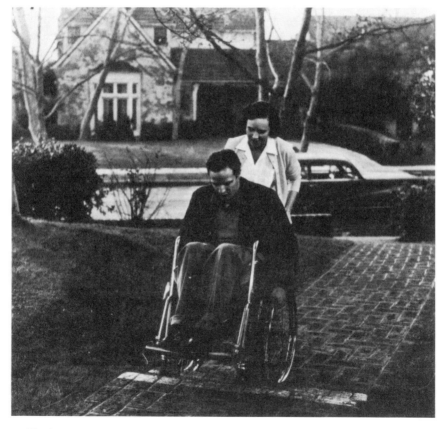

The last scene.

people don't like us," remarks one patient, "because we remind them that their own bodies could go—snap!—like that!" There's an acute psychology here, an awareness of a truth that is perhaps more sour for the healthy than for the victims: that the lame and the halt are testimonies to the fragility of this life, that in an irrational world we are all of us prey to cruel chance, and that one need not have been at the battle lines to suffer loss. A stroke, as the doctor points out, may afflict anyone in the comfort and security of his own home; an errant truck can cripple a casual pedestrian in seconds; a visitor at a swimming pool may slip and be plunged into crippling dependency. The basic theme of the film, then, is one of universal courage—courage in the face of utter hopelessness.

The film never cheats: Ken is indeed doomed to the wheelchair, but he is not doomed to unhappiness and bitterness. In spite of him and his wife's own family, Ellen's persistence and the doctor's helpful honesty enable him to return home and accept her offer to help him up the first awkward step to the house. The film's final shot shows Miss Wright at the front of the house, helping Brando negotiate his wheelchair up the first step. This highlights the theme of his acceptance of being needy. Her need is not clearly indicated by the script, but in Teresa Wright's sensitive performance there is a loving self-sacrifice that never descends to the easy, sappy heroics or synthetic sentiment of much movie characterization.

Several scenes, under Zinnemann's sparse and clean direction, linger in the mind long after one has watched the picture: the montage of paraplegics' exercises, the water therapy, the carefully worked out routines with braces and weights. These sequences avoid heart-tugging cliché by emphasizing not the ease with which a man shifts from a resentful isolation to engagement, but the innate desire for life—the best sort of life on whatever terms—that resides within all people. And when Brando and Wright return to the new home on the wedding night, the sudden distance between them is obvious in the room. She tries to fill in awkward moments by bringing a bottle of champagne, and Zinnemann shot the scene with an admirable economy and understatement: the couple appears against a background of walls and chairs which frames them in tight, medium-close shots. The camera pans so slightly to allow her to exit the room that it seems this sad young couple will never, in fact, have any necessary physical distance between them: the atmosphere isn't intimate, it's just cramped. The static nature of the scene perfectly corresponds to his physical condition. And the escape from the oppressive and apparently hopeless situation is not really an escape at all: thus the film moves relentlessly to Brando's return to the hospital, and his manic smashing of the windows with crutches.

Equally memorable is the final sequence with Sloane: for the first time, the doctor discloses that his own wife had died from a spinal injury sustained in an auto wreck many years earlier. "I would give anything to find her waiting at home for me," the doctor says with a distant, dry-eyed glance, "to find her waiting, in a wheelchair." He makes Brando understand that he has expected more of Wright than he should of anyone. She, after all, is human, too, with all the weaknesses, needs and strengths that he has. It would be easy for scenes like this to be played for fraudulent emotionalism, but the performances and low-keyed direction infuse a certain unromantic realism and genuine feeling to the scene. This is augmented by a slightly low camera angle and subdued lighting effects.

Brando's sullen tenseness is nearly always right. He conveys the quiet bitterness and mixture of feelings with unsentimental poignancy, but there are moments when he seems a trifle too calculated, and there is an emotional warmth lacking that could have invested his scenes with Teresa Wright with a deeper feeling.

"Marlon Brando was terribly insecure when he did this picture," recalled Fred Zinnemann. "He had never been before a camera up to this point, and he didn't trust people. He was completely enclosed within himself, so totally identifying with Stanley Kowalski"—the man he portrayed in Williams' *A Streetcar Named Desire*—"that he approached the part of the paraplegic veteran as Stanley."

Teresa Wright, on the other hand, had a decade's screen experience when she came to this project. It was very likely her performances for Hitchcock (in *Shadow of a Doubt*) and for William Wyler (in *The Little Foxes* and *The Best Years of Our Lives*) that most influenced her keen sense of timing and subtlety. The role—which would have been diminished by many other actresses in the sheer awesome shadow of Brando's glowering— thus moves us most when there is a shading of tenderness and confusion.

The minor performances, however, do not always further theme or plot. The role of Norm Butler, for example, seems gratuitously written and gets entirely out of hand when, sup- posedly in his cups, Jack Webb bitterly quotes Hamlet's speech about death and sleep.

Yet *The Men* suggests that there are other aspects in the demonstration of manhood than winning a political war; the war with one's own spirits is the real test of manhood.

Kramer and Foreman had extensive army film experience, and Zinnemann's work at MGM from 1937 to 1942 (during which time he made numerous short films) had taught him to survey facts quickly, vividly and economically. There is a richness of feeling in Zinnemann's work, and his two later films for Kramer (*High Noon* and *The Member of the Wedding*) are remarkable, too, for their deceptive modesty and meticulous attention to detail.

It's worth dwelling on that precision, for Fred Zinnemann is a director oddly neglected by both academics and cultists. Con- sciously eschewing auteurism ("I don't worry about stamping my signature on a film") Zinnemann is nonetheless more than an expert craftsman. He in fact does have significant and consistent concerns, as he has admitted: "Certainly there are themes that fascinate me, such as the conflict of conscience." He has dealt with this most notably in *The Nun's Story* (1959) and *A Man for All Seasons* (1966). The latter has been the source of keen debate among critics, most of whom claim that it is simply a filmed play, all its virtues deriving from Robert Bolt's scenario; its faults, critics like to point out, lie in the director's unimaginative use of the camera. The public, however, has responded much more enthusiastically to this film.

Zinnemann's masterpiece is arguably *The Nun's Story*. Robert

Anderson's screenplay for it, based on Kathryn Hulme's novel, is a tender elegy to the fading traditions of European convent life and a great celebration of the primacy of conscience. The triumph of the conscience runs through the best of Zinnemann's work, too, and it's easy to understand his attraction to a cinematic treatment of this book. He has an instinctive understanding of the extent to which people can be victimized by their environment and traditions, which, with supreme irony, act as stencils against which people discover and refine the best in their own natures.

There is a wonderful moment in *The Nun's Story* which is relevant in this regard. Audrey Hepburn, as Sister Luke, has told her religious superior, Edith Evans, that she has decided to leave the convent life and return to secular living. Evans, as a woman of preternatural compassion, kindness and wisdom, is seated next to Hepburn, in front of a floor-length window in the cloister of the mother-house convent. She is clearly saddened at this news, but her admiration and love for her younger colleague are stronger than her disappointment. "When I go from here," says the older nun quietly and with great grace and dignity, "I shall take you with me in my prayers and keep you always in my heart." Tracing the cross on Hepburn's forehead, she rises and walks away. Hepburn is now seated alone, against a window streaked with a gentle autumn rain. Suddenly the rain lashes the panes more heavily, and the camera dollies back swiftly, stopping so that now we see in long shot the black-clothed nun, emotionally drained, the rain forming a pathetic fallacy for the dimensions of her life at this moment.

There's a tender rightness about moments like this in Zinnemann's films. The shot of Gary Cooper and Grace Kelly before the grandfather clock, relentlessly ticking toward high noon, is another. And the triptych of Ethel Waters, Julie Harris and Brandon de Wilde huddled to Miss Waters' breast as she sings in *The Member of the Wedding* is another. The director's unfailing sense of rhythm and composition give an intimacy the stage version never had. It is the same sense of intimacy and involvement with which he enriched Bolt's story of Thomas More and Kathryn Hulme's factually based account of a woman's religious struggle.

It was, then, a rare combination of talents—a script rooted in reality, meticulous and deeply felt direction and admirable production values—which invested *The Men* with motifs that are emotionally valid and made it a film that is also a timeless human document.

Teresa Wright and Marlon Brando.

CHAPTER 5

The $5,000 Nose—
Cyrano de Bergerac, 1950

Stanley Kramer caught *Cyrano de Bergerac* on the rebound.

Edmond Rostand's French tragicomedy had been a very popular play since its premiere in 1897 and had been performed with great success throughout Europe and America. It was filmed in Italian in 1909 and 1922, and in French in 1946.

The curious situation that resulted in Kramer's acquisition of the rights to the play began in 1936, when Ben Hecht was commissioned by producer Alexander Korda to write a screenplay. Hecht completed the task, but by the time Korda was able to mount the production on the lavish scale he envisioned, there was an unpleasant development. Because of his espousal of Zionism and his violent criticism of Great Britain during the heat of the battle over Palestine in the 1940s, Hecht was bitterly regarded in England after the war. Korda, therefore, fearing a boycott or even a strike against any project in which Hecht was involved, thought it unfeasible for him to use the American writer's script. But he still shared, with Rostand's estate, the rights to the play, and he had invested almost $200,000 in retaining those rights, commissioning the script and in various preproduction details. Plans had been tentatively announced, in fact, for Garson Kanin to direct the film, and for Laurence Olivier and Vivien Leigh to star.

When the Hecht version was abandoned in autumn 1948, Korda turned to Orson Welles with an offer. Welles was editing his film of *Macbeth* and made several trips to London for consultation. It was subsequently decided that he would write, direct and star in the long-delayed *Cyrano*. For reasons which to this day remain unclear, this plan, too, never became reality.

This made the way clear for Stanley Kramer, who had had a keen interest in the play since his earliest days in Hollywood. In the winter of 1948, Kramer dispatched his attorney, Sam Zagon, for conferences with Korda in London and with executors of the

Mala Powers and José Ferrer.

Rostand estate in Paris. In a matter of days, Kramer had purchased worldwide rights for what *Variety* called a "bargain-basement price." Korda, no doubt, was glad to be rid of what he considered a doomed project; and Kramer was glad to have the rights to the play. Little time was lost in planning his own version, which was made and released in 1950. It was well received by critics, and it won the best actor Oscar for José Ferrer, who had played the role on Broadway in 1946. In spite of his adventuresome performance, however, and several ingenious technical experiments, *Cyrano* remains essentially a tiresome, creaky play which is not much improved by a truncated transference to the film form.

The story of *Cyrano* is the story of a witty, deadly swordsman, Cyrano, whose attractive dash cannot compensate for his grotesquely prominent nose. He falls hopelessly in love with his cousin Roxane (Mala Powers)—so hopelessly, in fact, that, in total conformity to the romantic tradition, he sympathizes heroically with her love for the handsome but inarticulate soldier Christian (William Prince). Cyrano promises to look after his friend Christian, he coaches him in the language of love, and even encourages their marriage, which means his permanent estrangement from Roxane. The men go off to war, and Cyrano writes Christian's love letters to his wife. Even after her husband is killed, Roxane does not know the truth about the author of the sentiments that thrill and inspire her, for Cyrano keeps his secret for fourteen years—until his dying moments, in fact. The heartbroken and suddenly enlightened Roxane then declares, "I have never loved but one man in my life, and I have lost him—twice!" Cyrano, nobly, dies.

Carl Foreman, who based his very faithful screenplay on the Rostand original and the well-established English translation by Brian Hooker, faced many problems. The original, after all, ran four hours; José Ferrer's Broadway version required three hours. But Kramer knew that a motion-picture audience would find such lengths intolerable, and he insisted on a two-hour film. "In addition," Carl Foreman said just before the film's release, "there was the problem of words—thousands upon thousands of words—most of them beautiful, some archaic and obscure, a great many repetitious and overexpository. I found it necessary to perform major surgery on the beginnings of each of the five acts, for in every instance Rostand had paused to recapitulate and set the stage anew. Surgery and suture were necessary, we felt, for space, tempo and cinematic movement."

A hefty challenge, this—and one which most critics felt was met successfully. Arthur Knight, writing in *The Saturday Review of Literature* called it the first really successful translation of a play to the screen. There is no doubt that the script starts with a zesty energy and moves smoothly from high point to high point. The play is opened up, to include tortuous Paris streets and wide vistas of countryside and battlefield, and close-ups, two-shots and fighting scenes occasionally vary the rather cramped, conventional theatrical action. But they do not, unfortunately, enlarge or vitalize what is essentially a predictable and static work. No doubt the filmed play had more impact even on critics in 1950 than it would have today. A quarter century of film progress makes it look distressingly dated now.

What is quite interesting, however, is the use of the Garutso Balanced Lens, which helped perfect deep focus and was a stage in the development of motion-picture photography that has been surpassed. "The reason we used the Garutso lens," Kramer said, "was to get Cyrano's large nose in the foreground in perfect focus and, forty feet away, have another protagonist clearly visible, too." The nose—on which five thousand dollars was spent—is in fact a character in the story, and Franz Planer's camera treats it like the intrusive, obnoxious thing it is. " 'Tis a rock, a crag, a cape—nay, rather a peninsula," cries Ferrer in apparently insouciant self-mockery. "When it bleeds: the Red Sea!" And the camera, fearing a slash from the man's lively sword, cautiously half-circles the nose, peering, appraising, politely aghast. In this regard, of course, the film does in fact enrich the emotional texture of the play, since the gradual close-up, the sudden cut to or from an object and the skillful editing of reaction shots do enliven the pace and engage the eye. Director Michael Gordon, whose perhaps best-known work this is, seems to have remained undecided about the predominant tone of the film: there is a diffidence about scene and character, as if we are to be impressed with the sets and costumes, not with the humans who inhabit them. There is, however, a wonderful cinematic fandango that the camera performs as Cyrano duels to the death with an overbearing nobleman while simultaneously composing a poem.

By the time of *Cyrano,* Kramer had a reputation for producing films on comparatively low budgets: both *Champion* and *Home of the Brave* were made for less than $500,000. But no one could believe that he could produce a costume melodrama, with numerous interiors and exteriors and the services of a major Broadway star, for what he announced—considerably less than a million dollars. The skeptics, however, reckoned without the talents of Rudolph Sternad, who had been Kramer's production designer from the start. For *Champion,* Sternad had designed a million dollars' worth of sets for $25,000—which shocked just about everyone. *Cyrano* was budgeted at $850,000 and, with the standard 10 percent of budget allotted for sets, Sternad could then use more than three times the amount he had for *Champion*—but the sum was still very much less than required for such a lavish spectacle. As a matter of fact, he spent only $50,000, having devised ingenious methods for cutting costs and yet maintaining a sense of historical accuracy.

Sternad found that the script had seven basic settings: the theatre, the convent garden, the pastry shop, the cardinal's terrace, the streets, the plains of Arras and Roxane's garden. He built exact scale models of mobile sets, which had two to four sides each, and whose walls, ramps and balustrades were all interchangeable. These he arranged and rearranged, after consultation with the director and cinematographer, trying to forestall problems of camera movement. Eight sets were then constructed for a single sound stage, each mounted on wheels and with puzzle-like configurations. This is perhaps why virtually the entire film is made up of medium shots: since the sets were far from lavish and had limitations which would not allow for long shots, their modest dimensions could not be revealed.

Composer Dimitri Tiomkin set himself a difficult task, too, when he announced his intention to compose music faithful to the seventeenth century. With the flourish that marked his career, Tiomkin rushed from Hollywood to New York, where he visited the Metropolitan Museum of Art and studied French musical instruments: period harpsichords, serpentine horns and miniature violins, called *pochettes*, which dancing masters once carried in their pockets. He decided to assemble the kind of modern orchestra which could most closely approximate the sound of these instruments. "Polyphonic music began to be played at this time," Tiomkin recalled before he began to compose. "The human ear tried to expand its range. People began to hear lower notes. The spinet, for example, had very little range, so the harpsichord came in."

Tiomkin returned to Hollywood, and between May and September of 1950 he composed, orchestrated and directed sixty minutes of background music for the 113-minute film. The final score calls for an orchestra consisting of a harpsichord, two or three harps of different sizes, a large woodwind section, flutes in unusual combinations, oboes and bassoons, two occarinas, French horns, violins and violas, cellos, xylophones, chimes, mandolins, battle drums and lutes. The final effect was enthusiastically praised by film and music critics, and the score remains one of Tiomkin's best.

But it is José Ferrer's performance which really triumphs. It remains the role with which he has been most identified, too: his manner is quick with wit and sadness. He swaggers, boasts and covers his shame with a veneer of braggadocio. His rich bass voice conveys every nuance of the poetic and philosophical speeches, and there is a sense of loneliness that is almost palpable. In the duel with the meddler, during which he flashes a rapier and composes a ballade, in the fight with a band of ruffians in the street, and in his wooing of the youthful Roxane and in his death scene, he is not only an actor performing, he is an actor playing a character who is himself always performing. Ferrer suggests that there lurks in Cyrano a psychological need to compensate for his ugliness by being a querulous swashbuckler. Around and through Rostand's arch romanticism he creates a deeply human soul who in fact lives in a decaying and grotesque society that seems to have concentrated all its cruelties into his dreadful deformity.

Mala Powers and William Prince.

"When it bleeds—the Red Sea!"

Yet in spite of the ingenious sets, rich musical score and commendable leading performance, *Cyrano de Bergerac* is not saved from a fatal lethargy. The vast cuts made in the text are not, finally, vast enough; the talk is endless and endlessly florid, and the intimacy of the film mercilessly discloses just how antique and flat the work is. A whole generation of students probably struggled through it, but today the picture seems bloated, confined and unmoving, and the technical experiments and memorable performance seem somehow tainted and diminished.

CHAPTER 6

"There's something emotionally wrong here. . . ."—
Death of a Salesman, 1951

With the film production of Arthur Miller's play *Death of a Salesman*, a pattern seemed to emerge in Stanley Kramer's career. This was the third of seven plays he brought to the screen, and in retrospect he has some regrets about this: "I have built in my own mind now a kind of defense mechanism against the translation of produced plays into films. That may be because I have not been lucky with them." In spite of the Ferrer Academy Award for *Cyrano de Bergerac*, in fact, that film brought forth from the public what the producer himself called a "disastrous reaction." This occurred simultaneously with a new development in Kramer's career.

"The reason I started to bring some plays to the screen was really almost accidental. As an independent producer, I had doled out shares of ownership in my company. I was making about one film a year, I was the boss and I called all the shots. My partners, George Glass and Carl Foreman—and earlier, Herbert Baker—and my lawyer, Sam Zagon, said, 'If you're making only one film a year, where's the Promised Land?'

"At that time a man named Sam Katz was with Paramount

Pictures, and he wanted to be the most important executive in the film business. He saw me and considered me a new wunderkind, the new Irving G. Thalberg. Most of all, he saw me as a tool, a wedge through whom he could reintroduce himself to the industry—he had been dismissed from MGM. So he came to me and offered to give me and my group a sum of money if we included him. Because he was thick with Harry Cohn at Columbia, he promised we could make a multipicture deal at that studio!

"I resented this deeply and was suspicious of Katz. But my partners saw the chance to make a dozen pictures in two years as a great source of financial security. I agreed to go along with

Cameron Mitchell, Fredric March, Kevin McCarthy.

their wishes only if, at the end of a three-year period, we could be free of each other.

"You see, the bickering had started already. And soon six or seven of the people working with me were to be subpoenaed by the House Un-American Activities Committee. I was regarded as the professional liberal voice at the time, but I had some social ideas that some men who were themselves subpoenaed considered communist-inspired! They accused me of stealing their ideas and making them into films, and in living-room dialogues I was called a Red baiter, because I didn't have anything to do with their tactics! Some day I'm going to tell this whole story in my memoirs. . . ."

During the latter part of the 1940s and through the early part of the 1950s, the notorious House Un-American Activities Committee, which was born at the time of the country's severest anti-Communist terror, spread its mantle over Hollywood as well as the rest of the country. Writers, directors and actors who were believed sympathetic to Communist ideas and ideals, or who had any leftist associations, were summarily dismissed from jobs and found themselves unable to work anywhere in America. Many found some work by writing under assumed names, many had to go abroad to work. When the first chairman of this committee, J. Parnell Thomas, was imprisoned for embezzlement, the power shifted to Senator Joseph McCarthy, on whose staff was a young man named Richard Nixon.

Soon a blacklist was circulated, listing the names of artists to be excluded from Hollywood employment. Studios cooperated with this blacklist (although they vigorously denied its existence) until relatively recently in the history of the industry.

Stanley Kramer's involvement in these unfortunate proceedings—filled as they were with paranoia, selfishness, betrayal—was never more than marginal. His partner, Carl Foreman, ran afoul of the committee, was repudiated by Kramer (who subsequently bought Foreman's share of partnership in the Kramer company) and dismissed by him. After contributing screenplays for *So This Is New York, Champion, Home of the Brave, The Men, Cyrano de Bergerac* and *High Noon,* Foreman worked in Britain, where his most notable achievement was as collaborator on the script for

The Bridge on the River Kwai, although his name does not appear on American release prints. Foreman has remained in England, where he has written, produced and directed films.

Edward Dmytryk, on the other hand, was one of the so-called "Hollywood Ten"—a group who, when called before the committee to give evidence, defied its authority. Dmytryk was cited for contempt of Congress, dismissed by RKO Pictures, and departed for England, where he made three films. Returning to America for passport renewal, he was arrested, fined one thousand dollars and given a prison term. In 1950, he appeared once again before the committee, recanted and was at once hired by Kramer.

"At any rate, I agreed to undertake this massive multipicture deal. I agreed to play the part of a new Zanuck. So Foreman and Glass became my associate producers, and I brought in directors of all kinds. The most brilliant one was probably Irving Reis, who directed *The Four Poster* for me. I used Fred Zinnemann twice after *The Men*, and Laslo Benedek for *Death of Salesman* and *The Wild One*. I brought back Richard Fleischer after *So This Is New York*, and had Edward Dmytryk direct four films. Dmytryk wound up on both sides of the political fence at the end. . . .

"To be honest, I chose to do a number of plays because it took some of the responsibility away from the people who, in my own arrogance, I didn't completely trust—writers, for example. Plays are a safe commodity, and that's why I chose to produce lots of them in their screen versions. I knew what they were, and the screenplays turned out to be, basically, just adaptations.

"This was the least rewarding time of my life, to tell the truth. I was unhappy every minute."

Kramer's first film for Columbia under this cinematic new deal couldn't have alleviated his gloom very much: the oppressive and depressing *Death of a Salesman* had been highly praised on Broadway. It is among the best-known and most frequently performed American plays, and is given frequent revivals in major cities throughout the world. Humorless and relentlessly gray, it tells the story of a traveling salesman who wanted to "make it big" all his life and who passed on empty dreams of success to his sons. After thirty-four years selling for the same company, Willy Loman confronts the replicas of his own delusions in the wasted lives of his grown sons, and when the emptiness of his values begins to press on him, he careens toward madness. Despondent, he yields to the hallucinatory voice of his late brother, who urges him to suicide.

The play has been called an American tragedy—even, by some, *the* American tragedy. This appraisal is based, perhaps, on the human sadness which the play describes. But it's also based on an improper understanding of what constitutes tragedy. It would be more accurate to say that what happens to Willy is *pathetic* and, as his wife, Linda, indicates, "attention must be paid."

While attention is paid to the slow disintegration of a quite unnoble (not exactly ignoble, but surely unnoble) character, however, it must also be paid to the fundamental thesis of the play and film, which is not entirely wholly satisfactory in the rendering. Willy Loman seems more of a "case" than a man suffering from an authentic tragic flaw. He has always been a small, unimaginative man, pathetically driven to follow an image of himself that never really existed. He is, in other words, a man without the heroic qualities that would make his disintegration and downfall authentically tragic. "Putting upon his puny shoulders the burden of Mr. Miller's large and indignant theme," wrote an anonymous New York critic at the time, "results in a kind of overwriting, and now and then overstatement."

Miller is concerned with the undoing of a man's soul by the dreams of fraudulent glory and success to which most of us Americans have been encouraged: financial success, family and social legacies, and the benefits of being not only liked but, as Willy says, "well liked" by those who are in a position to give a boost up the ladder. Miller's play thus indicted with bitterness all the presumptions about the fabric of American middle-class life. No doubt the play was considered stern stuff when it premiered on Broadway in 1949: a complacency was setting into the gut of postwar America. Free enterprise, success and the ascent up the ladder of social and financial success were assumed to be our most valuable assets. This grim parable shocked

Mildred Dunnock rehearses with director Laslo Benedek.

theatregoers, revived the theatrical tradition of the play with a social conscience, and, with the mesmerizing performances of Lee J. Cobb and Mildred Dunnock, gave bite and substance to a dark and unpopular issue. Unlike the same author's later work *The Crucible*, which raised the question of freedom of the individual conscience and provided a fairly clear parallel to the McCarthy witch hunts, *Salesman* is emotionally sterile because of its lack of economy. It does not justify the stridency of its scenes between the father and sons, nor of Willy's inevitable mental collapse, since it does not show us enough of the characters' inner life, nor of their fundamental psychology.

Laslo Benedek's direction rightly concentrated, therefore, on the performances, and the marvelously expressive features of the principals were all lit with exquisite skill by the cameraman, Franz Planer. It would have been impossible to maintain Miller's dense content and claustrophobia and simultaneously change the play by opening it up. What we have, therefore, is simply a filmed play. This bestows the asset of documenting fine performances, and the liabilities of a certain photographic stasis.

The film overcomes this stasis three or four times with some brilliant technique, and it is astonishing to realize that this technique did not become a model for other films in this regard. There are several flashbacks to earlier days in the life of the Loman family: when the boys were in high school, when life seemed simpler and the complication of Willy's inflated ego was not yet quite so crippling and when, tragically, his son found him in a cheap hotel with a prostitute. These moments are handled without the customary and clichéd flashback devices— the rippling dissolve or the montage of calendar pages.

In its seventeen scenes, the play jumped between past and present quickly and smoothly, using convenient and traditional lighting cues for such changes. But Kramer wanted something different and insisted from the start on the avoidance of stereotype. With designer Rudolph Sternad and editors Harry Gerstad and William Lyon, a clever but difficult solution was devised. The time wanderings of Willy's confused mind are conveyed by means of juxtaposed sets, elongated perspectives, eerily apposite lighting effects and subtle gradations in lens apertures. Willy, for example, goes back twenty years by walking a few steps: the camera dollies close to his face, there is an imperceptible cut, then the camera reverses and the scene has changed. Or, entering his kitchen at night for a snack, the flick of a light switch illuminates the backyard of the Loman home years earlier. Or again, two carefully matched cuts to Willy on the floor of a restaurant washroom transfer the scene to a hotel room many years earlier. These transitions are handled with unusual skill, each cut matched so flawlessly that when the film is studied at an editing table, it's necessary to watch the sequences frame by frame to appreciate just how seamlessly the changes are made, and how slightly the camera angles change the angle of the person photographed, so that the background and setting seem to alter magically! There is never, in any of these examples, any loss of pacing or tension, any flagging of interest.

Fredric March, who had originally turned down the offer to create the leading role on Broadway, gives a fine performance. In fact it's almost too fine: his sensitive and intelligent face, his blazing eyes and throaty guffaw make a viewer aware of a forced characterization, not of a character arising organically from an actor's preconsciousness. He is simply too smart a presence to portray so naïve a character. His Willy is extravagantly loony, and it's really a kind of ironic relief when he smashes his car and dies.

"I made a mistake in wanting March for the role," Kramer admitted. "He was a wonderful actor, but there's something emotionally wrong here. I was making six or seven films that year, however, and I was rushed and frustrated, and I chose March because I loved and respected him, and knew he'd turned down the Broadway version."

There was no mistake, however, about Mildred Dunnock repeating her stage portrayal of Linda Loman. With her thin, pained face, virtually limned with the years of quiet inner struggle and anxiety over her failed husband, and her wide eyes filled with the acceptance of hopelessness, the actress turned a soap-opera stereotype into a warm and living person, highly individualized and never incredible. There's a particularly poignant moment when she berates the two boys for their insensitivity to their father's condition: "He's not the finest character," she cries, her high-pitched, metallic voice edged with bitterness. "But he's a human being, and a terrible thing is happening to him. So attention must be paid!" It's perhaps the most arresting line of play and film, and Miss Dunnock delivers it with a glaring, demanding challenge that never masks her own grief. The simple nobility of Linda Loman lingers in the mind long after the film ends. It is a performance that deserves to be ranked with Sara Allgood's Mrs. Boyle in Hitchcock's *Juno and the Paycock* and Jane Darwell's Ma Joad in Ford's *The Grapes of Wrath*. It is a figure full of grandeur and compassion and

Mildred Dunnock and Fredric March, during a break in shooting.

humanity, one who contains in microcosm much of the feeling that is elsewhere lacking in both play and film.

"*Death of a Salesman* destroyed me emotionally when I first saw it," Stanley Kramer told me. "The reason for this is the fact that I was raised by my grandparents. My grandfather often said to me, 'Always have friends.' He was a traveling salesman and he also said to me, 'I go to Hartford and I have it *made.*' He was really the prototype of Willy Loman. I was eighteen before I realized how foolish all this was. So I went to see the play years later and it really cut me off at the knees. That kind of thinking isn't at all important. What's important is to take a stand on something."

CHAPTER 7

Offense: Actor—
My Six Convicts, 1952

Films about prisons and convents always reach a wide audience. There's guaranteed box office in entering behind forbidden walls, penetrating the secrets of a sexually segregated society, peering into the routine of special kinds of men and women. There's also something reassuring about such films: we're not as restricted as the characters in them, a fact which instantly becomes precious as we depart the theatre.

When the subject of a movie is prisons and prisoners, there's bound to be a lot of shouting, snarling speech, banging on bars and general mayhem on the sound track. Depending on when the film is produced, there's also usually a certain attitude about the criminal and society. Other films, like *The Big House, Brute Force, Duffy of San Quentin, Cell 2455 Death Row* attempted a tidy balance between conservatism ("We must keep society safe from these dangerous men") and a healthy progressivism ("Something must be done about deplorable prison conditions, which make men more criminal than before they entered"). Today, of course, after *Fortune and Men's Eyes* (1967) and *Short Eyes* (1977), we're accustomed to harrowing, bloody depictions of the horrors of prison life—uncosmeticized stories of human exploitation and official indifference. The films of yesterday only hinted at such quotidian realities when they were aware of them at all.

(Perhaps the most notable depictions of life-style exploitation, ironically, were the films about women's prisons. *So Young, So Bad* and *Women in Chains* were two of the nastiest examples, but they were so shrill and offensive that now they offer themselves as ready-made for parody—and were, in fact, parodied in a recent minor play, *Women Behind Bars*.)

Occasionally a very strong prison scene stands out in a film

John Beal and Harry Morgan.

otherwise concerned with a small- or big-time crook, and it's usually a scene connected with a grimly upsetting treatment of capital punishment. It's hard to shake off the memory of James Cagney, shrieking (offscreen) his fear of imminent death by electric chair in *Angels with Dirty Faces*. It was a double twist, a deliberate feigning of cowardice to prevent becoming a cult hero to younger thugs—but it was also possible that his barking façade had finally cracked, and we were seeing, for the first time, the man behind the tough exterior. Susan Hayward made the blood run cold—and secured an Academy Award for herself— during the final moments of *I Want to Live*. She was strapped into a gas chamber and breathed the lethal fumes, and the scene took the picture from crime melodrama to anticapital punishment tract.

For any filmmaker interested in some deeper sociological perspective, therefore, it's ready-made in this type of film. Dr. Donald Powell Wilson had published, in 1951, a best seller about his work at Leavenworth Federal Penitentiary in the early 1930s, for the United States Public Health Service. His book told of the extraordinary incidents surrounding his three-year period as staff psychologist, testing inmates for special skills and working toward a program of vocational rehabilitation. The prisoners, it seemed, tested and helped him as much as he tested and helped them.

By the 1950s, a prison psychologist was still unknown in many places. This fact touched Stanley Kramer's sense of social responsibility—and he also felt that the book had possibilities for a commercially successful film. "The prison psychologist was a hot idea for that time," he recalled in 1977. "Not all places had one, you know. I know the film seems outdated today and a little naïve. But I don't mind doing something that seems a little outdated, if the main theme holds up." In discussing this film, Kramer was defensive about it from the start—and with good reason, for the picture, in spite of noble intention, is peppered with stereotypes. Had there not come later films like *Fortune and Men's Eyes* and *Short Eyes*, perhaps *My Six Convicts* would remain entertaining and even enlightening, although I doubt it—the film generalizes and whitewashes and romanticizes prisons and prisoners. Since films have got much tougher and grimier and the public much more aware about the truth, this 1952 movie seems an unregenerate product of a pale society. With *Eight Iron Men* and *The Juggler* it forms a trio of extravagantly dull films which give no indication of the sort of class product Kramer contributed, the same years, with *High Noon* and *The Member of the Wedding.*

The problem with *My Six Convicts* is that it is a 104-minute concatenation of trite incidents involving trite characters. With one exception, all the prisoners are depicted as lovable rascals who can be won over if they're just trusted a little, treated like men, given some sense of responsibility and approached as if

The doctor and his six convicts, in a mess.

they were all fair targets for easy rehabilitation. Even Gilbert Roland, who can look sinister with little difficulty, turns out to be an attractive, wisecracking Latin (with the eye-rolling name of "Punch Pinero"), and at any moment you expect to see him leap on a horse and rustle up some cattle, return with a pretty girl and a good cigar and seem bored. Among the other convicts, only Millard Mitchell, as a sort of poor man's Charles Bickford, manages some interesting moments. He's cast as a safecracker, and the warden recruits his talents to open a jammed vault door in the bank of a nearby town. In return for this favor, Mitchell gets a twenty-four-hour furlough, and the sequences—clearly calculated to give the audience a furlough from the prison, too— have a breezy, good-natured humor. Henry Morgan (who soon after changed his name to Harry Morgan, to avoid further confusion with the radio/television comedian who had appeared in Kramer's *So This Is New York*), plays the unregenerate Dawson, who plans the desperate prison break at the film's finale. He snarls darkly and convincingly, which is about all that is asked.

As the prisoners' doctor-psychiatrist, John Beal projects a bland middle-American earnestness. Later in his career, Beal developed an interesting theatrical talent; recently he played the elder Tyrone in a revival of O'Neill's *A Long Day's Journey into Night*. But after a series of insistently charming roles in the 1930s, his look of boyish innocence was becoming a handicap. Here, he seems to have entered some new realm of hypernaïveté, and so it's hard to take seriously his initial discomfort with the prisoners and, as well, his final success in winning them over to himself and rehabilitation.

To direct the film, Kramer chose Hugo Fregonese, a young Argentine actor-writer-director who had come to Hollywood in 1945 from an independent group called Argentina Associated Artists. The scenarist, who could do no worse, was Michael Blankfort.

The cast and crew of the film spent nine days at San Quentin, California's medium-security prison. Warden Clinton Duffy (who himself was immortalized in *Duffy of San Quentin*) had grown up inside the walls of that institution, as son of a guard. His first official act—and a historic one it was, too—had been to abolish the ugly cells for solitary confinement. Duffy was pleased, probably for reasons of public relations, to welcome the Kramer crew to the prison; it may well have been in deference to the warden's constructive reputation that prison conditions seem far more humane than we know them to be.

San Quentin guards were the extras for the film, and the real convicts had to be photographed in the distant background, so there would be no possibility of their real identity becoming known. This accounts for the conspicuous lack of depth focus, or use of the Garutso Balanced Lens, about which everyone was so pleased in the making of *Cyrano de Bergerac*. For the members of the cast, the nine days seemed like months, and the atmosphere was often tense. Shortly after shooting the scene of

John Beal, at San Quentin.

the attempted break, for example, two inmates tried to make life imitate art. Like the sequence, however, it was a futile gesture.

Actors and technicians had their hands stamped with invisible ink each morning on arrival and were carefully checked on departure so there would be no problem about who was leaving. Each was issued a prison identification card, and in the space marked "offense" was printed the word "actor." There seemed to have been more tension and humor during the location shooting than in the finished film. . . .

Before the release of *My Six Convicts*, Stanley Kramer had written: "To make a place for himself, the independent producer has to *add* something to the industry's output. He cannot be a small-scale echo of what the majors are doing much better than he." That is the ultimate reason for the failure of the film. Mark Hellinger had produced a brutally realistic prison drama in 1947—*Brute Force*, directed by Jules Dassin and strikingly photographed by William Daniels—and, until the brutality overreached itself in the 1960s and 1970s, *Brute Force* remained perhaps the best in this subgenre of conflict.

Arthur Franz as the sniper.

CHAPTER 8

A Dandy Defrocked—
The Sniper, 1952

Stanley Kramer sponsored touchy subjects in his films. He didn't avoid them in life, either. After *My Six Convicts,* he hired as director a man who'd recently been jailed.

"I was blacklisted after my film *Crossfire* in 1947," recalled Edward Dmytryk, one of the so-called Hollywood Ten. "I had made a couple of films in England, but couldn't find work in America. In 1950, I returned and made a second appearance before Congress, was sentenced to jail and came out the day before Thanksgiving. It was then that Stanley Kramer contacted me and offered me the chance to direct several pictures for him. As soon as I felt able to work, he signed me to a four-picture deal."

His first film back in Hollywood was *The Sniper,* scripted by Harry Brown from a story by the film's associate producers, Edward and Edna Anhalt. It's the story of Eddie Miller (Arthur Franz), a psychopathic woman hater whose complex, troubled past has turned him into a sniper-assassin of young women. At first we see him fighting his compulsion to kill: he deliberately burns his hand in an effort to be committed to a hospital's psychiatric ward, but the doctors are too busy to inquire into the reasons for his "accident." From this point, he and his victims—a nightclub pianist, a girl he meets in a bar, a woman he sees on television, a girl he meets in a park—are all destined for tragedy. Led by Lieutenant Kafka (Adolphe Menjou) and helped by the wise city psychologist, Dr. Kent (Richard Kiley), the police track him down, and he is taken alive.

Because of the timeliness of its theme and the keenness of its technique, *The Sniper* is a consistently interesting film. With the recent Los Angeles sniper shootings still fresh in the public mind, the Kramer project could have been merely a cheap thriller, designed to exploit the public's fears. Instead, it's a discerning study of a madman who emerges neither as an abhorrent monster nor as a character to be coddled. Nor is the complexity of the theme oversimplified by means of easy textbook answers to the causes of the young man's aberrant condition.

"You'll catch him," says the psychologist wearily, as the search continues. "And they'll kill him and everybody will forget about him—until the next one comes along. Then it'll start all over again. Listen, a few years ago, a man was arrested in New York for the murder of a child. A judge of the State Supreme Court estimated that he had undoubtedly killed fifteen others. They executed him for one, but fifteen were dead. This isn't an isolated case. It happens everywhere. Put these people away when they're first caught. Get a law passed!"

The film does not go further: no alternatives to police action are outlined, nor is there any new plan for the kind of psychiatric treatment for this type of deranged killer who appears in society all too frequently. It simply pleads for the institutionalization of them—not their imprisonment which, as we have seen in more recent history, simply leads to an earlier release and the likelihood of the repetition of such crimes. The message, at the end, seems muddled, but that's perhaps because the issue is a complex one, involving legal, medical and psychiatric studies.

Parallel to the psychiatric theme is a strong and tense police story, however, which has compassion for the sickness in the

On the set—Edward Dmytryk, director, wearing zippered jacket.

Frank Faylen, Gerald Mohr and Adolphe Menjou.

man's soul and for the tragic victims, but is also tough and multileveled in the manhunt account. This aspect of the picture seemed especially to have appealed to Dmytryk, and it is easy to understand the reason. In spite of the obvious differences between the situations of a deranged killer and that of a political outcast, they have in common the fact that they both experience the force of official power, and finish at the mercy of a society which must defend itself from those it deems hostile. "This was the first intelligent treatment of the hunt for a homicidal maniac," the director said. "And since I dream and read and rehearse in terms of the film's cuts, I tried to preserve pacing in order to clarify without oversimplification, and to build suspense without forcing the film's climaxes arbitrarily." It is this careful attention to rhythms that makes *The Sniper* a film that does not have a morbid tone, despite its grim subject: there is no accent on the sensational aspects, and the film is played for the eerie deadliness of its facts, not for hysteria.

Much of this has to do with the sharp and sensitive direction, and the photography of San Francisco by Burnett Guffey: the film looks as though it were happening around the corner from anywhere. "I was surprised to hear from several university students," Dmytryk said, "that I am considered one of the founders of the *film noir* in America. At that time, I didn't even know what *film noir* was!" There's no doubt, however, that the picture has some of that style—dark settings, odd (almost surrealistic, or at least expressionistic) lighting and angles for a tale stressing dark mental passageways that are as gloomy and forbidding as the bayside streets of San Francisco.

The casting is creative, too—and this was entirely Kramer's. Arthur Franz had the crew cut, boyish good looks and clean appearance that had established him earlier as the sort of chap you'd expect in a television series' family. But here, in the title role, his dark eyes and brooding sulkiness are caught by the camera—almost subliminal reflections darting from his eyes—and there's nevertheless a softness and pathos that surface at just the right moments. Dmytryk recalled the extraordinarily malleable features of this actor, which were put to good use in two later Kramer-Dmytryk works. Franz's career was never a particularly exciting one—he was low-keyed, and his presence and acting style looked a bit flaccid and underdeveloped next to Marlon Brando, to whom every young male was inevitably compared at this time. But there was an interesting and attractive ambiguity in his manner, and the director exploited it, especially in the opening and concluding scenes.

These scenes are remarkable, and they stick in the mind long after the detective-story aspects are forgotten. The film opens at night with a long panning shot in the sniper's apartment. The camera, at a low angle, leisurely passes from an empty bed, past a window to a chest of drawers, to an open door, and finally comes to rest on the troubled face of the sniper. This cinematic gesture is reversed at the film's conclusion when, barricaded with his weapons against the arresting officers, he is finally taken, bloodlessly. The reversal now of the opening shot reveals not his anxious features, but an odd look of relief, as if the terrible ordeal were just now ending for him, too.

The generally subtle and understated camera movements are punctuated by several aptly startling ones. The director is especially proud of the moment in which, after the sniper meets a girl in a bar, he follows her to her home. The camera stays outside. One sustained violin note is heard on the sound track until the shattering moment when the gunshot is heard, and the next murder—this one entirely unexpected and unprepared by the fabric of the sequence—pierces the sound track. "We simply overlapped it," Dmytryk explained. "We looped the note's sound so that it could be heard for a longer time than a violinist could play it." This is part of the film's clear concern for what the director called psychological suggestion through the visual. "It all seems very obvious to me," he said, "but I guess some people aren't clear on what effect they want until they get to the shooting of the scene. I know what I want before we ever arrive on the set."

Another key moment occurs in the sequence in which a building painter spots the sniper on a roof and shouts to the police. He is gunned down by the sniper, and the camera follows the trajectory of the paint can—not the painter—as it falls to the ground and splatters, an explosion of white against the gray street. It's an isolation of detail that simply and effectively conveys the idea of plunge into chaos, and the subversion of normal life.

The Sniper is remarkable, too, for the curiously satisfying casting of Adolphe Menjou as Lieutenant Kafka. Menjou had been a dapper leading man in the twenties who was perhaps the prototype of the polished, sharp-spoken character-actor version of William Powell. In this role, he is not, as Gilbert Seldes

Arthur Franz, over the rooftops of San Francisco.

pointed out in *The Saturday Review of Literature* when the film was released, a bigot committed to routine, but is experienced in it, and he is compelled to defend the routine against the frightened and angry citizens who demand an arrest. "His turning to the city psychologist," wrote Seldes, "and his slow conversion to the idea of preventive action are a tribute not so much to the force of circumstance (the failure of the routines) as to the force of intellect, and that is rare in the movies."

"*The Daily Worker* knocked hell out of me for using Adolphe Menjou," Dmytryk recalled. "Menjou was one of Hollywood's leading Red baiters, one of the most reactionary men who ever lived. This meant, to them, that I'd sold my soul to the devil and gone far right. Which is ridiculous, because I'm not that way at all. Menjou was simply an excellent actor, and I knew he could play a down-on-the-heels cop with old clothes that were too baggy for him. I wanted to cross-cast him." And so he did. It was one of Menjou's last really memorable performances, and a strangely effective one for the actor who had long been regarded as Hollywood's best-dressed man.

"I loved making that film," said Edward Dmytryk. "It was astounding: we made it in eighteen days—and that included the location work in San Francisco and the stage work in Hollywood. We were rushed. But everything seemed to work well."

Everything did indeed work well.

The Sniper is more than a facile cops-and-robbers melodrama, and less than a pretentious psychological case history and a plea for social reform. It's a film that emphasizes reason and intelligence, and it has those qualities in its production values as in its themes.

Gary Cooper and Grace Kelly.

CHAPTER 9

Harry Cohn Steals a Masterpiece—
High Noon, 1952

"We already had the title—it was one we dreamed up for the working title while we were secretly preparing *Home of the Brave* a couple of years earlier. So when Carl Foreman suggested a rousing little Western thriller he'd read in a magazine, we finally had the chance to use it!" Stanley Kramer was recalling the origins of one of the classics of the modern screen, *High Noon*. "It was based on John Cunningham's story 'The Tin Star,' and we had to buy the rights to that. So Foreman went and bought it for us, because if I had negotiated the deal, we would have had to pay a whole lot more. As it was, Foreman got it for something ridiculous, like about $25,000.

"We made the film on the Columbia ranch, called it *High Noon* and had to fight everybody all during production and post-production. Everyone thought Cooper was too old to be playing a marshal. And no one had heard of Grace Kelly or Katy Jurado. Besides, we weren't sure what kind of Western this was going to be at all. It was such a quiet film, really. And it wasn't expensive, either. So everybody got nervous. . . ."

From such humble beginnings came one of the most admired

and controversial films of the decade. It's a story in which very little happens, and a great deal is implied. Marshal Will Kane (Gary Cooper) is about to retire from his job in Hadleyville (population four hundred). His young bride, Amy (Grace Kelly), a Quaker, deplores violence, and so the couple have decided to retire to another town and open a small store. At the same time, however, they learn that Frank Miller (Ian MacDonald) is returning to town, seeking vengeance: the marshal had arrested and sent him up for murder five year earlier. At first, Kane decides to leave town, heeding the advice of the townsfolk. He returns, however, believing that the gang will hunt him down even if he should leave the town, which will itself then very likely come under the deadly, controlling vengeance of the gang. Three members of Miller's gang are in town already, gloating, awaiting the boss's arrival on the noon train and planning their revenge against the marshal.

Kane turns to the people for help in forming a posse. One by one, however, they disappoint him. Each man has an excuse: some, like the young deputy (Lloyd Bridges), turn away, jealous of his position and authority; others believe any conflict with the gang will end tragically for them; still others flee in simple cowardice; even Amy does not remain, unable, by virtue of her strong pacific religious convictions, to understand his code of honor.

High noon approaches. After writing his last will, Kane goes to meet the desperadoes alone. In the final shoot-out, he's victorious, and is in fact helped by his wife, who's driven back to his side by her love and admiration. She's also been sternly counseled by Helen Ramirez (Katy Jurado), an older, wiser woman who was once Will's mistress, then mistress of the murderer, and now has a dubious affair with the young deputy. Helen is, as John McCarten wrote in *The New Yorker*, "a woman who has certainly lived mighty fully in a settlement of four hundred souls."

At the end, the four villains lie dead, and the marshal and his bride at once leave town, silently. Contemptuous of their fickle loyalties, Will throws to the ground his tin star.

Kramer's previous films had all been "inside movies"—pictures which, for reasons financial as well as thematic, emphasized interiors and cramped, enclosed spaces. Even *Home of the Brave,* which occurs largely in flashback on an island jungle, has a restricted, theatrical feeling, and the battlefield sequences of *Cyrano de Bergerac* are simply the necessary breathing spaces, inserts to another fundamentally theatrical exercise. But in *High Noon* Kramer ventured into the wide open spaces—although the film, which benefits hugely from inspired direction by Fred Zinnemann, does not, in the final analysis, give a typically Western feeling of expanse, of journey, of the vastness of the

As the clock approaches noon . . .

land, which is usually the setting for a big story about conflicting forces.

In fact, it is not easy to restrict this film to the genre of the Western, for on examination there is much that is uncharacteristic of that form. It is, as Kramer pointed out, a very quiet film: there is very little violence (just two brief fistfights) until the final, inevitable shoot-out. And, far from endorsing the comfortable view of pious prairie pioneers, there's a sharply critical attitude toward the supposedly simple folk of a century ago: they're shown to be just like people of any era, capable of a pathetic cowardice and of abandoning their loyalties as quickly as their Sunday go-to-meeting clothes. Nor are there tribes of savage Indians lurking just behind a boulder (as in John Ford's classic *Stagecoach,* for example); there is no vast panorama in which men and animals move in an epic journey (as in Howard Hawks's *Red River*); there is no sense of spectacle or of colorful, unspoilt nature.

The Hadleyville of *High Noon* is thus no romanticized refuge from the evils of encroaching civilization, which is part of the structure of the Western. The saloon here is not the community meeting place, but an area where petty jealousies and prejudices and cowardices stand out clearly. The marshal is not heroic by conscious choice: he sees his position as the only possibility and is not above weeping, when alone in his office, at the hopelessness of his situation. As played with a sense of accidental heroism by Gary Cooper, Will Kane emerges as a man whose options have dwindled like his friends. He finally confronts his enemies with the kind of stoical acceptance of the probable outcome that suggests that his life, now that he's been abandoned by wife and comrades, is worth much less in any case. *High Noon*, then, is not a Western about sheepmen against cattlemen, or ranchers against oilmen, or rustlers against settlers. It's a film about interiority, and about that quiet point deep inside the soul where the act of heroism is the logical and perhaps sometimes the only possible outcome of the habit of being true to oneself. It's probably the most un-Western Western ever made.

"Of course a lot of people are entitled to credit—Fred Zinnemann most of all, who's a brilliant director," said Kramer. "And I had a very good film editor, Elmo Williams. He said in a recent piece that when he showed me the first cut of the film I was so aghast I didn't know what to do with it. Well, I was certainly aghast—there were problems—but I knew what to do with it. I was the one who did the final cut of this film—I alone, and I stand by whatever flaws or virtues the film has to this day."

High Noon was produced when Kramer was working as an independent at Columbia Pictures, although this film was to be released by United Artists. "I was editing *High Noon* at another independent studio, at night and on weekends. Since I was at Columbia doing other films Monday through Friday, Harry Cohn"—head of Columbia—"summoned me to his office and said he wanted to see the film and maybe buy it. I refused and told him he wouldn't understand it. Naturally, he didn't like that very much!

"Three weeks later, on a Sunday morning, I went to the independent studio to finish the editing. Dimitri Tiomkin, who was composing the score for the film at that time, met me at the gate and asked me why I'd relented and let Cohn see the film. I was shocked, since I'd done no such thing! It turned out that Cohn had sent his limousine, with phony instructions 'from Stanley Kramer' to pick up the film and bring it to Cohn's home for private screening, then return it to this studio before I arrived. Monday morning I went to Cohn's office at Columbia and called him a thief. He shrugged and said, 'It doesn't matter, since the film's a piece of crap anyway.' "

The "piece of crap" won a handful of Academy awards and was an international success.

In the first cut of the film, there had been no music at all. Kramer then commissioned Tiomkin and lyricist Ned Washington to replace the frequent gaps of silence with an appropriate song. Their first attempt was unacceptable. To show Tiomkin what kind of ballad he had in mind, Kramer then took an old Burl Ives recording of an American folk song, played it for mood music and ran the picture for Tiomkin. Soon after, "Do Not Forsake Me, Oh My Darlin' " was submitted.

"The preview, held in Inglewood, was a disaster," Kramer admitted. "There was a fifteen-minute scene in which the deputy and his girl are outside the town. It was totally extraneous and didn't work at all. But the worst thing was the recurrence of the ballad: it was used at every silent bridge—every time Cooper walks through the town, from place to place. The fourth time they heard the ballad, the audience started to laugh, which got me nervous, because I knew there were at least six more uses of it coming up! So right after this disastrous preview, I told Tiomkin to cut down the use of the ballad, and I knew I also had more cutting-room work to do. Tex Ritter sang the song at the beginning of the film, and as a reprise at the end, and we wound up with only four uses of the song during the film. We also cut the out-of-town sequence. Finally, everything came together."

(The ballad, in fact, was one of the great hits of the decade. Frankie Laine, who recorded the commercial release version, gave it the highest and most elaborate compliment he'd ever given to a tune: "That's a bitch of a number!")

The running time of the film (about eighty-six minutes) is the span of time in which the story occurs—from ten-thirty until noon. To keep a sense of pacing in this really quite actionless story, there are no dissolves. The passage of time is indicated by frequent cutting to various clock hands, closing like scissor blades toward noon. Particularly effective are the shots of deserted streets in broad daylight: it's a kind of inhabited ghost town that Zinnemann created. The streets are dusty paths which seem to lead nowhere. And the low-angle shots of the empty railroad track, on which the noon train will shortly bring its deadly passenger, is the film's compelling substitute for the marauding Indians, grasped holsters or the continuous stereotypical mounting of horses—conceits one encounters in so many lesser Westerns.

"The entire picture is the result of a team effort," Fred Zinnemann told me. "The visual concept of the film, however, was entirely mine: included in it are the railroad tracks stretching to the horizon, symbolizing the menace; the restless figure of the marshal moving about the town in his search for help; and the idea of letting the action slow down by degrees during the approach of the train by gradually increasing the camera's speed was also part of my concept, which is homogeneous and logically constructed. The film was indeed brilliantly edited by Elmo Williams, but no one, including him, has the right to claim creating any part of it."

The film's single most memorable shot is that which begins as a close-up of Cooper, alone in the street, about to meet his enemies. Without a cut, the camera rises in a single, breathtaking reverse high-crane shot, thus stressing the man's physical and psychological solitude, abandoned, certainly frightened, but implacable in his decision to confront destiny. It is this single shot which indicates the major concern of the film—the theme of honor defended. "This shot, and the various shots of the clocks were part of my concept, too," said Zinnemann.

The marshal becomes here the prototype of all solitary men who have to face an issue while others rationalize themselves out of it. Those who had celebrated his wedding and praised him for saving their town now manufacture a batch of handy reasons for refusing to help. The theme of honor is poignantly located, too, in the problem faced by the young bride, who must wrestle with the dilemma of fidelity to her conscience and to her husband. Kane's former woman tells Amy where the right path lies: "You must stand by him, Mrs. Kane. You must because no one else will." A bit facile, perhaps, but in context it works.

The courage which the film examines happens almost by accident: the community cowardice becomes the glum cyclorama against which heroism emerges by default, as if the town had to come up with *some* human gesture of grandeur. The citizens of Hadleyville, says the uncompromising script, desperately want law and order. And this, it seems to me, is the point of the last strange gesture of the film—which, by the way, angered many critics and viewers. The scene in which the marshal removes his tin star and tosses it to the ground has been seen as contempt for the voices of law and order who were in 1952 naming many in Hollywood (Carl Foreman among them) as dangerous to society—members, supposedly, of the anarchic American Communist party.

But this interpretation seems to me myopic. The issue is perhaps almost diametrically opposed to this: no citizen is worthy of liberty who is not willing to fight to preserve it. The gesture is an indictment of the town, whose representative leader and defender Kane can no longer be. Authority without support of those it defends, says *High Noon*, is meaningless.

There's also a related subtheme: the contrast between youth and mature middle age. It's evident in the rivalry between Cooper and young Bridges, who looks very much like a smoother, more untried version of the lined, now tired marshal; evident, too, in the immediately striking age difference between Cooper and Kelly, she creamily young, bonneted and unwise in the ways of human perversity, he gray with age and fear and

The final shootout.

heartsick over his dilemma, anxious for peace and frankly unable to comprehend the easy morality of his fellows. Also, the contrast is clear in the confrontation between the dark, mature, Latin face of Jurado and the young blond bride played by Kelly. What links all these contrasts in the dialogue is the constant talk about growing up. As they wait for their leader at the station, the Miller gang joke about the habits of grownups. Jurado chides Bridges about not being grownup. Cooper says Bridges can't be the next marshal because of his immaturity. The subtheme highlights further the marshal's mature manhood, a measure by which everyone's maturity may be gauged.

Gary Cooper, whom the Academy voted best actor of the year for this performance, found in himself new resources for conveying a sense of muted anguish. In the film's single moment of real sentiment, he sits at a desk in the office, buries his head in his arms and weeps. It's deeply affecting, probably because Cooper's normally laconic manner didn't prepare us for this. You get the sense of a man coming into touch with unsuspected possibilities in himself and simultaneously losing touch with those around him. His plain angularity, the lines of gravity and premature old age, seem etched more deeply in this film. The walk seems rightly calculated and too full of bravado—thus there's the creation of a real-life character, exaggerating his own manufactured courage.

Grace Kelly was not so satisfactory. She'd appeared in only one previous film, *Fourteen Hours,* in which she'd had a very small role. "I'd seen her in an off-Broadway play," Kramer said. "She was a very beautiful lady and I thought she had the makings of a great star. So I took a chance and offered her this part." The actress, now Princess of Monaco, has no illusions about her performance here: "When I saw the picture, I was extremely disappointed with myself. In fact, I jumped on the first plane out of Hollywood and went back to New York, begging Sandy Meisner to give me more acting lessons!" Very soon, of course, she blossomed into a formidable talent: her three roles for Hitchcock show a deepened dramatic ability, and in 1954 she was herself awarded an Oscar, for her sensitive portrayal in *The Country Girl.*

As elsewhere, Fred Zinnemann demonstrated his meticulous control of camera, actors and the subtle links that film can draw between setting and character. The sharpness of Foreman's script thus comes through unblunted—perhaps also because personal courage is an issue that has concerned Zinnemann throughout his career.

After a quarter century, *High Noon* has lost little of its power to intrigue the viewer, to suggest directly the spiritual issues which in fact the Western genre has always had at its root. It has a clear-sighted intention about human honor and frailty, and it sets up relationships between major characters with an entirely credible premise: love, implies the script, does not in fact conquer all. In fact, the wedding and inchoate binding of Will and Amy are not described in dewy, romantic terms. Quite the contrary; their future will involve them, very likely, in more dilemmas of conscience. It is sometimes painful, always inevitable, usually productive of inner growth, this kind of personal struggle.

High Noon is, however you think about it, the sort of film that states its solemnities with a rare kind of cinematic humility, and that is probably most responsible for its endurance.

CHAPTER 10

Happiness, Aggressively—
The Happy Time, 1952

Speaking of his next venture for Columbia, a cinematic rendering of Samuel Taylor's play *The Happy Time,* Stanley Kramer called it the story about "the coming of age of a teen-age boy, his first reaching for maturity on everything from the intellectual plane to the first sex manifestation. Further, we strove to illustrate the frank, above-board viewpoint on things basic, such as sex, by the continental mind, as contrasted to the hush-hush and guilt school of thought." In this regard, the film tries to be a gently human—even noble—statement, an anti-Puritan tract dressed up as a domestic comedy. As tract, it comes close to succeeding. As domestic comedy, it's dangerous for diabetics.

The happy time is the era just after World War I. The place is Ottawa. Young Bibi Bonnard (Bobby Driscoll) is about to celebrate his twelfth birthday, and his inchoate manhood has all sorts of family influences: that of his loving parents (Charles Boyer and Marsha Hunt), who have a spirit of patience and unself-conscious sacrifice and easy gentility that is found more often on stage and screen than in real life; that of Grandpa

Bonnard (Marcel Dalio), a very old man with a very young heart, whose amorous pursuits are shown as charmingly raffish; and—this being a large family—there is also the dubious influence of Uncle Desmonde (Louis Jourdan) who, from his travels, has amassed a vast collection of ladies' garters. Finally, just across the road is still another Bonnard brother, Louis (Kurt Kasznar) who doesn't pursue women at all, but is in fact pursued by his shrewish wife and his whiny daughter. For refuge, he curls up, most days and nights, with a water jug that holds cheap wine. Quite a variety of influences on the child! All that's lacking is a nymphomaniacal aunt or a gay brother-in-law. But it's 1924 in the film (and 1952 in real life), and there *are* limits. . . .

Kurt Kasznar, Bobby Driscoll, Marcel Dalio and Louis Jourdan.

Actually, there are all the ingredients for a play from the middle period of Eugene O'Neill, or one of Tennessee Williams' steamy veranda melodramas. But Taylor's comedy of manners, which had a modest success on Broadway, is built in the tradition of *Life with Father* and *I Remember Mama*—and with a twist. It baldly decries Victorian ideas about sex, and ends as Papa tells the boy about love and sex—a little homily which is careful to avoid the anatomy lesson, and just as careful to avoid either endorsing or condemning the amorous misadventures of Grandpa or of Uncle Desmonde, or the bibulous retreat of Uncle Louis. More than taking a stand with the angels, this story is on the side of the saints. The only problem is that everyone who wanders through the story seems quite close to an oozy kind of natural sanctity.

The problem with the film's good intentions is typified by the fact that the maid of the household, just like Mama Bonnard, wears gowns by Jean Louis. It gives the film a too-pretty, starched, overdressed look. Thus the conventions of their lives, which can be accepted on the distancing stage, don't come across as ingenuous in the film's intimacy. By enlarging the boy's innocence and by showing the lovably roguish ways of other men in the house, the happiness seems merely calculated, not natural. And this militates against the gently universal lesson of the film as much as Jean Louis' lovely, expensive gowns. Young Driscoll's eyes are always so wide with boyish charm and delight that one suspects the presence of tiny toothpicks at the corners of his lids. And Boyer's benevolent smile, like the ungrownup ways of his own father and brothers, seems alternately just plain stupid or determinedly irresponsible. It's fine, in other words, to be a happy family in a happy time, but the Bonnards are aggressively happy. From what could have been an unpretentiously amusing little *documentaire* about tilting over into adolescence there comes a bloated chunk of saccharine.

Kramer was, by his own admission, playing it safe by transferring a slew of plays to the screen in the early fifties. But in retrospect this was a dull period: *The Happy Time* and *The Four Poster* and *Eight Iron Men* are perhaps the lowest points of his career. There is nothing specifically cinematic about any of them, and the endless talk and restricted acting spaces, instead of creating intimacies for the revelation of human problems, end up merely claustrophobic settings from which the audience is glad to be released.

A further problem with *The Happy Time* is the baldness of the options presented: we and the boy seem faced with either unbridled but damnably good-natured lasciviousness on the one

Bobby Driscoll and Marlene Cameron.

hand, or a sort of angry repression on the other. Against these extremes, Boyer, as the embodiment of balanced wisdom and—although we can only infer this—of sane experience, shows his son The Enlightened Way to grow up: seeing sex as Part of Life, whereas Uncle Desmonde, it is implied, sees life as part of sex, and Grandpa sees life and sex as virtually synonymous. (Never has so old and frail an actor as Dalio seemed weighted with such an affliction as this astonishingly geriatric case of satyriasis.)

There are, however, two nicely paced and amusing sequences which, momentarily at least, let air into the film. The first is a schoolroom episode. Wrongfully accused of drawing "a wicked picture" by his principal, the boy is punished daily until Papa and the uncles come to his rescue.When their rational arguments about a boy's healthy curiosity fail to placate the stuffily outraged academic, Jourdan sighs that all this is too bad, since he doubts the neighbors will be pleased to hear that the principal patronizes burlesque houses. Fighting fire with blackmail, it seems, is all right if family honor and a boy's innocence are the stakes.

The second occurs at the local theatre, where Papa plays violin for the silent movies. On the screen is Rudolph Valentino as *The Sheik*. The boy notices how his companion, the new family maid, responds to the star's languid sexuality ("Come ride with me into an exciting new dawn," proclaims the florid title card). That night, determined to please the maid (the first female to spark the boy's confused erotic instinct), he creeps into her bedroom—it must be associated in his mind with the sheik's tent!—plants a bold kiss and rushes out. The maid, of course, is certain that Uncle Desmonde is responsible for the stolen kiss, and she promptly empties a water jug on the sleeping playboy. This little bit of farce leads to the wedding of maid and uncle: it's the same kind of logic which will slow down (but not dispatch) Grandpa with a heart strain. And the family tradition of all this *toujours l'amour*, etc., will be continued, as we see in a rather too cute twist at the final fade-out. Young Bibi kisses the girl next door, twelve-year-old Peggy (Marlene Cameron), whom before he had refused to acknowledge. Fearful no longer of the rival maid's potential embraces, nor of her own recently removed dental braces, Peggy is free to accept the new attentions of the boy.

Director Richard Fleischer hadn't the subtlety to handle all this rather obvious material, and so what could have been wryly amusing becomes a confused, parodic parable. For all its good intentions about the desirability of maturing free of neurotic sexual guilt, the film exploits the playboy uncle's slightly greasy approach to sex as conquest, and the tired convention of a goatish grandpa's insatiable appetites. Then, as if to confound the censors, it abruptly concludes with a speech about sex and love. "The picture should prove suitable for the family," said one trade report at the time, "although it is somewhat risqué." Well, that kind of comment shows you where we were in 1952, and how apt the theme of the film really was: *The Happy Time* is about as risqué as *Snow White*.

It's interesting to compare the rather calculated style of *The Happy Time* with the awakening to sexuality that is detailed in

Kathryn Sheldon, Jack Raine and Bobby Driscoll.

the early films of François Truffaut—*Les Mistons (The Mischief-Makers)* and *Les Quatre Cent Coups (The Four Hundred Blows)* especially. The actions and motivations of boys tottering on the brink of adolescence are not simplified, and there's a richer humor in the incidents. The organic, Gallic wit relates budding eroticism to the rest of life. No one—Truffaut's boy characters least of all—thinks sex is all of life, and their knowledge of women and of themselves grows logically out of experience. No need for a formal talk with Papa. Nor does one suddenly wake up to adolescence: you sort of slide into it, in Truffaut's more natural world, without much fuss or psychologizing. Boyer and Jourdan should've known better.

This kind of healthy nonchalance is what is missing in *The Happy Time*. It works so hard at being good-natured about sex that one finally sniffs a moldy prurience lurking just beneath the surface. Even Boyer, supposedly the prototype of the sane and balanced man, looks here like a bored bourgeois husband. I can't help thinking French Canada would have been, with this family's pedestrian eccentricities, a little more happy if they'd gone back to France for some lessons on understated family living.

Rex Harrison and Lilli Palmer.

CHAPTER 11

Uncommon Commoners—
The Four Poster, 1953

Jan de Hartog's two-character matrimonial comedy *The Four-poster* was doing brisk business on Broadway when Stanley Kramer's film version of it was released. (There's an inexplicable difference in the renderings of the title: on Broadway it was *The Fourposter*; on the screen, *The Four Poster*.) This was no hurried cinema treatment of a hit play. In fact, Kramer bought the screen rights and began production even before the play opened in New York. What was filmed under Irving Reis's direction was de Hartog's first version, which had actually been a catastrophe in London. There were major changes in the New York version—most of them having to do with basic shifts from a serious to a comic tone—and audiences who attended the play in New York and then saw the screen version really saw two quite diferent works.

The Four Poster is the story of a marriage. In eight episodes, we follow the marriage of Abby and John from their wedding night, in 1897, to old age and death. The entire action (what little there is of action) takes place in a series of bedrooms, in each of which an imposing four poster is a symbol of Abby and John's unity and the strong individuality of each. The episodes detail the awkwardness of the wedding night, the early days of John's financial struggles as a writer, the birth of children, the loss of a son in World War I and the marriage of a daughter, the excursions into infidelity and the inevitable reconciliations. From the laughter and tears of quite ordinary occurrences, in other words, the play distills a certain recognizable, if basically predictable, pattern of human behavior.

The major differences in the narrative of the New York stage version and the London/Kramer version are easy to describe. In the first place, there is in the latter an awkwardly melodramatic poisoning scene in which John has prepared a lethal brandy for Abby and himself, having just been informed that she has a terminal illness; in addition, they have serious financial problems. His loving instincts prevail, however, and he smashes the brandy glass from her hand as she is about to offer a toast. They will, then, live together as long as is naturally possible.

Second, in the film there is the use of the ending from the original London version. After Abby's death, we see John feverishly working to finish his memoirs. Suddenly, his wife appears before him, as radiant and beautiful as on her wedding night. Feeling he is tricked by his vivid imagination, John tries to banish the apparition. Moments later, however, she reappears—this time as the young wife, then as the turn-of-the century matron, then as the gradually graying companion, and once again as the beautiful virgin bride. Finally, John understands: Abby has come for him. She kisses him, and there is a sudden metamorphosis by means of a quick cut. John enters the room—he is once more the young groom! He picks up his bride, announces that "this is the beginning, it's time to start again." The four poster is empty now. The chair by the fire is abandoned. They leave the room, entering into the mystic diffusion of eternity. It is indeed the beginning.

None of this happened in the revised New York stage version, which stressed the comic tone and deliberately avoided the sentimental touch, much less the overtly mystical subtheme. Yet there is an irresistible rightness to these last moments in the screen version. It's not only the last-minute, welcome release from the claustrophobia of a single room. There's also the

One of the famous cartoon interscenes from *The Four Poster,* created by John Hubley and Stephen Bosustow.

The fatal glass of brandy, rejected . . .

perfectly natural (if slightly sentimental) suggestion of what must come to the minds of all persons who live devotedly together through many years of struggle, namely, that love is eternal even if this life is not. The metaphysics of this final sequence is a little muddy: is the script opting for a personal immortality in spirit, in a life beyond the grave? Or is there a kind of Oriental generalized belief in the absorption of spirits into the cosmos? Or a hint of reincarnation and repetition? No matter the option: emotionally the scene is quite touching.

What's bothersome in this filmed play, however, is in fact the talented twosome. Abby and John are supposed to be warmly commonplace people, and their basic simplicity is necessary for an audience to identify with and care for them. But never for a moment do you really have the impression that Rex Harrison and Lilli Palmer are a simple, homey couple. Her pellucid beauty is mesmerizing, her European charm sparkling, her refinement almost royal. And he seems to be projecting more of his own personality, with its benevolent pomposity intact, than that of a struggling writer. In other words, the preternatural attractiveness of this couple are distractions in what is to be a common style of character and life. There's just nothing common about this pair, no matter what modest settings they're in. They have an air of worldly brilliance and convey a lively, glittering life, urbane and audacious. The couple seems, in their playing, successful denizens of high society rather than a couple living mostly in cramped quarters.

The film's interest lies chiefly in the gaily animated cartoon sequences which act as interscenes, bridging the time gaps between the eight episodes. Created by the team who produced *Gerald McBoing-Boing* (director John Hubley and producer Stephen Bosustow), this cartoon cast signals the passage of time with renderings of a wedding party, the changeover from horse to horseless carriage, a Paris holiday, the suggestion of the holocaust that was World War I) and the crazy roaring twenties. These bridges set the mood for each successive episode and give the two characters a visual and thematic link with the outside world—which otherwise we have to take on faith. This couple seems as involved in society as Carthusian hermits.

These cartoon inventions are quite diverting and highlight the egregious flaw of *The Four Poster:* for after the first ten minutes of this photoplay, we realize that outside the cartoon sequences we are doomed to this localized talk, talk, talk between one man and one woman. Even if the talk were *always* stimulating, *always* devilishly clever and philosophically and psychologically provocative and acute, it would be hard to accept so much of it in a medium from which we expect motion and action to advance the narrative. This couple talks endlessly about doing things, about having done things, and about plans to do things. We see none of the action, and the confinement to the bedrooms—which at first promises an emotional intimacy—quickly becomes monotonous, then suffocating. *The Four Poster* is, in the final analysis, just pictures of very pretty people talking, mostly with the aim of soothing their respective egos. More than once, a viewer is inclined to crawl under the canopy, pull up a distancing blanket and snooze through an episode . . . or two. . . .

Bonar Colleano and Richard Kiley.

CHAPTER 12

A Case of Terminal Torpor—
Eight Iron Men, 1952

A pattern is emerging, and as Stanley Kramer admitted later, it was not an entirely good one. *Eight Iron Men,* adapted by Harry Brown from his Broadway play *A Sound of Hunting,* was the producer's sixth film that originated on the stage. Unfortunately, preproduction hopes were inflated, and in many ways the film marks a low point in Kramer's career. Even Edward Dmytryk, who directed, has no illusions about the picture; twenty-five years later he said without embarrassment, "I have to admit that I remember absolutely nothing about the making of *Eight Iron Men.*" Just as well, for certainly it marks no advance in his career, either.

Featured in the original New York cast of the 1945 play were actors named Burt Lancaster and Frank Lovejoy. The latter's first important screen role was in *Home of the Brave,* and Kramer hoped to have once again the actor's pleasing combination of severity and understated warmheartedness. He had hoped, too, to have Lancaster, but that actor had received better offers (which is not hard to imagine) and so was not available. Lovejoy proved to have an incompatible schedule, too. These two absences are regrettable, for while the presence of an unfamiliar cast makes it easy to accept them as soldiers, it also makes it difficult to identify emotionally in any significant way.

In addition, the design and direction are far removed from documentary—they even occasionally veer into the romantic-fantastic—and a well-known face would have provided a locus for the transference of emotions. It's interesting to contrast this film with Kramer's earlier story of beleaguered soldiers, *Home of the Brave.* That film's success derived from its sharp treatment of a known social issue and the enlargement of characters to type without a loss of specificity. *Eight Iron Men,* however, lacks a pointed social theme, an engaging narrative and sharply drawn characters, and seems infected with a dreadful boredom. The endless talk is not alternated with sufficient action, and the occasional flashes of wit and sentiment are weak as momentary punctuations in so garrulous a film. In fact, the picture is a good example of the inadvisability of casting nonstar performers, a risk ordinarily affordable only when there is an exceptional script or when the premise is very unusual.

The story involves a combat squad in a bombed town. Despising every minute of the dirty war in which they're engaged, a group of soldiers (Bonar Colleano, Arthur Franz, Lee Marvin, Richard Kiley, Nick Dennis, James Griffith, Dick Moore), in spite of their cautious captain's orders, deliberately risk their lives to rescue a comrade (George Cooper) trapped in a shell hole. Except for a very few moments of escape, we're trapped in this crumbling bunker with the men: we exit only when they do, which is briefly. Even then, the rifle fire, mortars and artillery—and the inhospitable, chilling rain—drive them back to their grimy home. The bitter irony of their dangerous waiting and attempts to save the buddy occurs when the man is finally dragged back to safety. "I was comfortable out there," he whines. Explaining that he had given himself a shot of morphine to kill the pain of a sprained ankle, then curled up peacefully and gone to sleep, he says he would have been quite happy to wait out the siege and limp off later, or even die. Totally ungrateful for the sacrifices made on his behalf (and even for his share of a fruitcake which was, with considerable discipline, saved for his return), he trudges on with his comrades as they leave the bunker at last.

Scenarist Harry Brown was an old hand at these war stories, having written or collaborated on *The True Glory, A Walk in the Sun, Arch of Triumph, The Sands of Iwo Jima* and *Bugles in the Afternoon* before he contributed to *The Sniper* earlier the same year that *Eight Iron Men* went into production. Unfortunately, Brown mistook monotony for grimness this time round: in striving to create the depressing atmosphere of an army bunker, he succeeded in simply drawing up a gallery of soldiers broadly representing personality types (the Brooklyn tough guy, the sensitive youth, the joker, the romantic adventurer, etc.). In fact, you have the sense neither of types nor of very specific individuals.

Kramer's press release for the film announced that "behind the screen of indifference and selfishness, and the veil of self-preservation, there is in every man the virtue of love for one's comrade—which comes to bear only in the presence of imminent danger." A noble sentiment, but one which is all but trivialized by the bitter ending, which in fact implies that such love may be wasted because it is not always reciprocated. In the final gesture of the film the staff sergeant, played with typical barking bravado by Lee Marvin, spits on the bunker just as the crew of loyal, iron men (and one limping, plastic one) move on to the next combat zone.

"I don't really think this was a film about war," said Dmytryk. "The war is merely a background allowing certain emotions to be liberated which under other circumstances wouldn't be." Those emotions, which are only suggested in the script (which keeps the enemy far offscreen) and indicated broadly by the merely adequate performances, range from fear and resentment to hope and affection, loyalty, suppressed eroticism and the release of certain delusive romantic fantasies. All these men have a great desire to belong, to be members of a self-sustaining group, and to be loyal to that group. That, after all, is what makes their perseverance in the rescue of the last man possible, and it is what makes this basement bunker the new home for a sudden *ersatz* family. In this regard, the men find themselves becoming quite domestic in their depressing new abode: a laundry line is hung, a makeshift kitchen arranged, a few crude drawings and photos find their way to the dripping, moldy walls. And, quite organically and with no hint of exploitation, the men seem to establish a family: one mothers the group, preparing

A soldier's fantasy.

meals and wearing an apron—an image which is at once sad and funny, since his uniform is already soiled with mud and blood and soot. The men cheer one another, they fight, they engage in petty arguments, they make stupid bets, they even enjoy a little dancing together. The film clearly wants to idealize the possibility of human solidarity even in the midst of the horror of war, and this is, thanks to the direction, what comes through from the script—when it is not drowning sense in the vapid dialogue.

The talk revolves mostly around family and food, amorous adventures at home, hopes for the future, military matters and cherished memories—and this is how the film affects attitudes instead of projecting them. Issues are talked to death, as in *The Four Poster.*

In addition, loyalty is sledgehammered into incredibility: "We came up here with eight men and we're going back with eight men," boasts Marvin. "That's the way we do things in this part of the army. We're gonna go out there and get him!" This, of course, is like the stereotypical moment in antique serials which drew cheers from all the neighborhood kids on Saturday afternoons.

But the talk is manly proud in another way, too—the way of confrontation. "I came up here with a company and I'll be lucky to leave with a platoon," complains the captain. "I kept my squad together," replies Marvin airily, with defensible arrogance. These dust-ups between staff sergeant and captain are kept to a respectful minimum; the film, in the final analysis, is about fidelity and honor, and it doesn't want to get itself bogged down in a discussion about insubordination or rudeness to an officer.

Eight Iron Men is not without inventive, classy moments. These, as you might expect, do not occur within the gloomy reality of the chamber-bunker. One of the leading men, affectingly played by a young actor named Bonar Colleano, often drifts into romantic fantasies, and at such moments the entire texture changes. These dream sequences show Dmytryk at his best: in one, the soldier imagines himself in a vast house filled with gorgeous women. Instead of the brief shots and abrupt cuts which prevailed in the bunker scenes, Dmytryk now directs the camera in long, fluid shots and a brightness that seems almost blinding in contrast to the dreary dirtiness of the real-life situation. In a dramatic point-of-view shot, the camera cranes up a flight of stairs as the man, dreaming, imagines himself handsomely dressed and translated into this wonderful new setting. Then, without a cut, the camera proceeds to find lovely, waiting arms in several rooms. The sequence rivals the best moments in films like Fellini's *8½* and *Juliet of the Spirits*. And Dmytryk is everywhere careful to retain moving point-of-view shots for the fantasy wedding, in which the slight diffusion of light and the sparklers atop candles give the proper romantic-fantastic glow.

The rest of the picture, alas, is deadeningly routine, and the

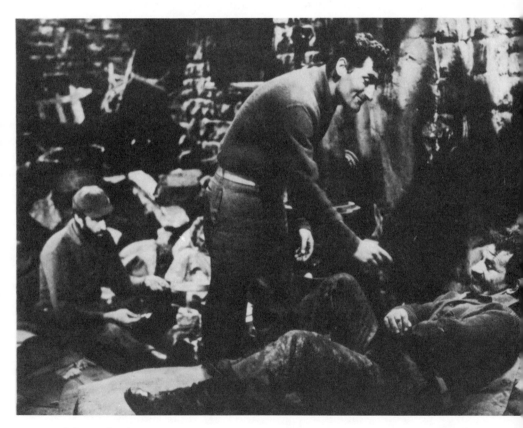

Life in a bunker.

machine-gun fire and strained talk of men under pressure cannot redeem it from terminal torpor. Even the reporter for *Variety*, trying find good words, decided that "it will best serve as a companion feature."

The theatre pieces filmed by Stanley Kramer in the early 1950s have the look of being made on the cheap. They're mostly examples of the least entertaining kind of B-picture, and it would have been hard to predict that in a few short years he would himself be directing big-budget, big-star films, or that he would only once direct a play. And when he did, it worked. *Eight Iron Men*, one of his Columbia "quota quickies," is best left to the archivist. An expert on trivia, however, may find it interesting—and come to think of it, that's precisely what it's about.

Julie Harris, Brandon De Wilde, Ethel Waters.

CHAPTER 13

"God Is My Director!"—
The Member of the Wedding, 1952

Among a group of gifted American writers from the South—a group called the "Gothic school" by Tennessee Williams—can be included William Faulkner, Flannery O'Connor, Truman Capote, Williams himself, Katherine Anne Porter, perhaps Eudora Welty and Walker Percy. And certainly—maybe even quintessentially—Carson McCullers. These writers document in fiction the pain of life, the suffering of souls sensitive to the fundamental mystery of the universe, to what is unknowable, to what fills them with dread.

Before her death at fifty in 1967, Carson McCullers produced a small library of deeply affecting, disturbing works: five novels, two plays, some short stories and a few poems. The theme of all her work was the theme of her life—the awful experience of loneliness, the congenital inability to sustain deep emotional relationships, and the conflicting need for such relationships. This complex is fictively best described in her delicate and fragile mood piece of a novel, *The Member of the Wedding.* Published in 1946, it became a small classic at once. Very likely the gentleness of the writing, the wistful evocation of adolescence, the simultaneous celebration of it and the mourning for its passing, appealed to many people who were disillusioned but still hopeful after the war. The author herself soon set to work on a theatrical version, and that, too, was hugely successful: it won the New York Drama Critics' Circle Award for the best Broadway play of the 1949–50 season.

According to Virginia Spencer Carr (in *The Lonely Hunter: A Biography of Carson McCullers,)* the play's producer, Robert White-head, began negotiations with several Hollywood independents for the screen rights in August 1950. At the same time, the New York stage version was returning handsome profits to the investors. In February 1951, a deal was settled with Stanley Kramer, by which the screen rights were purchased for $75,000 plus 10 percent of the profits. McCullers' share of this sum was approximately $40,000 (but no additional percentage profit, for the screen version was not financially successful). By early summer, the three principal players from New York—Ethel Waters, Julie Harris and Brandon de Wilde—had been signed to repeat their roles for the film. And Fred Zinnemann, who had done so well for Kramer with *The Men* and *High Noon,* was engaged to direct. The play closed in New York on March 17, 1951, after 501 performances, and the company (with some temporary substitutions along the way) immediately went on national tour until May 1952. At the tour's conclusion, the actors arrived in Hollywood to begin filming. The result is Kramer's most successful filmed play of the fifties, an important document of the original performances in a tender, elegiac play—perfor-mances which are all the more valuable now that two members of the cast are dead.

The Member of the Wedding is Frankie Addams (Julie Harris), a highly strung, confused girl of twelve who lives in a small town in Georgia. Her only friends are a six-year-old cousin, John Henry (Brandon de Wilde) and a warmly wise surrogate mother, the black cook Berenice (Ethel Waters). Neither child nor woman, Frankie feels keenly the loneliness of her life—a loneli-ness partly caused by fate (her mother is dead, her father preoccupied with his modest business as a watch repairman, her only brother away in the service) and partly caused by her own ornery eccentricity. Aching to belong to someone or something—

she's not sure which, and doesn't understand the strange admixtures of the need for friends and the awakening of a young girl's sensuality—she seizes on her brother's imminent wedding as the beautiful and romantic thing that will make her life perfect. She falls in love not only with the young couple (Arthur Franz and Nancy Gates), but fundamentally with the idea of the wedding, that archetypal social symbol of union and belonging. Neither Berenice nor bespectacled, owlish John Henry, speaking as a kind of chorus to her sometimes subdued, often hysterical words, can understand Frankie's insistence that she will go away with the couple on their honeymoon, to live with them and always be a member of their wedding. She cannot do this, of course, and she does not. Shortly after the bitter disappointment of being left behind, and a brief foray into one of the town's grimy back streets, she returns home, where John Henry is soon spirited away in death by a swift childhood illness. Because his mother, Frankie's aunt, will come to keep house for the Addams family now, Berenice leaves. As the story ends, Frankie prepares to make new friends and tentatively steps over the border into adolescence.

The film is successful where so many other filmed plays are not, precisely because, in the sensitive hands of director Fred Zinnemann, specifically cinematic devices are exploited in order to achieve dramatic effect. The entire action of the play takes place in the slightly depressing, ramshackle rear kitchen of the Addams house, and it is here—over the kitchen table, near a cupboard, at the sink—that Frankie and Berenice and John Henry share their confusions and lonelinesses, young hopes and old memories, childish confusions and odd flashes of maturity and vision. With little modification, the set for the film was built to match the theatre's three-walled set. Only very occasionally do the characters leave the kitchen, and when they do it is not simply to open up the movie. Scenarists Edward and Edna Anhalt have gone back to the novel and adapted key scenes (Frankie's attempt to leave with the wedding party, and her journey into town at night), and these illuminate the human tragicomedy which is articulated so delicately in the kitchen conversations.

More basically, the success derives from Zinnemann's sen-

Preparing for the wedding.

Arthur Franz, Nancy Gates, Julie Harris.

sibility about the photography and interpretation of the human face. He certainly had significant talent to work with in the leading trio, and his rightful insistence on the close-up is the cinematic manner of conveying the intimacy which the play conveyed through personal presence, tenebrous lighting and the muting of set and performance. (This is partly the reason, too, for Zinnemann's success with Robert Bolt's play *A Man for All Seasons.*) McCullers called *The Member of the Wedding* "an inward kind of play," and it is a real inwardness that Zinnemann captured on the faces of his players. His camera studies the marvelous mobility of Julie Harris' features, the wondrous combination of angularity and sensitivity in her bodily movements. Around the kitchen table, he has arranged as counterparts to her tomboy awkwardness the innocent face of the young de Wilde, with his wide eyes and ingenuous smile. There are splendid moments here, when the boy is caught whisking a fly away from his ear or wiping his spectacles on a soiled jumper. And, too, there is Ethel Waters, her eyes taking in the two young ones with absorbing warmth and wisdom; her smile banishes gloom from the gray set; when she sings "His Eye Is on the Sparrow," as they nestle against her ample bosom, it is enough to stop all the tears of the world.

It's this insistence on the telling, simple reaction and the revealing gesture that illuminates the inner corners of a character, and few directors know this as well as Zinnemann. His camera is intimate without cramping or prying, so that even when it scarcely moves at all, the frame is filled with an animated tableau or, alternately, a trio of unforgettable human faces that suggest the whole human race.

The climax of the film—and a moment which improves on the simple reporting of it in the play—occurs when Frankie hides in the back seat of the honeymoon car. Her brother and his bride try to persuade her of the impossibility of her joining them, and she finally has to be dragged from the car, kicking and screaming, by her embarrassed father. It's a hysterical, frenzied moment. And yet . . . and yet you can't help feeling that a trip away from the small town would be a welcome part of her growing-up process. All that's left to her now is to wander the darkened alleys of the town, alone, that night. And it is only because she comes very close to real trouble there that she returns home, subdued.

Her house and family are not things to which Frankie feels she belongs—and this brings us to the major theme of *The Member of the Wedding*. "Shush, just now I realized something," she says to John Henry. "The trouble with me is that for a long time I have been just an 'I' person. All other people can say 'we.' When Berenice says 'we' she means her lodge and the church and colored people. Soldiers can say 'we' and mean the army. All people belong to a 'we' except me.

"Not to belong to a 'we' makes you too lonesome. Until this afternoon I didn't have a 'we,' but now I suddenly realize something. I know that the bride and my brother are the 'we' of me. So I'm going with them, and joining with the wedding ... I love the two of them so much because they are the 'we' of me."

This theme of belonging to a "we" in order to be whole has a logical progression in *The Member of the Wedding* and in its three distinct movements.

In the first part, Frankie Addams feels stirrings of dissatisfaction with her life. She describes situations, friends and even herself with words like "queer," "curious," "puzzling." She is plagued by a feeling of being ostracized: older girls don't want such a tomboy in their clubs; she plays only with her young boy cousin, she's self-conscious about her sudden spurt of height. As she pours out her complaints to Berenice and John Henry, the kitchen becomes at once her sanctuary and her prison. It represents the entirety of her past life, in one single place.

The journey of adolescent initiation continues in the second part, where she calls herself, with wry affection, F. Jasmine Addams. Now she plans for flight as escape, and it falls to Berenice to bring the dreamy girl back to the ground: "Me is me and you is you and he is he," she tells the child with simple, encouraging realism. But the girl is far from the kind of natural maturity which accepts the dignity (and concomitant isolation) of the individual. Her gown for the wedding, meant to be glamorous, is merely ridiculous, and soon she has a rude awakening to the present.

Finally, in the third movement, after the necessary trauma of being rejected as honeymoon companion, she is willing to be called Frances; her disillusionment is accompanied by a new wisdom about the limitations of her age and of life itself. As critic Lawrence Graver has written, the ending reveals the author's ability "to mourn for maturity as well as to praise it." In

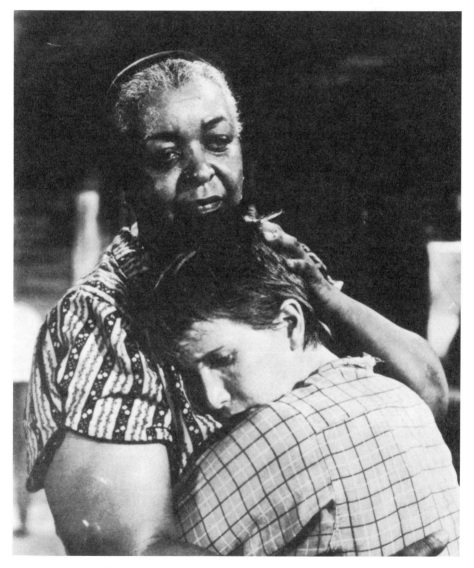

The final comforting.

this regard, it is interesting to observe that *The Member of the Wedding* is no easy, sentimental folk tale about the passage to incipient adulthood. Berenice and John Henry are equally isolated individuals. (McCullers saw every individual as finally walled off, although only the most sensitive souls realize this.) John Henry, an oddly androgynous child who is quite comfortable dressed in Berenice's Sunday clothes, seems almost too frail for this world, and must die, by virtue of the emotional rigor of the theme, before he too can confront the pain of passage. And Berenice, finally, will leave the Addams home. She is no stranger to loneliness, either, deserted as she was by her last husband and abandoned by her aimless stepbrother who's always in trouble. She is not even saved by her wisdom, common sense and innate dignity. The pain of passing hurts all equally, although the film concludes with her singing "His Eye Is on the Sparrow."

All this is carefully articulated in the dialogue. "I hardly have anything to do," remarked Fred Zinnemann during production. "This is a drama with long sustained scenes in a confined set, depending heavily on dialogue. The actors' performances are what makes it come to life." And years later, recalling Ethel Waters' monumental playing, he said: "Ethel was a wonderful, sad woman. Between scenes, she'd sit in her dressing room and listen to her old records. But she was also a very headstrong lady. If she took three steps to the right and I'd ask her to move to the left instead, she'd stand perfectly still, point to the sky and say, '*God* is my director!'" For all that stubbornness, this is almost certainly the role for which she is most remembered. After fifty years on stage and in films, Ethel Waters died in 1977, close to eighty years old. She fulfilled every promise she had made to herself as a child, promises which are detailed in the 1953 autobiography which draws its title from the song she sings in *The Member of the Wedding.*

Brandon de Wilde, whose only stage experience prior to this work had been a single line in a Sunday-school drama and his grade-school portrayal of a carrot, made nine more films. He was thirty when he was killed in a motorcycle collision.

Julie Harris has had an uninterrupted career of great distinction in the theatre.

And Carson McCullers, after living her final years in a terrified twilight of loneliness and creative frustration, died of a massive cerebral hemorrhage. For some time she had lived as a tenant in her own home, afraid of company, afraid of solitude. Visitors during the last months say she frequently turned aside to carry on a brief conversation with Frankie Addams.

Kirk Douglas as the juggler.

CHAPTER 14

Kirk Douglas, Juggling and Snarling—
The Juggler, 1953

"Everybody was working to create a new country, and there was a unique spirit of cooperation. Everyone struggled together on everything involved with the film, too. And it wasn't only a question of money. We all planted trees. We all worked on the kibbutzim."

Edward Dmytryk was speaking of the third film he directed for the Stanley Kramer company, *The Juggler*, which was the first Hollywood feature film photographed in the young nation of Israel. "We did all the location shooting there, but about half the picture—all the interiors—had to be filmed in California because of the lack of proper equipment, lighting problems and the like. I did that film in order to see Israel, a country that was pulling itself up and doing wonderful things for the world. Although I myself am not Jewish, I felt deeply concerned, and was glad to go there first for location scouting and then, with the cast and crew, for the filming late in 1952."

Unfortunately, however, the spirit of the young Israel does not come through in this little picture.

The story of *The Juggler* is the story of Hans Muller (Kirk

Douglas), a famous German entertainer who, after his imprisonment under the Nazis and the death of his wife and child in
concentration camps, arrives with the busloads of refugees in
Haifa, Israel, in 1949. Terrified of confinement and paranoid in
his attitude toward all men in uniform, he knocks unconscious a
policeman who simply asks him for necessary identification
papers. Thinking the officer is an SS guard, and believing he has
killed him, Muller flees across the countryside. On his journey
he meets and befriends a teen-age boy (Joey Walsh) with whom
he travels to a cooperative farm near Nazareth. En route he gives
the boy juggling lessons. When they wander into a minefield,

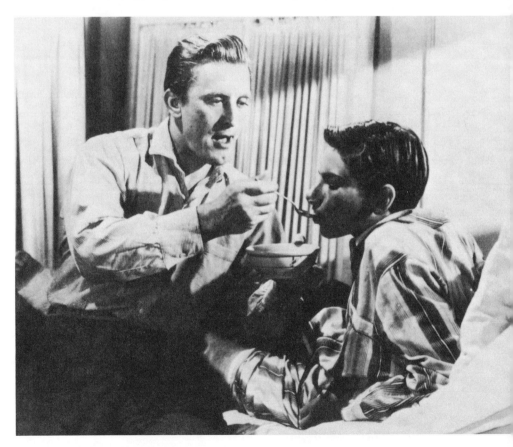

Kirk Douglas and Joey Walsh.

residue of the recent war, the boy suffers a broken leg in the resulting explosion. He recovers in the home of a beautiful Israeli girl (Milly Vitale) who has lost her fiancé in the war. Muller and the girl fall in love (surprise!), but she senses that the man is deeply disturbed and in need of psychiatric help. The police finally arrive, and with the girl's assistance they convince Muller to give himself up and accept necessary therapy. She will wait for him until he is well; then they will begin a new life together in this new nation.

Michael Blankfort, who wrote the screenplay from his own novel, has in fact constructed a story that is more chase drama than ethnic or historic statement. What happens, in fact, could occur anywhere, and, as Otis L. Guernsey, Jr., has pointed out, "it is doubtful whether the adventures of a psychopath, however pitiable, are quite the right glass through which to view modern Israel."

As a chase story, there are two serious problems with *The Juggler*. First, the dialogue does not establish sufficiently early just what are the nature and cause of the man's illness. As a result, his paranoia and his violent reactions do not elicit the audience's sympathy, merely our wonder. Because the man's history is revealed only later, our sympathy must be withheld, no matter how charming the travels in which he engages, no matter that he's earnest and kind to children. What we have here, in fact, is *The Sniper* with a new and timely sociological twist.

The second major problem is that the healing of Hans Muller will supposedly be effected by the understanding love of his fellow countrymen (the sympathetic police included) and by the love of a good woman. This is a rather fatigued melodramatic cliché, and it depends for its urgency on whether or not we can accept this understanding love as the counterstatement to the awful history of suffering which the man has already endured. Such intention in real life—just like the intention of reel life here—is fine, but it's unlikely that they're going to easily solve the man's illness, or remove the danger to which he exposes so many people—uniformed men in particular—who may at any time be the objects of his psychotic rage!

These two problems alone are enough to deflect the viewer's

concern away from the joys and problems of an inchoate nation. Hope, compassion and brotherhood are singled out as the great values (it's not likely that anyone's going to argue with that), but the script ignores the subtler realities and strengths of the very environment it has chosen to celebrate. Thus *The Juggler* presents a loving but not fully limned picture of Israel, aimed at entertaining by means of a chase thriller rather than provoking thought or documenting struggle. None of these omissions are compensated for by the film's unregenerate sentimentality, with scenes such as that in which the boy, in a leg cast, has to be spoon-fed by the heroine, now a surrogate mother. Why can't a grown boy with a broken leg feed himself? Just to provide a reason for her to be there when the juggler peeks in on his young friend—it's a sort of family, get it? The film is uneven in tone and at times like this it tends to overthicken, like untended matzoh-ball soup.

When it chooses to celebrate the young Israel photographically, however, the film gives a pleasant enough tour of the countryside. Roy Hunt's camera floats engagingly over the landscape, revealing glimpses of a newly planted valley, picturesque village streets and squares, a campfire dance sequence (with lively ethnic music for this, by George Antheil), an old woman selling papers and beaming with local pride, and a refugee carpenter, pleased to discover that he can find work. But these seem like arbitrary intrusions into the chase story, and I can't help thinking that while originally they may have formed the pictorial "message" of the film, they have been finally relegated to subsidiary, even exploitive, status. What is remarkable, of course, is that they are presented without specifically religious emphasis, so the story (as well as the pride) is at last nonsectarian.

The tour of the new Israel is best when it arises organically from the story—as, for example, when the couple goes mountain climbing, and we're given a lovely view of the hills and valleys in the background. It's not so good when the characters, riding through the countryside, say things like "Here we are in Jerusalem!" and, later "Another ten minutes and we'll be in Nazareth!" After a while, you expect one of those sonorous travelogue narrators to take over, perhaps concluding with something like "As we leave the sun-drenched hills of Israel, and our friends scurry away from the police . . ."

Still another problem is Kirk Douglas.

"Kramer occasionally did things that were naughty," said Dmytryk, "and casting Kirk Douglas was one of them. I went location scouting in Israel, and when I came back he said he'd signed up Douglas for the role. I was very unhappy about this because Stanley otherwise lets the directors have a say in casting. For this reason, I really didn't enjoy making *The Juggler* very much. My previous two films for Kramer"—*The Sniper* and *Eight Iron Men*—"I pretty much had my way, and the actors were good to work with. But Douglas is a very difficult man, perhaps the most difficult man in the industry. Wasn't it Thomas Wolfe who said, 'I finally found out that creation is a battle you fight inside yourself'? I always wanted to say that to certain insecure and difficult actors.

"When it came to shooting a certain scene, for example, Douglas wanted to revise and question everything we'd already worked out in rehearsals. He'd do this for hours, causing endless delays and bringing us right back to where we'd started before rehearsals!"

Personal problems aside, Douglas simply isn't right for the role. His idea of conveying a psychopathic state is simply to widen his eyes more, clench his teeth, mutter more threateningly, and thrust his cavernously dimpled chin at the camera, as if to compensate for his basic "tough kid" appearance. He's so strident in the role that he throws the film out of focus; it's also unbelievable that a German could pass himself to Israeli Jews as an American, although that's the writer's fault, not the actor's.

This is, then, ill-advised casting in a mismanaged script, since the character of Hans Muller *could* have been deeply affecting—especially without the damp love story. Blankfort seemed to have in mind that the juggling represents Muller's desire to keep things (and self) in constant motion—always in the air, never locked up, as he was in the German prison. "You've locked yourself in," says the girl, about his psychological state, when the police finally catch up with him, and it is her strength and compassion at this moment that stand for the hope of the new land. Unfortunately, it takes quite a lot of emotional juggling for the audience to feel deeply into a situation that is shown so late, and is so shrilly put across. The single asset in this regard is Dmytryk's great, racking close-ups, in which the camera brutally details the man's concentration camp memories.

"These were cheap films," said Edward Dmytryk. "They were B-pictures Kramer and I made—at least before *The Caine Mutiny*. But they were done with class and style and basically good subject matter, even when things went wrong. Stanley read every part of every script and got involved in every aspect of production. But he made only minor changes, and never arbitrarily. He certainly supervised the editing, but there was nothing of an unusual nature, at least in my case.

"Above all, Stanley Kramer is very intelligent and very reasonable and rational. He's an easy man to go to and talk with

Kirk Douglas and Milly Vitale, on location in Israel.

and work with. I've worked with producers who weren't so good. You could always discuss and argue with Stanley, but the discussions were always sensible. He's really an eminently reasonable man, and a gentleman, too. I enjoyed working with him as much as with anyone because he was never a problem. Except once—when he cast Kirk Douglas as *The Juggler*."

Peter Lind Hayes, Tommy Rettig, Mary Healy.

CHAPTER 15

A Nice Little Nightmare—
The 5,000 Fingers of Dr. T., 1953

The 5,000 Fingers of Dr. T., to Stanley Kramer's great surprise, has become something of a cult film in recent years. Part of this has to do with the fact that this Technicolor musical fantasy, most of which is set in a boy's dream world, is screened only rarely: there's always a certain fascination for the arcane, after all. More positively, however, it does have a coterie of ardent admirers—those who find its imagination enterprising, its music and lyrics sharply satiric, its sets and costumes vastly different from anything in a Hollywood film at the time, and its mélange of styles and oblique nastiness a daring change from most colorful children's fare of the early fifties.

The producer, who is inclined to be his own severest critic, remembers the film with keen regrets. "It was one of my favorite properties, and one which I very much wanted to direct myself. Columbia Pictures wasn't ready for that yet, and there wasn't enough money to do what should really have been a musical extravaganza. We set the story in a boy's imagination, and the theme in fact becomes imprisonment *within* that imagination."

The title gives little indication of what the story's about: for years I'd imagined something like a cheap British Gothic-horror film. Actually, it's a satire on a staple of American domestic comedy, the fact that little boys loathe piano practice and lessons, and would much rather devote their nonschool hours to baseball.

Little Bart Collins (Tommy Rettig, late of television's *Lassie*) falls to sleep over his piano practice and imagines himself in a hellish underworld which is presided over by the formidable Dr. Terwilliker (Hans Conreid) and his band of lackeys. There's a mile-long, two-decker piano, at which the comic fiendish doctor plans to trap five hundred boys whose hands will thenceforth belong entirely to him, whose wills and talents he will completely control: "Think of it! Five thousand fingers! And they're mine, all mine!"

In this dreadful place Bart finds his mother (Mary Healy), who has been hypnotized—like all adults—into doing the musical will of Dr. T. And there's his pet dog, too, and the local plumber, Mr. Zabladowski (Peter Lind Hayes), come to rescue the boy from this fate worse than school. After lots of chasing and singing and dancing, the boy wakes up at his piano. Life, it turns out, isn't as bad as his dream. Why, Mr. Zabladowski is just beginning to notice how attractive his widowed mother is!

The entire conception of the film was Theodor Geisel's. As "Dr. Seuss," he was a well-known cartoonist and author-illustrator of numerous wildly imaginative children's books and of several movie cartoons. "I took piano lessons," he told *Time* magazine when the film was released, "from a man who rapped my knuckles with a pencil whenever I made a mistake. I made up my mind I would finally get even with that man. It took me forty-three years to catch up with him. He became the Terwilliker of the movie." In spite of this honest disclaimer, John Beaufort, writing for *The Christian Science Monitor*, felt it was a pity "that the makers of the film could not have scored their point about the rights of small fry without seeming utterly to condemn the study of the piano." Well, perhaps it's not so universal a statement as that in the intention, but Beaufort is right in seeing an anticultural diatribe in the final result.

For the film, Geisel worked closely with Kramer, with Allan

Hans Conreid and Tommy Rettig.

Scott on the screenplay, and with Frederick Hollander, for whom he wrote the lyrics for several bouncy tunes. With production designer Rudolph Sternad he worked on the fantastic sets and costumes for Dr. T.'s subterranean castle—a place equipped with topless sky ladders, sliding doors, passages leading nowhere, split staircases, labyrinthine pirates' coves, etc. In fact, these sets are the most interesting aspect of the film, and the occasions when Franz Planer's camera dollies round them are the moments when the film comes closest in style to German expressionism—a style with which Planer was familiar from his earlier work in Germany. There are clear reminiscences of the stark, nightmare angularities of Robert Wiene's *The Cabinet of Dr. Caligari* (1919), as well as of the 1930s' Gothic-horror picture, which flourished briefly before its swift decline to kitsch and camp.

The somewhat dyspeptic critic for *The New Yorker* wrote that "the sets . . . are discouragingly lacking in the kind of nonsense we have come to expect of Dr. Seuss. A junior draftsman might have tossed them off in a spare moment while planning Levittown." No doubt, as Kramer has admitted, the sets were intended to be far more lavish. But in fact they are not supposed to be entirely nonsensical. It's important to remember that the film is a journey into the imagination of a young boy: the horrors of the grownup world—localized in the painful obligations of music lessons—are not, *for him*, nonsensical at all. And while the aim of the film is to amuse, entertain and beguile children as well as the accompanying adults, there is just the proper tinge of the dreadful to all these sets, just the right drop of ghoulish horror that no junior draftsman—especially the unimaginative sort responsible for Levittown—would design. Not only are they oddly shaped and colored, they also have all kinds of malevolent, torturous devices which, by the wonderful rules of film comedy, never really hurt those they momentarily entrap. Thus the boy and his dog, and his mother and the friendly plumber, may be for an instant caught in situations which provide the viewers with red-herring suspense, but we never for a second doubt that they're going to get out of all this quite intact.

This, of course, is where the problem of the film emerges.

The 5,000 Fingers of Dr. T. compromises, since a child's nightmare world would be somewhat more terrifying. The whole dream is really too sophisticated, even for Tommy Rettig, who

seems awfully astute and prepared for all of this, and who seems
as if he wouldn't mind piano playing after all. If this were a
cartoon feature, the fantastic would be more evident. As it is, the
realism militates against fidelity to the child's nightmare world.

This issue of depicting the fantastic in terms realistic brings to
mind the Disney films, which portray the most witty-grotesque
renderings of children's imaginations. In fact, the Disney influence can be felt in several places in this film. There is, for

In the land of Dr. T.

example, a pair of Siamese twin flunkies, joined by one long white beard, who go about their chores on roller skates. There's also a bizarre ballet (staged by Eugene Loring) in which a prisonful of captive kids writhe in abject torment, having to listen to all sorts of variations on musical scales and practice material. And there are the songs, too: "The Kids' Song," well calculated to make every adult feel like a bully, and "The Dressing Song" and "Dungeon Elevator" and "Victorious" and "Hypnotic Duel." The villains are an odd mixture of Disney creatures—pirates, heavies straight from the fairy tales and *The Arabian Nights,* scientists dabbling in the secrets of the atom (how timely can you *get!*) and cheerleaders for a rival football team.

Dr. T's 5000 fingers, busy.

All these elements recall a typical feature-length Disney cartoon (*Pinocchio, Alice in Wonderland* and *Peter Pan* come readily to mind). And the ballets, the theme of serious music and the age-old battle between adults and children, somewhat simplistically equated as the battle between authority and independence, recalls major sequences in Disney's classic *Fantasia.* The only notable difference apart from the realistic genre of this film is the absence of a glowering, Disneyesque villain—Hans Conreid's Dr. T. is finally more comic than deadly.

But this isn't the only influence which, consciously or not, operated on the making of the film. Lewis Carroll's Alice reached her Wonderland by drowsing over a history lesson; this little boy nods off over his piano. And in his world, as in Alice's, things are oddly shaped, grotesquely under- or oversize, and curiously endowed with their own spirit. There's even a modern ballet, which has the kind of flare and zest that Loring gave to his ballet *Billy the Kid,* and which seems to have been inserted for the edification of the adult audience. If that's not the reason, it subverts the entire premise of the film, which is to release kids from forced attention to matters cultural!

Composer Frederick Hollander called the film "an unusual child's opera for adults," which may be too great a claim but has a measure of truth. (I can't help wondering what's "unusual"— the child or the opera?) There is something of Gilbert and Sullivan in this production, especially when it is blatantly lyrical or deliberately satiric. Nevertheless, in a way that Hollander probably could not foresee, there are basic inconsistencies with this and a child's imagination.

Hans Conreid is a wonderful Dr. Terwilliker, tall and funny-menacing. His voice has a throatily gleeful male witch's quality, and it has extraordinary rich variations in timbre. He was about the same time the voices of Mr. Darling and Captain Hook in Disney's *Peter Pan.* Tommy Rettig is entirely credible as the son of Mary Healy, which means he's pleasant and attractive and not very exciting. Peter Lind Hayes seemed to wander through the film more confused than the boy.

But the direction seems not bold enough, nor sufficiently and straightforwardly mischievous. "Roy Rowland was perhaps not the right director," Kramer said years later. "The picture required a tougher man. The idea of the film is not a gentle one. It's an attack on a life-style, but you wouldn't know it from what you see: too many good things were cut out of it. Originally, it was much longer, but Columbia foresaw problems in the distribution, so the editing was severe."

One rainy day during shooting, Rowland and Kramer and a large crew were trying to supervise the scene in which almost five hundred boys play *Chopsticks* on the monstrous double-decker piano. By the time the shot was ready, the boys had gone outside into the rain and gorged themselves on hot dogs from the nearby commissary.

"Have you ever tried to get five hundred rain-soaked boys, with stomachaches, to play a giant piano?" asked Dr. Seuss sometime later.

Not recently, to tell the truth.

CHAPTER 16

Sir Gawain on a Motorcycle—
The Wild One, 1954

"It would be nice if I could say that it was all an original idea of mine," Stanley Kramer said of *The Wild One,* "and that I had understood and captured a tear in the fabric of society before other producers, and then set out to make a film about it. The truth of the matter is that I read a story in *Harper's* called 'The Cyclists' about a group that ransacked a town. It touched my sense of social responsibility, and I thought it would make a good movie."

The true story behind the magazine piece occurred during the weekend of July 4, 1947, when four thousand members of a motorcycle club roared into the hamlet of Hollister, California, and tore the place apart. They ran their machines into cafés and bars, destroyed furniture and mirrors, and drank virtually every drop of liquor in the town. Two days later, they roared off. According to *Life,* they said later, "We like to show off. It's just a lot of fun." Six years later, Kramer put his film into production. It was the first film to deal with the problem of gang violence in America. And, *Life* observed, "It also helped create an image of motorcycling that nonviolent bike riders have been trying to live down for a quarter of a century now."

The film is about Johnny (Marlon Brando), leader of a motorcycle gang that disturbs the peace of a nameless small town somewhere in middle America. He meets and is attracted to Kathie (Mary Murphy), but any relationship is impossible: he's a drifter, a wanderer; she's a nice girl with a stable if dull life. The chemistry is right; the alchemy would be disastrous. Finally, the townspeople set upon Johnny because his gang has become rather too rambunctious, with their high jinks and encounters with another rival gang. Johnny and his pals leave town after charges have been pressed but dismissed by a kindly official who happens to be Kathie's father. She is left behind,

The arrival of the motorcycle gang.

with only his motorcycle insignia to represent the memory of knowing him.

"I gathered together a band of motorcyclists—a gang just like the one that made the newspapers earlier," Kramer recalled. "Brando and I talked to them, and then the writer Ben Maddow was brought in. But he was subpoenaed by the House Un-American Activities Committee"—it was that sad time in Hollywood— "so John Paxton took over the script.

"These guys were a new breed, and there weren't many of them around. They came from every stratum in society. They all had girls and were living like nomads. A lot of the dialogue is taken from our actual conversations with them. All the talk about 'We gotta go, that's all . . . just gotta move on' was something we heard over and over. And one of the most famous lines in the film came from my conversation with them, too. I asked one of these kids, 'What are you rebelling against?' and he answered, 'What have you got?'

"Well, we ran into trouble with the censors, who said it was an anti-American, Communist film! In the original version, we told the truth about the incident—that no charges were brought against the boys because they brought so much business to the town! But the censors said this was unsuitable. They made us cut it out, and some readjustment was necessary." Still, the image of small-town America is far from rustic/charming. As Jeanine Basinger has pointed out, "The greed and hypocrisy of the local merchants and lawmen are striking today. This uncharacteristic bleak portrait of American life is found throughout the films of the 1950s."

Although *Sight and Sound,* the most prestigious British film journal, called the film important ("The adolescent gang stands as a symbol of revolt. *The Wild One* shows the collapse of a society's defenses under strain"), the British Board of Film Censors in fact banned public screenings for fourteen years. They felt that it might incite young men to riot, and that it glamorized juvenile delinquents. American distributors and theatre owners, too, were nervous about the clientele it might attract. "But there was no glorification of violence," Kramer insisted. "We simply showed that this was the first indication that a whole set of people were going to divorce themselves from society and set up their own standards." They became, of course, the ancestors of the 1960s' disaffected youth.

Brando, sullen and silent, epitomized an entire subculture that was fast spreading in America at the time—the drifting gang—and it is a phenomenon that has maintained its identity, at the fringes of polite society, to this day. A recent, lonelier form of the motorcycle traveler, and one whose rage derived from specific dissatisfactions with society, was the *Easy Rider*, which was more influential even than *The Wild One*. Both films are sort of a subgenre of the American Western.

With his leather jacket and slightly bloated cap, raunchy in his jeans and large sunglasses, Brando looks like a latter-day Lone Ranger, with a similarly blurred identity. There's something oddly boyish and unformed about Brando here, and he's a very different man from the paraplegic of Kramer's *The Men*. His voice is too high-pitched, his face is too clean-shaven and fleshy to indicate he's really dangerous. It's not that any great innocence or purity of soul is suggested—you can sense a real cauldron of sensuality underneath all that ragged garb. It's simply that his motorcycle could really be a scooter. But perhaps that's too patronizing a judgment on a film that's a quarter-century old and has, let's admit it, dated somewhat. As John Coleman wrote in England's *New Statesman* when the film was finally publicly released in 1968, "the sets are studio-bound to an embarrassing degree. The sequence in a forest glade where Johnny and the nice bar-girl (impeccably lipsticked Mary Murphy) have a hesitant sexual exchange seems almost capable of incorporating Dorothy Lamour from behind a prop-bush: it's all that grass-matting and indoor lighting that does it." Things like that, and the relatively mild rapscallions (compared to today's hell raisers) have made the film in some regards a period piece.

Trying to justify his life of wandering, Brando remarks: "You don't go to one special place. You just go." And when the girl asks, "Johnny, what are you rebelling against?" he makes the quick reply, "What have you got?" The rebellion—here, as with James Dean in *Rebel Without a Cause*—is a diffuse thing, amorphous, generalized. In this regard, the film is part of its own

time. Life in that decade was very much concerned with conformity to specific social and democratic ideals, and everyone was
urged to band together against the danger of a Communist takeover—the Reds, it was often felt, would creep over the window
sill any moment unless we maintained severe vigilance. Young
people's rebelliousness, never quite formulated or given a cause,
was a reaction against this fetish for conformity. Thus the
townspeople in this film are shown to be even more violent than
the gang, pinning Brando down and subjecting him to a vicious
beating because they're both resentful of his unorthodox freedom and fearful of where his free-lance living may take him—
perhaps, finally, to the freedoms which America has always
offered its young. This they could not tolerate, and so they
threaten him with worse than a beating unless he leaves town.

The Brando character is very closely identified with the man
himself, the new, unorthodox young method actor: he was a
challenge to everything the Hollywood establishment represented, in life as in art. His deportment in Los Angeles was
notoriously ungracious, or at least unconventional, at the time.
He and his buddies in the film, for whom we can easily
substitute the young method actors he inspired, are only just
tougher than the earlier Dead End Kids. They are the satellites
surrounding Brando, who's always in total control. He can calm
any situation. He has an answer for everyone about everything.
The camera reinforces this sense, for in many confrontations
with townspeople or lawmen, it's kept quite low, and thus the
viewer feels strongly the intimidation tactics of Brando's gang,
and the facility with which the people's insufficiencies are
demonstrated!

But a great deal is revealed about the character, and about the
sort of pained man he stands for, in his unlikely relationship
with the girl. It's problematic, of course: she represents everything to which he's opposed—the life of home and family, of
stability. She's frightened but attracted; he teases her about her
conventional life-style. But when his gang teases her and threatens her with assault, he rescues her. Like an heroic cowboy (or a
latter-day Sir Gawain), he takes her away on his shining cycle to
the edge of town, where his subsequent kissing is brutishly

passionate, and where he reminds her that he's not the sort of gentle man she's looking for.

It's important to note that he never smiles at her (until the very last shot of the film) and that this is at once the problem and the reason for her odd attraction to him. The fact of her virginity is communicated without much subtlety: "I've never ridden on a motorcycle before," she says with wondering admiration, gazing moist-eyed at the phallic motorcycle. Her ride has all the joy of a horseback journey for her. "I wish you were going someplace. We could go together." But he senses the romantic fallacy of this more acutely than she, and rejects such

Mary Murphy and Marlon Brando.

crazy dreaming, although he's disturbed by it, aroused by it. It's not hard to see her as the unrealized and unacknowledged anima—the feminine counterpart in the masculine psyche. Conversely, Brando's black garb and his stiff, unremittingly dark mood counterbalance her simplistic innocence and dippy good cheer about the charm of the drifter's world. In effect, he's her animus, too.

Fundamentally, however, *The Wild One* treats the nature of the male gang, the social embodiment of a wild principle in men, whose instincts are passionate but unfocused. Thus, they're wanderers. The gang's activities are more mischievous than felonious, and the film is very much concerned with society's fear of the marginal man—the different one, the outsider, the man at the fringes. This is what makes it really an anti-Fascist tract, a declamation against easy judgments about acceptable conduct, and director Laslo Benedek has emphasized this whenever he had the chance. It's forcefully highlighted, for example, when a rival gang comes to town, led by Lee Marvin, whose apelike swaggering, smelly cigar, ugly stubble and vulgar loud talk make Brando look like an Anglican archbishop. In the inevitable fight, the two crash through the window of a store that sells men's tuxedos—the formal wear is a neat contrast to the gangs' studied casual attire.

The ultimately disturbing thing about Brando's crew of grown kids is that they don't steal or kill, and that they show a far more ready open-mindedness than the adults whom they upset, and who tilt toward fascism. The people seem to be in desperate need of being upset, and it's just someone like Brando who can jar their preserves. He mocks social presumptions and smugnesses needing to be undermined. The problem, however, is that he hasn't the requisite social grace to establish himself with any authority, and thus to beat them at their own game. He's doomed to marginality, and at the end he's forced to withdraw into further isolation from the dubious civilization round him. We're left quite unsure as to the quality or the locus of victory.

It's at the conclusion that we become aware of precisely how close *The Wild One* comes to the classic Western, and how much Brando is the doubtful hero-villain, and Murphy the civilizing

schoolmarm. Freed from a charge of disorderly conduct on condition he leave town, he can't even express his thanks to the sheriff or to the girl. There's the vaguest of smiles as he leaves— depositing his insignia as memento and trophy, rather like the Lone Ranger's silver bullet. It's the crude/tender relic of an enigmatic transient with some villainous strain but a whole lot of untapped good, too.

Brando represents the archetypal wild one. He stands for everything that is primitive and untamed in the masculine psyche, and which will survive, in spite of a repressive and highly ordered society. His pain is deeply felt, and so keenly that it must be muted in the expression; his love is unclear, and so is thwarted, but that's as much the fault of an overregulated society. His confusion is a confusion of identities, of the inability

The beating of Johnny.

to cope with the multiple possibilities of polite society. He'll always be the wild one, the man who can kiss only crudely, at the edges of town, and whom you can never imagine sitting calmly in a two-bedroom townhouse, feet comfortably on a hassock, smoking a pipe while his wife knits.

Brando has never depended on a gamut of expressions to convey an inner state, just as the modern antihero can't release an array of evident emotions. Everything's inside and has to be inferred from the occasional blink or tilt of the head. You have to work to get through to him. He oozes sex, but in his eyes there's something infinitely distant, sad and dispassionate in his posture toward life. His slow blinks simultaneously betoken boredom and muted sensualtiy, his laconic raising and lowering of the eyebrows give him the look of a man who can never be surprised by anything this side of the grave, but who's certain to let you know he finds you considerably less interesting than you find yourself.

Fred MacMurray, Robert Francis, Van Johnson, Humphrey Bogart.

CHAPTER 17

Bargaining for Battleships—
The Caine Mutiny, 1954

When Stanley Kramer brought to the screen Herman Wouk's Pulitzer Prize-winning novel *The Caine Mutiny*, it had already become the basis for a powerful play which enjoyed national success. By the time of the film's world premiere (in June 1954, at New York's Capitol Theatre), the whole story, therefore, was well known to many. Such a situation can be an advantage for a producer, since he has a ready-made audience. But it also can be a severe handicap, since certain elements of suspense are short-circuited, and both critics and public will inevitably make comparisons, often not basing assessments on the specific demands of film, but on facile ideas of what is "faithful" to book or play.

The critical reaction to the film was mixed, but audiences liked it, and it was a considerable hit that year. The film begins with an odd epigraph: "There has never been a mutiny in the United States Navy. The truth of this story lies not in its incidents but in the way a few men meet the crisis of their lives." Stanley Kramer explained the origin of this strange disclaimer: "The epigraph was agreed on with the Navy in exchange for aircraft carriers, destroyers, combat boats, the use of Pearl Harbor and the port of San Francisco, and anything else we needed technically—with the proviso that on the screen we do not say that the film was made with the cooperation of the United States Navy! In fact, this was the only film made with the complete cooperation of the Navy for which they didn't want credit—and insisted on the opening disclaimer."

This agreement was the result of a good deal of preproduction struggling. Before Kramer told director Edward Dmytryk to begin principal photography, he had submitted to the Navy virtually all the plans he and Harry Cohn, head of Columbia Pictures, had for the film. Rear Admiral Robert Hickey, information chief of the Navy, wrote to the producer: "I believe your production would plant in the minds of millions the idea that life in the Navy is akin to confinement in a psychiatric institution." Necessary cooperation, early on, was thus dependent on the filmmaker's agreement to several modifications in Stanley Roberts' scenario: (1) The omission of the word "Mutiny" from the title. It's not hard to imagine the amused reaction of millions of Americans who had read a novel called *The Caine Mutiny,* and then found the film version advertised as *The Caine Incident,* a title which was seriously considered. Happily, Kramer prevailed against this demand. (2) The correction of the inference that the *Caine* was not a carefully managed ship at the outset (although there never was, of course, a ship with that name). (3) The improvement of the intelligence of the enlisted men, who must not seem dull or unclever—much less, unkempt. (4) The softening of Captain Queeg's cowardice. (5) The presentation of the officers of the ship as "ordinary, well-trained, neat, efficient people rather than a bunch of scurvy misfits." There were other demands, and specific objections to scenes and lines of dialogue. Because Kramer and Columbia needed Navy cooperation, they had to consider (and argue about) demands that would, in the final analysis, have totally changed the action and purpose of the film. That the changes were kept to a minimum, and that the film script was accepted and the producer received official cooperation is little short of miraculous.

The story is set in 1944. It follows Ensign Willis Keith (Robert

Francis) as, after his departure from Princeton and from a possessive mother (Katherine Warren), he enters the Navy and is assigned to the *Caine*. There, he meets a decent and courageous senior officer named Steve Maryk (Van Johnson) and another officer, aspiring novelist Tom Keefer (Fred MacMurray). At first the young ensign had hoped to be on a carrier or a battleship: this is "just a beaten-up tub," as Captain DeVries (Tom Tully) admits. In his zeal, Keith finds the captain lazy and incompetent, and fails to see his humanity and understanding of men's needs. But although he has the chance for a transfer, Keith chooses to remain on the *Caine* rather than seem like a malcontent. "You will live to regret staying here," says Keefer sarcastically.

At first jubilant when Captain DeVries is replaced by Captain Queeg (Humphrey Bogart) he, and gradually his mates, are dismayed to discover that the new leader is a sick man, paranoid, obsessed with petty details and on the verge of

The beginning of Maryk's doubts . . .

complete insanity. The first sign of his illness occurs when the captain recounts an earlier war experience: "The way those subs ganged up on us, I. thought they had it in for me personally." Gradually, the man's megalomania, his compulsion about the crew's neatness and his habit of rolling two steel balls between thumb and forefinger all lead the perceptive crew members to the realization that they're in for trouble with such a man at the helm.

And so they are. In a typhoon, the captain is paralyzed by fear into making poor judgments. Invoking Article 184 of the Navy Regulations—which involves the relief of a commanding officer by a subordinate, under special circumstances—Maryk takes over. He is, of course, brought to court-martial, and this is the second climax of the film. What at first appears to be a lost battle for Maryk turns into a victory, as Lieutenant Barney Greenwald (José Ferrer) reveals the captain's madness right in the courtroom. The accused is acquitted; the ensign has grown up and can now marry a girl he has dated while on leave. But Maryk and Keefer, uninvolved and unsympathetic, are the objects of Greenwald's outspoken scorn at the evening's "victory celebration." He berates them for their lack of concern for a sick man and for their blithe ignorance of those who had earlier defended the country and were now victims of such strain—like Queeg. The film ends by claiming an inherent heroism for most naval officers.

Not since *Gone With the Wind* had the public been so excited about a movie based on a recent and popular book. Magazines round the country ran several stories on the production and imminent release of the film, and publications as different in tone as *Variety* and *The Christian Science Monitor* were publishing features and interviews before the New York premiere, detailing the difficulties of making the film and the anticipated response from audiences across the country.

"Twentieth Century-Fox and MGM had gone to the Navy when the bidding for the book was open," Kramer said. "The Navy flatly said, in the beginning, that they simply wouldn't have anything to do with a project like this." Then, when Kramer had secured the rights, subtler negotiations began. He had taken an option on the book which gave author Herman

Wouk $12,000 to work with Stanley Roberts on a treatment that would mollify the hurt feelings of the Navy about the intention to make a film about a mutiny. (Wouk was to receive an additional $48,000 when production began.)

One of the first problems confronting Wouk and Roberts was the Navy's objection to Queeg's status. The Navy wanted Queeg to be a reservist rather than an Annapolis graduate, class of 1936. The writers wouldn't back down on this, however, and later compromises enabled them to retain Queeg's original history. Even more to the credit of the Navy's sense of balance and humor, reported *Newsweek* somewhat smarmily, was the fact that the Academy's class of '36 reserved two vacant chairs at a reunion banquet for the fictional Captain and Mrs. Queeg, and that the same class provided Commander James C. Shaw as the film's technical adviser.

For having agreed to an opening disclaimer and no mention of

The moment of mutiny.

official assistance, Kramer was lent two destroyer mine sweep-ers—the *Thompson* in California, and the *Doyle* in Pearl Harbor. "I was practically in command of Pearl Harbor for three weeks," recalled Kramer with some amusement. Then, in order to synchronize production with the ships' maneuvers, the company went with the *Thompson*, long in drydock, on its postrepair trial runs. In Hawaii, they went aboard the *Doyle* for a trip into tropical waters. (Although it was the original intention to steer that ship into a gale for the bad-weather footage, it was finally decided that the typhoon would be artificially created in the studio. Thanks to the extraordinary efforts of Lawrence W. Butler, the special effects for that sequence have the look of authenticity and real danger.)

In many important ways, *The Caine Mutiny* is a very different film from anything Kramer had previously attempted. Up to this time, his reputation had been based on films which were really modest, black-and-white pictures with offbeat castings, tight shooting schedules and surprisingly low budgets. This, however, was a wide-screen Technicolor spectacle budgeted at two million dollars. "One penny beyond that, or a minute beyond two hours' length," recalled Edward Dmytryk, "and Columbia had the right to take over the film for editing."

In addition, it had a grade-A, stellar cast and a shooting schedule of almost three months. Thomas Wood, who inter-viewed Kramer during production, found that the producer's attitudes had shifted somewhat by this time: not opposed to making money by satisfying the public's taste for "blockbust-ers," Kramer allowed this film to be directed almost entirely by practical considerations. With all the preproduction publicity and nationwide interest in casting, it became clear to Kramer that only the biggest names would be acceptable to people.

"Kramer would cast all his previous films very modestly," said Dmytryk. "He'd slap a director on the back and say cheerfully, 'Oh, you can do it'—implying, 'without big stars.' But *The Caine Mutiny* was different. Kramer saw how big names meant big box office, and he never forgot this when it came to the films he directed himself, beginning just after this picture.

"I don't know why he picked me for it," Dmytryk continued.

"He had mentioned it to me before I left for Israel to do *The Juggler*. This was going to be a very big picture, he said, and I told him I certainly was very interested in it. But up to that time I'd done only B-pictures for him. This was an exciting new development in our relationship.

"But it's a disappointment in my career, to tell the truth. I insist it could have been a classic. It did get an Oscar nomination for best picture"—and nominations, too, for Bogart (best actor) and Tully (best supporting actor)—"but Kramer, who (with Dore Schary) is the most publicity-conscious man in the industry, got high-handed with Harry Cohn, and in fact had to toe the line. The film should have been much longer. Stanley Roberts' original script was about 190 pages, even without the romantic subplot involving the ensign and the nightclub singer. It should have remained that—a three and one-half- or four-hour picture—and it would have been more logically developed, the characters would have been further fleshed out. It would have been perfect."

(The romantic subplot has an interesting detail, too. The girl, called "May Wynn" in the novel and the revised screenplay, was played by a former Copacabana entertainer named Donna Lee Hickey. She took the professional name of "May Wynn" for this picture, probably intending the deliberate confusion—May Wynn playing the role of May Wynn—to provide a neat joke for her new career. But the new career did not go farther than two additional films that same year.)

There is one quite significant difference between the novel and the film which in fact alters the meaning of the film as well as its structure, as critic Arthur Knight was quick to point out in *The Saturday Review of Literature* when the film was released. José Ferrer, in his tipsy tirade at the conclusion, reminds the officers—and audience—of the value of a peacetime Navy, scolding not only MacMurray (who gets the champagne tossed in his face) but everyone who stood by and refused to help when the sick captain was in trouble. This sudden shift in tone—which implies that the crew, unsympathetic to Queeg from the start, was at least partially responsible for the conditions which made the recourse to Article 184 necessary—turns the film to a safe endorsement of the system, rather than the critical questioning of it which was quite clear in the novel. "It's a hell of a yarn," said Admiral William M. Fechteler, former chief of naval operations, after reading Wouk's book. "But I wonder how the author collected on one boat all the screwballs I have known in my thirty years in the Navy!"

The film's most obvious screwball, of course, is Captain Queeg. At the Navy's urging, Queeg became in the film a more sympathetic character than he appeared to be in the book. He is here depicted as a battle-fatigued veteran who has seen so much action that now his mental health has been affected. As in all feature films the sequences of *The Caine Mutiny* were necessarily shot out of order. It's altogether astonishing, therefore, to note in the final product Bogart's gradual delineation of mental breakdown, the slow retreat into madness, the finally crippling paranoia leading to collapse on the witness stand. "In his mouth," wrote Arthur Knight, "the meaningless clichés and strange circumlocutions that give the first hint of his true nature still have the ring of natural speech." But as the captain begins to crumble, Bogart slowly abandons the cool confidence of his innumerable melodramas and his image as a "tough guy," until, in his forlorn and frozen pain in the pilot-house at the height of the typhoon, the poisonous red of the emergency lights transforms his face into a demonic mask.

But this virtuoso performance paradoxically reveals another flaw in the picture. Nowhere is it adequately explained how such a madman could have got so far—even in government service. Surely the condition would have been noticed by officials or subordinates before it reached this critical point?

The movie, for all its slick handsomeness and first-rate production design, is also sometimes, as *Time* magazine put it, "a little cold and loud where it needs the flare and hiss of honest anger." And there is that annoying finale, in which the emphasis of the entire work has been shifted from the case history of a psychopath (with anti-Navy overtones to the story, too) to a forthright cheer for the Navy and for a paranoid commander—an effect, as Arthur Knight noted, that was heightened by the blaring, Movietone-News marches in Max Steiner's score.

In addition, the handling of Ensign Keith is unsatisfactory. In the book, Wouk used the sensitive young man's point of view to tell the story of the ship, its captains and crew. But the film has its own point of view, quite independent of Keith, and the ensign becomes another—and somewhat wooden—character. Just because he figured so prominently in the novel, and because the writers tried to remain as faithful as possible to it, Keith gets an inordinate amount of attention. The romantic scenes are unconvincing and irrelevant, too.

But *The Caine Mutiny* is by no means dull. It was a bold attempt for Kramer to turn a popular book into a film that

José Ferrer, Van Johnson, Fred MacMurray: the trial.

would sharply divide critics and audiences. "Perhaps," suggested Philip T. Hartung in *Commonweal,* "Wouk's sprawling novel was almost too hard to film—especially if the finished product had to please everybody, including the United States Navy."

The film was the last Kramer made for Columbia Pictures under his contract, which expired in March 1954. He had had several disagreements with Harry Cohn (an experience in which he was not alone), and he did not associate with Columbia again until *Ship of Fools,* a decade later and several years after Cohn's death.

Instead, he returned to work at United Artists, for whom he directed his first film—also based on a best-selling novel of the time.

CHAPTER 18

Kramer Directs—

Not as a Stranger, 1955

"One of the things I regret about my life is all those years I had to be a money raiser, a producer. Some people say I should have stayed a producer, that I was better at it than directing. But to tell the truth, I was ill equipped to be a producer. I always wanted to be a director. I had been training for it since my early days as an editor and a writer. And as soon as I could break away from producing and move on to directing, I did so." It wasn't a complete break, of course, for Stanley Kramer continued to produce all the films he directed in the second phase of his career. (And on three occasions he produced without directing.) But he had reached his goal, the director's chair, and nothing was spared in his efforts to make the first film a really big Hollywood movie.

Novelist Morton Thompson had died two weeks after he finished the manuscript for his book *Not as a Stranger*, the story of an arrogant doctor "who practiced medicine but didn't know how to treat people." It became one of the best sellers of the 1950s, and Stanley Kramer bought the film rights when the book was in galleys. He exerted a greal deal of care preparing the film

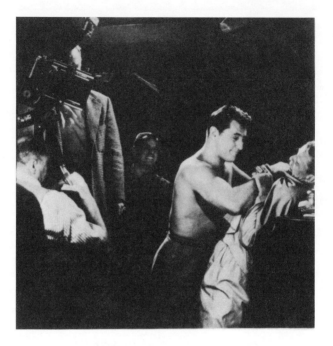

Kramer directing Robert Mitchum and Frank Sinatra . . .

. . . and what the movie audience sees.

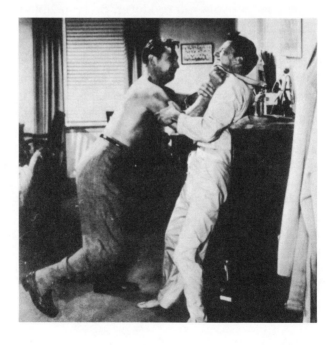

and signed four Oscar-winning actors to the cast. He also did meticulous medical research and immersed himself in the details of the book's background.

"I thoroughly enjoyed making this picture," he recalled. "It was the first open and respectable assault on the unsavory aspects of the modern medical profession, and it generated all those medical series on television. I could have directed some of those, too, if I'd wanted to."

The ambition of Lucas Marsh (Robert Mitchum) is the major theme of the story. It's his goal to become a great physician, and this is at once his chief asset and glaring liability. It drives him, on the one hand, to work tirelessly in school and to tolerate no shoddiness in colleagues or doctor friends; but it also leads him, on the other hand, to exploit the affections of nurse Kristina Hedvigson (Olivia de Havilland), who supports him before and during their loveless marriage until he has his own practice. Because of his lack of feeling, he is an embarrassment to his friend and fellow medical student Alfred Boone (Frank Sinatra), and to his mentor Dr. Aarons (Broderick Crawford). He is also unsympathetic to his poor, alcoholic father (Lon Chaney, Jr.).

Following internship, Lucas joins Dr. Runkleman (Charles Bickford) in a small-town practice, where he treats many diseases but few patients—his flaw remains his lack of compassion for others' anguish. This is especially true of his nonrelationship with his wife, to whose desire for a child he is indifferent. An affair with a local divorcée (Gloria Grahame) brings his marriage to a critical point, and his wife, after bearing his unwanted child, leaves him. Only when Dr. Runkleman dies (while Lucas is performing an emergency heart operation on him) is his character at last tempered with humility. At the end, he attempts to repair his broken marriage.

Edna and Edward Anhalt's script condensed a 972-page book into a tight, 173-page shooting script, and this resulted in some major changes. Lucas' childhood was eliminated, the plot was updated from the 1920s. The modern medical and surgical advances had, therefore, to be taken into consideration. The film's budget (nearly two million dollars) was many times that of Kramer's earlier black-and-white features, and it put him at once into the very big leagues. From the former Chaplin studios, where the film was prepared and shot, the producer-director and his cast went forth to local university hospitals, where they virtually set up shop in order to absorb atmosphere and learn to recreate attitude and detail. Mitchum and de Havilland, in fact, attended eight different operations. (Broderick Crawford, in the film's opening moments, announces to his students that they should watch carefully since he is about to perform the first autopsy they'll see. One by one, the students faint or turn away in disgust and shock. Only Mitchum, as the steely Dr. Marsh, is unfazed by what he sees. To prepare to act the part of a skilled knife wielder at this procedure, Crawford attended an autopsy at a local hospital. He promptly got sick.)

Much to Kramer's credit, there are four operations which have been dramatically recreated in the film, and which are discussed with admirable scientific accuracy: a laminectomy, a subtotal gastrectomy, plastic surgery on a hand, and an attempted repair of an aortal aneurysm. That Not as a Stranger maintains such a realistic texture and is so faithful in medical detail, is due to the technical consultation of Drs. Morton Maxwell and Josh Fields, and Marjorie Lefevre, R.N., as well as a dozen subtechnical advisers. In the operating-room sequences, Mitchum was assisted by a team of real surgeons, all playing themselves, all masked and appropriately anonymous.

These operating-room sequences are not incidental to the narrative. Since the film's major theme is the "lack of heart" in Lucas Marsh, there is structural reinforcement of this in the plot when his father dies of heart failure due to alcoholism; when his friend and mentor Dr. Runkleman dies—literally in his hands—of heart failure; and when his wife refers, as she frequently does, to his own emptiness of heart. This receives visual support when a human chest wall is laid bare, the ribs are cut away, and the camera shows the beating of a human heart. There's a stark documentary quality to this scene, as there is to the scenes of nurses passing instruments with rapid precision, the anesthetist turning his dials and monitoring his pumps and graphs that indicate every vital sign during surgery, and the fluoroscopic examination which follows the path of a pin's removal from a boy's chest. In sequences like these, the viewer becomes aware of the deliberate bipolar attitude of the film: admiration and wonder before modern medicine and the skills of gifted physicians and nurses; and rage at the frequently venal motivations of those in the profession. There is, in support of this latter idea, a running and blunt discussion of fee splitting, professional snobbery, neglect of the elderly and dying (who are insults to the talent of the physician, and who witness to the mortality of everyone), gross errors in judgment and the pressure of politics within the system. There's also mention of the widely practiced system of racial and religious quotas—especially regarding Jews— in medical schools at the time.

The film actually tells two quite distinct stories: the first is set in the medical school, and the climax occurs when Lucas' father is brought, dead on arrival, to the hospital and his son stares down at the body. The entire scene is shot in glaringly bright light, and this contrasts with the following scene in which Mitchum walks in dry-eyed reflection through his father's gray, dark, depressing cold-water flat. The second narrative movement begins when he goes to Greenville to begin his practice. There's a certain letdown at this point, perhaps unavoidable after the swift, wise-cracking breeziness which Sinatra, Crawford and Lee Marvin brought to the first part of the film, and in which the arrivals of ambulances, the sudden nighttime emergencies, the round of study and work gave the film a marathon pacing.

The second part of the film, however, locates its action and suspense more directly within the spiritual sickness and confrontation: the weakening marriage between the principals, and the short-lived affair. The film runs along more than two hours, and in the last forty minutes one perhaps wishes the hand of the editor had not been stayed.

Within these movements, however, the film is structurally admirable: the first part ends with the death of Marsh's father; the second part ends with the death of his adopted father figure (Bickford), which jolts the chilly Dr. Marsh into realization of his own frailty and mortality. The critics, almost to a person, were unimpressed by Robert Mitchum's performance. "He's considerably over his acting depth," wrote the critic for *Variety*, "and he's poker-faced from start to finish. The confinements of Expression A and Expression B hardly fit the interior drive, the confusion and furious ambition implied in the script." William K. Zinsser, in *The New York Herald Tribune*, complained that Mitchum "hardly changes expression, or conveys emotion, from beginning to end. It is a monotonous performance in a role that could have been intriguing." British critic David Shipman came closer to the mark, perhaps, when he noted that Mitchum's "careful underplaying" gave the film a center (although Shipman disdained the film itself).

In fact, the casting and performance of Mitchum seem to me inspired, for his archness and priggishness, his cold glances and subdued, laconic movements reveal precisely the emotional desert in which the man exists. His heavy-lidded sensuality has been for once more creatively exploited, and all that comes through is a sort of detached, defused passion that serves only his professional ambition. It was Mitchum's most financially successful film to date, too.

"Robert Mitchum was so difficult to photograph," said Kramer, "because he's such a powerful presence. Offscreen, he thinks it's weakness to care about something or someone, so he pretends he doesn't—which gives a nice edge to his role in *Not as a Stranger*." Apparently, Mitchum's reputation for on-the-set high jinks was sustained here, too. "Olivia de Havilland was at all times a real lady," Kramer added. "But she was surrounded by all these rowdy guys, who were also a heavy drinking crowd. During shooting, I imported Myron McCormick from New York for the part of Dr. Snider, the anesthetist. We were ready to shoot an operating sequence, and Mitchum's cue to McCormick was, 'Ready, Al?' Everyone was masked and poised for the scene. Then, McCormick suddenly screamed out, in a too loud and thick voice. 'READY!' And then I realized that I'd added another problem to my already problem group: McCormick was dead drunk!"

The critics had trouble accepting Gloria Grahame, too, as the steamy divorcée Harriet Lang. "She was so wonderful in *The Bad and the Beautiful*," whined *The Hollywood Reporter*, "but she seems to have gone into her blue period of acting. She seems bent on playing every scene without moving her upper lip, as though she were a British colonel stoutly holding Fort Chutney during the Indian Mutiny." And *Time* observed that she played the role "in a manner suggesting that someone has paralyzed her upper lip with novocaine." Stanley Kramer explained these criticisms. "In

Olivia De Havilland, off-camera.

fact, Gloria Grahame put tissue under her upper lip because someone told her a thrust upper lip was sexy! See what I had to cope with?" With the pencil-thin lipstick line, it became her trademark; but today it seems a self-contained parody, and the truth is that she was better in earlier films—Fritz Lang's *The Big Heat*, for example, in which she plays the hapless gun moll whose face is doused with boiling coffee by brutish Lee Marvin; and in Cecil B. Mille's *The Greatest Show on Earth*, she's a live wire of wisecracks and subtle lovelessness, splendidly paired with an acidulous Dorothy Lamour.

The climatic scene between Mitchum and Grahame—unfortunately unforgettable because of its dreadfulness—occurs one wild and windy night, when they meet in an orchard in back of her stables. While they stare longingly at each other, a dark stallion batters the barn door in an attempt to get to a mare who

At the premiere party: Broderick Crawford, Olivia De Havilland, Charles Bickford, Robert Mitchum.

frolics in the field. Mitchum releases the passionate stallion, and while it charges toward its mate in a furious crescendo of music and hoofbeats, Mitchum approaches Grahame and plants a desperately passionate kiss. Fade-out. The pop-Freudian imagery is a little hard to take, even for 1955, and the scene doesn't work: the humans, like the horses, seem merely to be standing on their hind legs really doing nothing, just full of sound and fury. Equine metaphors work occasionally: they worked for Shakespeare in *Venus and Adonis,* they worked for D. H. Lawrence on several occasions, and they worked for Hitchcock in *Marnie.* But the effect here is tired, mechanical and finally amusing.

Olivia de Havilland played the role of a Swedish nurse with a sweetly strong simplicity, and her performance is deeply felt, if only rarely credible. Her wide-eyed wonder and antiphonal repetition of phrases like "Ya, dis is goot" make her seem like a refugee from television's *Mama* show, but this is partially the fault of the script.

In his first film as director, Kramer tackled a bold subject with imagination and generally good taste. He and Franz Planer cross-matched their principal players and emphasized the physical contrasts between them: tall, burly Mitchum teamed up with slight Sinatra; de Havilland's high-pitched blondness with Grahame's pouting, puffy slinkiness. There are some inventive and classily mounted dissolves and pans to show Mitchum practicing with Bickford, and to show the arrival in his office of a variety of patients: the camera pans round a room, and each time, in a series of barely perceptible cuts, a door opens to reveal a new patient. During the final, fatal surgery on Bickford, the camera swirls up and about the frantic Mitchum, following the action like a busy operating-room nurse. As Mitchum becomes more anxious, the camera moves more swiftly. His frenzy is sensed in the turns and dips of the camera, not in any overstated acting or strident dialogue.

Even if the critics were unenthusiastic about the film, many audiences loved its story and its medical setting.

But nobody liked Kramer's next film, which he has called "a complete and utter bomb!"

Frank Sinatra, Sophia Loren, Cary Grant.

CHAPTER 19

Sinatra Walks Out—
The Pride and the Passion, 1957

"In fact, it was more than a bomb—it was a bust!" With admirable honesty, Stanley Kramer admitted the failure of the biggest film he ever made. *The Pride and the Passion*—more expensive, more ambitious, more problem-laden than all his other films combined—was undertaken with great earnestness and in the hope of adding to the film spectacles that were so popular in the 1950s. The result was disappointing. But what went into the making of the film is fascinating.

Based on *The Gun,* a famous novel by C. S. Forester, the film tells about a dedicated band of Spanish *guerrilleros* during the invasion by Napoleonic forces in 1810. Led by Miguel (Frank Sinatra), an uneducated son of a shoemaker, and aided by British naval Captain Anthony Trumbull (Cary Grant) who offers to lead the men to British support forces, the men recover a valuable lost cannon—huge in size and terrifying in its possibilities—and drag it two hundred miles across the Spanish countryside to Avila, where the French forces are headquartered. En route, they experience severe hardship, and many men die trying to bring the cannon to its destination. The goal is finally achieved, but only after the heroic deaths of Miguel and of Juana (Sophia Loren), a fiery and patriotic woman over whom both men had intermittently fought. Trumbull reverently kneels at the statue of St. Teresa of Avila within the conquered walls, and then moves on to make the final symbolic gesture of unity between English and Spanish forces which will spell the end of Napoleon's influence in Spain.

The film's title (never actually made clear) probably refers to the combination of Spanish virtues which it attempts to document visually and dramatically: the pride located in Miguel and the passion located in Juana. At least one critic, however, saw the pride as that of the Grant character, and the passion as that of the Sinatra character: they work together for the defeat of the French, but they clash over the woman. Thus, their unity and division become a microcosm for the hostilities which finally erupt in war between neighboring countries. This explanation for the title seems a bit precious and may give more significance to the characters than the script does.

One of the major problems with the film is, in fact, the script by Edna and Edward Anhalt. They had been collaborators and friends with Kramer and were also associate producers of several films. Natural choices for his first—and, as it turned out, his only—epic, the Anhalts worked closely with him in California and then traveled to Spain for the months of preproduction. However, the Anhalts' marriage was terminating, and this did not help for the maintenance of unity in the script, which was, in any case, to have been a joint effort. The script's problems were further exacerbated during a siege of bad weather in Spain, when Kramer was recruiting a platoon of Spanish extras, getting official approval to use historic shrines and monuments and organizing a vast and astonishing logistical operation. These preparations—and the deterioration in the script—lasted almost eighteen months in Spain, and were followed by three months of shooting there (a time Kramer called "the hundred days that shook Spain").

Aware of the sensitive Spanish feelings about their nineteenth-century "War of Independence," Kramer met with Generalissimo Francisco Franco before he started filming. The script,

The cause of all the trouble.

The long trek to Avila.

he told Franco, was careful not to mention that England was the salvation of Spain in her struggle against the French (a point on which most history books differ from this film). Because Kramer gave emphasis to the courage and ingenuity of the Spanish guerrilla fighters, Franco was well pleased and gave his approval (and some cooperation). It is not clear—either to me or to the director—just how much Franco's approval concretized itself in various *incognito* official assistances as the company made its way through the Spanish terrain.

And make their way they did, over thousands of miles of rugged country, first searching for just the right locations. Kramer and production designer Rudolph Sternad finally settled on twenty-five locations, each within a hundred-mile radius of either Avila or Madrid. They were delighted when they saw the famous basilica at El Escorial, the aqueduct at Segovia and the wall surrounding Avila. As location scouting concluded, it became clear that roads would have to be built to permit the passage of caravans for the crew, technicians and cast of thousands. Accordingly, $75,000 worth of road construction was undertaken, and the budget began to soar. (Could this have added to Franco's delight? It's unlikely the roads were torn up after the production company departed!)

At the same time, Kramer's small staff of a dozen was growing. By the time of principal photography, there was a staff of four hundred, and no one was idle. Many had the task of maintaining order and peace among the villagers who appeared in various scenes as the shooting progressed from place to place. Extras and animals were recruited as the company traveled, and the people of one Castilian town refurbished several of their wooden carts—the same as those used in Napoleon's day—only to be told that the original battered and used condition was in fact preferable! They had then to work doubly hard for several days to restore their "props" to the natural state.

Of the nearly ten thousand extras, five thousand were needed to stage a disorderly retreat across the bleak and muddy mountain top of Hoyo de Manzanares, forty miles from Madrid. The extras, of course, were excited about making their film debut. As the helicopter, equipped with the camera on a Tyler mount, soared overhead, they kept looking up and smiling. They moved over the hill in a blaze of green and red uniforms, smiling continuously until a voice shouted at them from above through a loudspeaker system, "Keep your heads down!"—a Spanish god's commands from on high. Several takes were always necessary for scenes like this, and it wasn't easy to keep the native assistants, who were doing the shouting, from becoming impatient.

Mules, burros and horses were bought from local farmers as the journey progressed, and a ranch was established at a central location to house and care for the animals. How different all this was from the single interior set for *The Four Poster* or the studio locations for *Home of the Brave!*

Part of the crew, directly under Kramer's supervision, chose and trained two hundred of Spain's best athletes to act as the *guerrilleros*. These men lived with the huge cannon day and night during shooting, and because of the unpredictable Spanish weather and the inevitable wear and tear on clothes, the costumes exceeded two thousand, for this group alone, over the course of twelve weeks. Seamstresses had to be present for each sequence, needle at the ready: the VistaVision color camera caught the slightest detail, after all.

"These men ran through fire, were blown off bridges into eleven feet of water and fell from buildings," Kramer told me. "At Robledo, where we filmed an especially difficult and dangerous sequence, I was nervous the whole time about the athletes' safety. The cannon was supposed to crash through the side of a mountain—which it did—and was then released by a cable, went through a 'brick' wall that was actually made of cork, careened across an open field and turned over on its side. It was marvelous, the way these men cooperated. It was as if they were actually fighting for their own independence. They took it as more than just a movie job."

During preproduction, Kramer had wondered just how he would film the battles. Since expenses were already mounting, and since the management of such an enormous cast and crew had built-in problems and dangers in relation to the cannon, he decided to film these battle sequences in a manner established decades earlier in the epics of D. W. Griffith: a minimal approach for a maximum effect. The French soldiers' presence is indicated by a simple silhouette against a long shot of the horizon or a sudden close-up of individual stragglers or prisoners. Death and destruction are conveyed by a long shot of a burning village. Bloodshed and torture are suggested by the look of horror on the face of a comrade as he makes his way through the bodies of the fallen. There are no massive close-ups of hand-to-hand combat. "I wanted to tell a simple story of human courage," Kramer said, "and there was no necessity to detail the dreadful aspects. The main character, after all, was the gun, and that was terrible enough."

The three years needed to prepare the film *The Pride and the Passion*, the use of ten thousand actors and extras, artists' fees and technical costs raised the price of the picture considerably. So did the explosives ordered from Italy, the autos and trucks driven in caravans from Germany, the technicians imported from Hollywood, the sound equipment, loudspeakers and walkie-talkies shipped from France, the lighting equipment and makeup men from England, and the crew of assistants, purchasing agents, traffic supervisors, secretaries and translators hired from Spain. Very quickly the budget exceeded $4,000,000. (The last sequence of the film—the assault on Avila—lasts about three minutes on screen and represents the largest motion-picture payroll ever distributed in Europe on a single day: 1,200,000 pesetas, or about $30,000.)

The travel needed to plan the film reflected the story itself, for fundamentally it's in the tradition of the "long trek movie," and it has all the clichés of that subgenre. Intercut with the tiring (and finally tiresome) journey are the obligatory scenes of campfire and flamenco dance, guitar singing, jokes at a makeshift meal and the expected romantic triangle. These scenes are the least satisfying precisely because they lack the bigness of the rest of the film, and because neither the pride nor the passion of the characters matches the grand scale of the gun or of the masses of people making their way across the country. The principal characters are not finely drawn, and because they seem so flat and one-dimensional, it's hard to generate much interest in what happens to them. This is not helped by monumentally ill-advised casting. Grant is stiff and uncomfortable as the English officer on perpetual reconnoiter; Sinatra, in bangs, seems always on the verge of breaking into song (which he never does) and instead affects a Spanish accent that makes everything sound odd. "Jew want more, don't Jew, Captain Trumbull? Jew are thinking of her, after Avila, no?" The mass of fighters seems so much more compelling and credible!

Several of the spectacular scenes posed special difficulties, of course. One of these was the French camp sequence in which the men, in order to clear a road for their cannon, have no choice but to wipe out an entire enemy encampment. This they accomplish by making balls of pitch and straw, igniting them and throwing them down on the sleeping French soldiers in the middle of the night. "We shot that night scene at night, which added to our problems," Kramer said. "People had trouble seeing, and the lighting was very hard, even for our gifted cameraman, Franz Planer. But Cary Grant and Frank Sinatra refused doubles for this scene. They actually ran through the camp and jumped on a powder wagon that was already loaded with barrels on fire. Therefore, we could do close-up shots of them, since there was no problem of doubles!" At this point, Grant and Sinatra were still excited about the picture, and the scene is really quite astounding. Later, however, as we'll see, their enthusiasm waned.

A second difficulty was the destruction of a vast section of wall surrounding the city of Avila. Naturally, the actual wall was not to be destroyed, so a cork one was constructed around it. The first time the director shouted "Action!" the explosives which were contained within the cork wall failed to work, and there was a whole new setup, requiring two extra days of work.

For this scene, Sophia Loren is to be killed in the explosion. The camera catches her running through the melee, terror on her face. The terror, it turns out, is authentic: at one point Loren—here making her American film début, after Ava Gardner had turned down the role—was so close to one of the exploding mines that the cork and sand momentarily blinded her. She stumbled, nearly fell, rubbed some of the sand out of her eyes and then continued the assigned run. Had she faltered and fallen at this point, the entire sequence would have been ruined, since the wall couldn't have been blown up again! She continued her truly panic-stricken flight until the exact point at which she was supposed to fall dead.

"We rolled the cameras," Kramer recalled, "and the gun came right up to the lens. It was a perfect composition. As everyone scattered for safety, I looked around and saw twenty-five Spanish crewman crying with joy that it all went so well.

"It was at this point that Cary Grant said to me, 'Let's go home. You get yourself a boxing ring'—he was referring to *Champion*—'and I'll get a boudoir'—a set he was accustomed to for his usual romantic comedies. 'We'll make two pictures for the headaches of this one.' And I must admit there were moments I was tempted. . . ." But Kramer pressed on, and his enthusiasm was for a while longer contagious. In an article prepared in Madrid for *The New York Times*, Jane Cianfarra reported that "people on the production who have no immediate business in the day's shooting turn up unexpectedly, muddy and red-nosed from the long cold walk through boggy terrain to the camera, explaining that they just thought they would like to see how things are going. And Cary Grant, arriving several days ahead of his scheduled appearance before the cameras for one particular scene, borrowed knee boots for the hike and then squatted for hours on the camera platform."

A third spectacular sequence was filmed in the basilica at El Escorial. The morning call sheet read: "No smoking will be permitted in the basilica or in the sacristy. The entire crew and staff are hereby notified that we have been severely warned against loud talk and profanity. Under no circumstances should any nails be driven into the floors or walls of the monastery. Absolutely no visitors will be permitted in the sacristy, and no Sunday work will be permitted—neither interior nor exterior."

This set of rules, issued by the production department, emphasizes what a unique movie event was taking place. For the first time, a motion-picture company had been given permission to photograph a dramatic sequence within the walls of the famed monastery of San Lorenzo de El Escorial. For everyone—monks, crew, townspeople—it was a great day. With thousands of hooded and robed extras carrying thousands of flickering candles, the cannon is dragged down the main aisle, camouflaged amid the trappings of a religious procession and hidden beneath the high altar. The sequence was alternately photographed from a point on the upper floor of the monastery, 150 feet in the air, and quite low on the floor, on a dolly just ahead of the cannon's point of view, as it were.

It's no use pretending that the story line of *The Pride and the Passion* is anything but hopelessly static and empty. But exciting visuals like the siege of Avila, the entrance into El Escorial and the adventures of the cannon make the film intermittently interesting.

The cannon, of course, is the main character and reason for the picture. In the novel, it's described as weighing 6,000 pounds, with a 40-foot barrel and cannonballs weighing 96 pounds each that have an impact weight of 9,000 pounds— enough to breach the thickest walls. "To create this monstrous weapon," reported a writer for *Newsweek* who was on the set, "production designer Rudolph Sternad steeped himself in the military machinery of the Napoleonic era and consulted a squad of armament experts. Once he decided on the design, a giant mold was constructed. With this, six separate guns were made up to cope with the brutal treatment the weapon suffers during its heroic journey to the walls of Avila." Each cannon was 14 feet high, had a barrel 24 feet long and wheels 10 feet high, and was made of a nonflammable plastic. Each weighed nearly a ton and was richly ornamented with figures, scrolls and inscriptions.

At one point, mounted on a raft for a river crossing, the cannon rushes downstream and is caught in the mud. Next sequence: the necessary rescue from this predicament (all this is carefully planned in the script). Then the cannon is hauled up a steep hillside, only to run away on the far slope and have to be rescued again. Dragged, hauled, cajoled, pushed and pulled across two hundred miles of Spanish countryside, it is the cannon that urges the people to acts of courage and heroism; it is the cannon that sustains the story and overshadows the actors. It seems to have a life of its own, as it cuts a path through a forest, eludes patrols, inspires bloody battles and is hoisted high above cliffs. As Grant says to the archbishop, "It's not merely a gun, it's the only symbol of resistance left in Spain!"

All of this is visually exciting and is designed to support a theme which, according to United Artists' press release at the time, was that "of human strength of body, mind and spirit; of human faith, poured into the symbol of a gun which brings a balance, bought by self-sacrifice, between the pride of discipline, tradition and schooled intelligence, and the blind passion for freedom of country, home and self, held together by Woman, who will always believe in the glory of both." A very noble—and hopelessly prolix—statement, and one which is hard to find buried in the script. It would have perhaps been more accurate to say that *The Pride and the Passion* is a colorful spectacle, and plot be damned (much less theme). It's difficult, for example, to see Sophia Loren as the archetype of Woman, since she is called upon to do little except dress (or undress) daringly, dance a wild flamenco number and thrust her lower lip now toward Sinatra, then toward Grant.

The reason the film fails to engage interest beyond the spectacular sequences is also that there were seven weeks' more shooting in Spain scheduled when work was halted. "Suddenly Frank Sinatra said to me, 'Hot or cold, Thursday I'm leaving the movie. So get a lawyer and sue me.' He just couldn't stand Spain, and off he went. Of course I didn't sue. We were already a million dollars over budget! When I got back to Hollywood, I solved the problem by two days' work in a studio with potted palms." Well, this really solved nothing, and the unfinished characters, even at their deaths, seem still woefully unfinished.

Kramer, who to this day is embarrassed by the film, is surprised that some critics liked it. Hollis Alpert said that it was "haunting ... and there are a lot of fine things in it. The spectacle looks real, and very much unlike the sleazy effects gotten by De Mille in several of his cardboard and plaster epics. To make peasants look ragged and like peasants, Kramer got the people and the clothes dirty. When a monster gun runs wild down a mountainside it is a real effect and not something worked out in a laboratory. . . . There were doubts about him as a director, there will be none now." *Cue* said it was "a grand spectacle," and *Newsweek* called it "one of the year's best films, fresh and engrossing, a rousing paean to the spirit of nationalism without overt flag-waving. Moreover, the film has pathos, humor, even a touch of religion."

Few critics, in fact, were very hard about *The Pride and the Passion.* But the public was. As another producer said about one of his own flops, "The public stayed away in droves." Kramer is right in placing it far beneath his best works, one of which immediately followed this. "For the first time I did a story in which 'the thing' transcends the actors," Kramer admitted. And that's precisely the fatal flaw in the film: it's about an object, not about people. And it is people, their problems and prejudices, their pride and their passions, that elsewhere engage the talent and commitment of Stanley Kramer. Because there is not a recognizable and deeply felt human dilemma here, the film fails to have the Kramer touch. It's lovely to look at, but it has no heart.

"I may look healthy," he said on returning to California for the editing, "but that's because of the suntan. Underneath, I'm a wreck. An absolute wreck."

Tony Curtis and Sidney Poitier, the defiant ones.

CHAPTER 20

"Bowling Green, Sewing Machine!"— *The Defiant Ones,* 1958

"After World War II, when I started on my own, the things that impressed me turned out to be issues which I thought lent themselves to dramatization. That wasn't always true, but it was true often enough. I did find, however, that nobody really objected to messages. Everyone knows the old cliché about messages and message films, and the exhibitors' objection, 'If we want messages, we can go to Western Union.' What they really objected to was messages which didn't make money, which is something else altogether! When they made money, they thought the message films were quite extraordinary and very welcome.

"Some films the liberals regarded as contributions to the body politic in terms of the history of the black man in America— *Home of the Brave* and *The Defiant Ones,* for example. Some people always said these films would never be shown in problem areas, but they always were. If the film holds up as a decent piece of work, it's shown wherever films are shown."

Kramer was answering his severest critics, those who disparaged even his best work—films like *The Defiant Ones,* which is one of his favorites and is perhaps one of the truly fine films to come from America in the 1950s. It's strong without being strident or naïve, tender without facile sentimentality; it's austere without having the appearance of being made on the cheap. And, without being the least bit annoyingly homiletic, it has a potent and timeless message.

The Defiant Ones is the story of John "Joker" Jackson (Tony Curtis) and Noah Cullen (Sidney Poitier), members of a chain gang who escape when a truck carrying prisoners crashes on a rain-swept highway. Linked at the wrist by a yard-long chain, the two are mortal enemies—each has a deeply rooted prejudice against the other's race. Trying to keep ahead of the sheriff and his posse of state troopers, the two cross swollen rivers, wild streams, swamps and woodlands. They dive into a dangerous clay pit, barely escaping discovery, and because of the heavy rains they climb out only after a long and painful struggle. In spite of the hardships faced together and the ultimate reliance on one another, the animosity between them grows.

Captured and bound by a mob that threatens to lynch them when they break into a small town's general store and seek food, they are quietly released by a sympathetic ex-convict (Lon Chaney). On the road again, they have a climactic and savage fistfight and are interrupted only when a cocked rifle is aimed at them by a small boy. He takes them to an isolated cabin where his mother (Cara Williams) feeds them, offers them a hammer and chisel to break their chains, and cares for Jackson's infected wrist wounds. That night, she sleeps with Jackson, and next morning, wanting to be rid of the black man, she directs him not to safety but to sure death in quicksand. When she admits this later to Jackson, he leaves her to find Cullen. The boy shoots him as he lopes off.

Jackson finds Cullen in the swamp and they head for the railroad on high ground, hotly pursued by the approaching posse. Jackson is by now so weak from loss of blood that Cullen must support him as they try to leap aboard the train. They fail, and fall beside the tracks. As the sheriff overtakes them, Cullen is cradling Jackson in his arms, singing a sad but wisely strong song of defiance.

* * *

The Defiant Ones may be studied as part of a tetralogy in the Stanley Kramer catalogue—four films on the theme of race prejudice, which started with *Home of the Brave,* later continued with *Pressure Point,* and concluded with *Guess Who's Coming to Dinner.* In each of these the issue is differently focused, in each the locus of hatred and fear is varied. In addition, each has a different social milieu, and the protagonists have different backgrounds.

In *Home of the Brave,* the setting is a Pacific island during World War II, the men involved are all army comrades, and the rarefied atmosphere, the problems of hysterical paralysis and the

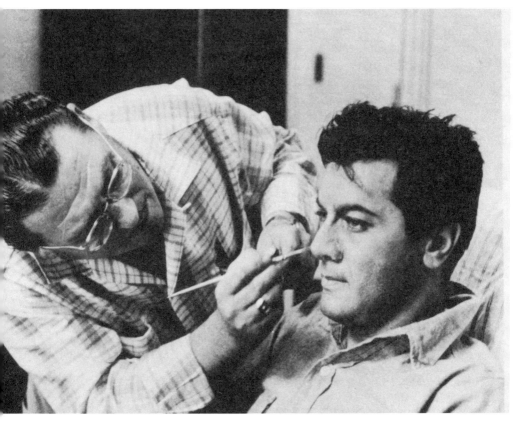

Tony Curtis becoming Joker Jackson.

smashing of group unconsciousness are the mental and spiritual barriers which provide a dramatic cyclorama against which the issue of spiritual brotherhood is worked out. The men clearly stand for types within each race, and the device of narco-synthesis and psychic healing suggests that prejudice is in fact irrational.

In *The Defiant Ones*, the protagonists are much more sharply individualized, and the human society is reduced from a company of soldiers to two men. It is important, in this regard, that the men here are convicted prisoners, that they are not shown as conveniently heroic, large-souled men, but rather ordinary law-breakers, crude, unforgiving, hard-nosed men without much of a past and with less of a future. Unlike *Home of the Brave*, the camaraderie is created and the humanity refined by the two men in process of airing their bitterness and discovering their common inhumanity to each other. In other words, they stumble upon their union as brothers without consciously realizing or articulating it: it arises rather spontaneously from their shared experience. In *Home of the Brave*, mental breakdown is the penalty for suppressing fears and ignoring the needs of brotherhood. In *The Defiant Ones*, men are chained because of and by their hatreds.

In *Pressure Point*, as we'll see later, these two issues of mental illness and imprisonment are fused: the deranged character played by Bobby Darin manifests his paranoia by joining the American Nazi party and by blaming Jews and blacks for his own insufficiencies. But in *Guess Who's Coming to Dinner* the issue comes, literally, closest to home. In this gentlest, least obvious and most unfairly criticized film in what I see as a linked series, the fragility of the genteel life is ruthlessly exposed, and the sentiments of well-educated, affluent and refined liberals are challenged when their daughter brings home a gifted black physician and announces their engagement.

From the stridency of *Home of the Brave* through the dramatic conflicts of *The Defiant Ones* and *Pressure Point* and the quiet tenderness and humor of *Guess Who's Coming to Dinner*, Kramer gradually developed a surer approach. By 1967, he no longer felt it necessary to describe the theme so loudly and dramatically. It is within the confines of the established upper class of the last film, where the liberalism is always conscious and even "chic," desirable, that he touches the Achilles' heel, and then offers a possibility of recognition of truth.

What links these four films is not only the black-white issue, but also the belief that what keeps men apart is their fundamental lack of knowledge of one another. With knowledge can come respect (thus *Home of the Brave*). With respect can flourish comradeship (thus *The Defiant Ones*) and the acknowledgment of one's needs (thus *Pressure Point*). The final goal must be love and the awareness that all men are members of the same human family (thus *Guess Who's Coming to Dinner*).

"Stanley was always a forerunner of terribly good things," Sidney Poitier told me in an interview. "He was the type of man who found it essential to put on the line the things that were important to him. In fact, he put his life and his career on the line many times. To produce a film like *Home of the Brave* in 1949, and then to direct *The Defiant Ones* in 1958 shows he was a man who made hard choices, choices based on his own conscience. He made one hell of a commitment to things when commitment was difficult for everyone. People have short memories: in the days he started making films about important social issues, there were powerful Hollywood columnists who could break careers. He knew this, and he said to himself, 'What the hell—I either do it or I can't live with myself.' For that attitude we're all in Stanley Kramer's debt. He's an example of the very best of a certain type of filmmaker."

The film's theme of prejudice is announced at the beginning, when the two men are in the prison van. Poitier's singing is annoying to Curtis, and soon unpleasant epithets are exchanged: *nigger, bohunk, honkey, spade,* and the condescending *boy.* Later, Poitier expresses the origin of these prejudices in the unhappy order of things in the world: "You breathe it in when you're born and you spit it out every day after." It's very important that these are ordinary men whose crudeness and orneriness locate them within the great mass of humanity. In a way, in fact, they are complementary personalities. Sam Leavitt's cinematography (which won the Academy Award for black-and-white photographing) emphasizes this complementarity by defining the two figures against diffuse, gray backgrounds, and by giving almost a three-dimensional effect to the sequences in the marsh, the clay pit and the woods.

Although both men have prejudices, each has strengths the other needs: the black man has a natural warmth and a certain ingenuity about coping with the crude backwoods of the deep South; the white man has a keen, savvy insight into human exploitation, and he's not about to identify the woman's sexual hunger with a promise of devotion. The complementarity is further highlighted when Curtis has to blacken his face with mud so as not to be seen in the moonlight—he thus becomes the man to whom he's chained! On at least two occasions each finds himself dependent on the other for help. When Poitier thanks Curtis for pulling him out of the rapids, Curtis replies, "I didn't pull you out. I stopped you from pulling me in!"

This act is reciprocated at the end, when Poitier refuses to abandon his former manacle-mate who's weak from the gunshot wound. Thus the film inextricably links their respective welfares. Iz the driving rainstorm, weary of frenzied flight, the men doze. Poitier sleeps with his head against the sleeping Curtis' breast. This scene of mutual unconscious comforting is reversed at the end, too, in the scene that is virtually a *Pietà* image, as Poitier cradles the wounded Curtis in his arms.

None of these sequences implies a simple, sweet reply to the issue of prejudice, much less any recipe for instant brotherhood. Caught by the sheriff in the film's final moments, the men will certainly be returned to prison—a place not likely to endorse any enlightenment they may have had in this brief sojourn into the world. But it's also unlikely that these two will revert to their former resentment and hatred. The shared experience has changed them.

Structurally, this is probably Kramer's most satisfying film, and the script—by Nathan E. Douglas and Harold Jacob Smith, who received the Oscar for best original story and screenplay—has an admirable balance and unity from start to finish. Most obvious, of course, is the framework of the journey within which the narrative occurs. The scramble for escape, the trek across the countryside, the episodes of danger and of safety—all these become the correlatives for the psychological and emotional journey the two men make. The film opens with Poitier singing; it concludes with Poitier singing—but it is no longer a needling, careless tune, it's a song of defiance. The camera cuts quickly to the face of the sheriff (Theodore Bikel), then back to Poitier, who with a triumphant smile seems to spit out the final, defiant lyrics: "Bowling Green, sewing machine!"—words with no literal significance, but sung in a tone of ironic victory. And on those words, and with Poitier's wry and mysterious smile, the film fades to conclusion.

In *Not as a Stranger*, Kramer had striven to document the details of hospital and doctor's office and to integrate a complicated story within a recognizable, common group of interiors. In

The final scene.

The Pride and the Passion, he set out to make a vast epic, so broad in scope that in fact it thinned the characters into virtual insignificance. In the third film he directed, he at last found the proper balance. There is no unnecessary footage, no clinging to the pretty or safe interiors, and the exteriors are hostile. In the faces of Curtis and Poitier, Kramer captured depths and complex reactions these actors may not have known they had. In the sequence in the clay pit, he has directed them and the camera in such a way that we feel the feebleness of their limbs against the slimy wet clay, and the scene suddenly becomes a metaphor of man's evolutionary struggle, and at the same time of the black man's anguished trek up from slavery. In the cross-cutting toward the end of the picture, as the posse gains on them, there is pure cinema in the manner of Griffith: the rhythm of the shots is correct, and the tension builds from their skillful arrangement. The film has an economy and a depth within its simplicity, and this is what makes it finally so moving a human document.

No other film by Stanley Kramer has such a curiously pacific ending. And films by other directors have only rarely matched it for toughness, compassion, conviction and a mature, unsquinting belief in the loveliness of the human spirit and the possibility of authentic human solidarity.

CHAPTER 21

The Hope That Springs from Despair—
On the Beach, 1959

Arriving in Australia from Hollywood for the filming of *On the Beach,* Ava Gardner looked about and promptly remarked, "I'm here to make a film about the end of the world, and this sure is the place for it." Kramer and the few other Americans who welcomed Gardner put her so much at ease, however, that she gave perhaps the best performance of her career. Some were surprised, too, at the discovery of considerable dramatic talent in Fred Astaire.

Made entirely in Australia (except for a few brief shots of San Francisco and San Diego), *On the Beach* was, like *The Caine Mutiny* and *Not as a Stranger,* based on a best-selling contemporary novel—this one by Nevil Shute. But unlike those two films, it responded to a very real fear of the 1950s: the possibility of nuclear holocaust. People who were in school at that time have vivid memories of Friday-morning sirens and drills; it was the time, too, when black and yellow "Shelter" signs appeared, and housewives prepared "bomb boxes"—supplies of bottled water and canned food to be stored in basements in case of emergency. These provisions would not have done us much good, most doctors claimed: had atom bombs been exploded in America, few would have lived to open canned food, and much of the rest of the world would eventually be affected by radioactive fallout.

This is the premise on which Kramer's low-keyed and high-powered film rests.

On an April morning in 1964, the American atomic submarine *Sawfish* under the command of Dwight Towers (Gregory Peck) arrives in Melbourne to prepare for an exploratory voyage along the West Coast of North America, which has recently been devastated in a nuclear war. The radioactive drift is expected to reach Australia in five months. Lieutenant Peter Holmes (Anthony Perkins) is assigned as liaison officer, and Julian Osborne (Fred Astaire), a nuclear physicist, is scientific aide for the trip.

Temporary survivors: Fred Astaire, Gregory Peck, Ava Gardner.

At a party given by Holmes and his wife, Mary (Donna Anderson), Dwight meets Moira Davidson (Ava Gardner), and soon the two date. But he alienates her by insisting that his wife and children, who were in America when the war broke out, may still be alive. This leads her to attempt a reprisal of her old affair with Julian. His new love, however, is a racing car.

Before the expedition begins, Holmes instructs his wife on the use of capsules that will, near the end, hasten a painless death for her and their infant. The crew of the *Sawfish* finds the American coast totally lifeless and so returns to Australia, where Dwight is quickly involved romantically with Moira. Julian wins the Grand Prix, but the victory is tempered by many drivers' deliberately suicidal crashes. Soon Dwight finds that radioactivity is beginning to affect his crew. Most of the men wish to die at home, and Dwight prepares to leave Moira. Meanwhile, a huge crowd gathers for a Salvation Army meeting. The songs, prayers and speeches have an old familiar theme, "There's still time, Brothers!"—i.e., to live, to repent. At the same time, Holmes and his wife prepare to face the end together; an Australian official (John Tate) and his assistant (Lola Brooks) discover that official formalities mask an incipient, doomed love; Julian ends his life in a garage, behind the wheel of his Ferrari. And Moria watches the *Sawfish* submerge. The crowds at the rally gradually diminish, and there is at last no sign of life in the Melbourne Square. Just a banner waving in the deadly breeze— "There is still time, Brothers."

The title is neatly concretized in the film: putting aside their cares for a brief time, Peck and Gardner frolic like schoolchildren on the beach; Perkins meets his wife at the same place; and there's a subtle allusion, as we watch the infrequent smiles on their faces, to the genesis of the race, to courageous and tenacious humankind crawling up "on the beach" and beginning a long climb to a civilization that is now on the brink of annihilation.

In their script, John Paxton and James Lee Barrett never overplay their hand: the dialogue is markedly free of the stereotypical speech of a disaster film, and the elliptical diction, always unhysterical, makes more stinging the people's dilemma.

The dialogue is always muted and suggestive rather than shrill and obvious.

But there are touches of humor, too—not intended as relief from the grim proceedings, but because the film is so comprehensive a treatment of *life*, not a calculated depiction of a terrible death: "Four hundred bottles of vintage port," complains an old gentleman at a club, "and only five months to go. Bad planning, I say." Always avoiding the cliché, there is in this story no crusty but benevolent sergeant from Brooklyn, no handy spokesman for God or country, no whore with a heart of gold who becomes a nurse or cares for neighborhood children, no exemplary old couple mouthing pious platitudes.

Gardner and Peck, on the beach.

"I needed an atomic submarine for the film, but the Pentagon told me, 'No: your story says an atomic war would wipe out the world, and that isn't so. Only about five hundred million people would be killed.' I told them that's the closest I'd like to get to a total wipe-out! So since I wouldn't change the script, we didn't get the atomic sub."

There's a frightening parallel between Kramer's recollection of government refusal to cooperate and the examination of a situation in which millions of innocents are doomed because of the recklessness and folly of some anonymous persons with the available instruments of annihilation. Astaire, drinking too much too fast, says that if there's any future history, it would record that "Civilization was destroyed by vacuum tubes and transistors—probably faulty ones, too." Since it was he who had built and exploded the bomb, his words have a bitter pathetic regret. "We're all doomed," he concludes, "the drunken lot of us, by the air we breathe." It's left to Ava Gardner to articulate the unfairness of it all: "Unfair because I didn't do anything. And nobody I know did anything." The tragedy was caused by others, leaders of many nations who "refused to cooperate."

The film was warmly appreciated by a Soviet audience when it was shown in Moscow in December 1959, the same time as the American premiere. A select group of twelve hundred Russians and a handful of foreign guests—Mr. and Mrs. Peck among them—attended a private screening at the Soviet Filmworkers Union. The Herald Tribune Bureau reported that the Moscow press praised the film's "opposition to atomic war."

The film, however, was never released for general audiences in Russia.

The British press was not very enthusiastic. C. A. Lejeune, in *The Observer*, said he deplored the film "because its effect on general audiences, who know they can't do much about the situation anyway, is so blisteringly miserable that it reduces one to a state of feeling 'What's the good of anything? Why, nothing,' the film seems to say." And Penelope Houston, writing in England's most prestigious film journal, *Sight and Sound*, remarked that the scene of the motorcar race "is an intolerably callous miscalculation: if the film can view the piled-up slaughter of this race-track with such equanimity, then its whole attitude of horrified anger at the prospect of the wider disaster becomes suspect." But, in fact, the point of that sequence is that the drivers are committing suicide, and to this they're brought by fear of imminent annihilation. The scene is also linked structurally to the frightened situation of many others, represented by Perkins and his wife, trying calmly to cope with a possibly noble way of expiring gently before they die horribly.

In America, the general critical reaction was a grudging admiration for the boldness of the theme and the confident, quiet tone of the film's message. But many observers, like the audiences for whom they wrote, found it all just too depressing, even when they had to admit that Kramer's direction of the material was astute, clear and terse. No one thought to see the picture as a logical variant on the theme of the previous Kramer work, *The Defiant Ones:* like that film, but not as intimately, *On the Beach* convinces us that people are strong and tenacious, that they are capable of goodness and of extending compassion and love. Outraged by racial injustice, Kramer felt equally deeply that, as one American critic put it, "it's a dirty, shocking slur on man's intelligence to conceive of his allowing such a possibility as nuclear holocaust to occur."

In fact, *On the Beach* is not a depressing film. It's a powerful and a moving and a thought-provoking film, but that's something else altogether. For some viewers, of course, any movie is depressing that does not reveal its significance without reflection or reviewing. On the contrary, a film (or any work) raising serious issues and refusing to give easy answers appeals to our maturity; it touches us at the deepest level of our humanity, and challenges our best instincts.

And that is just what this film does. Because Kramer consistently refused to detail the physical horrors attendant on nuclear holocaust, and because he kept the tone of the film quietly unhysterical, he directs camera and viewer to other concerns. He shows the real tragedy of war and death in the anguished faces of still healthy young people, considering suicide as the alternative to an agonizingly slow death from fallout. He locates loss and loneliness in the raspy complaints and the querulous tears of a middle-aged woman, unable to understand a universe which extracts such painful dues from those who had no part in causing global suffering. He defines a sense of cosmic delusion on the face of the scientist, who has fallen from the Olympus of fame to the empty fury of the racing car, courting fiery death because he's guilty for having loosed it on the world.

There's a sense of contemporaneity and commonness that makes *On the Beach* disturbing, too. We don't see weak, sick or dying people. We see only attractive, healthy people at parties and clubs, downing whiskeys and sipping vintage ports: it's easier to identify with them, after all. Kramer everywhere insists on the proximity of the tragedy (it's 1964, just five years away from the film's first audience), and the obvious identification is made more plausible and poignant because the people's concerns are our concerns: will an affair proceed happily? will the child survive? what will be the response of a former lover to a new knot in a relationship?

The faces of the principal actors, strikingly photographed, empasize the grayness of the world in which they are sole survivors. Never has Fred Astaire seemed so unlike the American Peter Pan that he has so long stood, or rather danced, for. Never has Ava Gardner's dark and sensuous beauty seemed so sadly doomed. And, perhaps most ironically of all, never has Gregory Peck's Lincolnesque earnestness seemed so pointless.

Lejeune objected that the film leaves a viewer feeling impotent to change the way things are, and because international politics don't allow involvement of the average citizen, the film reinforces a feeling of hopelessness. That reasoning, of course, makes it impossible to enjoy even a simple thriller or to justify any work which centers on a serious social issue. It is precisely because "there *is* still time" that the film rises above being a simple requiem for humanity or an extended meditation on futility.

It's important to see how these characters face the inevitable. In each case, there's a gentle, unsentimental love story which is the security against panic: the tender restraint of the passion between Peck and Gardner; the protective encircling of the young family by Perkins; the gruff and disappointed closet lover played by Astaire, who most of all regrets having squandered his affections; the sudden realization of love, grown in the soil of respect, as the admiral and his lovely assistant face the end with quiet courage—he asks why she's remained unmarried, and when told no one ever asked her, he invites her to share sherry, and he toasts "a blind, blind world." These are situations in which Kramer insists on the fundamental humanity of people under crisis, and he has given us an album of wonderfully alive portraits. Giuseppe Rotunno's gradual retarding of camera movements suggests not only the winding down of the world, but also the decrescendo of the commercial, the frenetic and the transient, so that our concern may be focused on finality.

Paradoxically, then, there is an affirming hope reflected in *On*

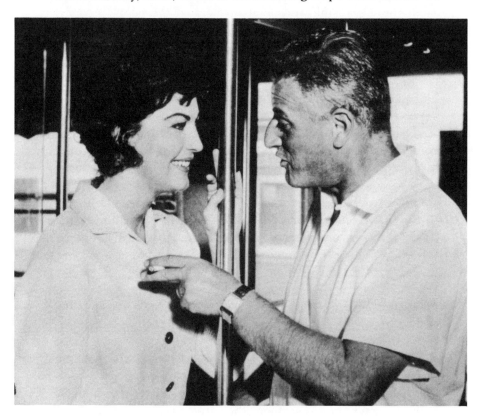

Star and director, on a Melbourne bus.

the Beach. There are no small people here because, in the face of irreversible crisis, there are no small feelings. Kramer clearly loves these characters, and he treated them with an almost religious respect—which the arbiters of the unseen war did not. Far from being a simple injunction to unspecified political action, the final shot of the banner fluttering in the deadly breeze seals a respect for life. And it's hard to imagine anyone leaving a theatre without wanting to be an agent of peace. "If you dodge this picture, you will miss one of the most moving and powerful films of this or any other year," said critic Felix Barker.

The people of *On the Beach* are under sentence of imminent death, and so their sense of life's possibilities is sensitized, heightened to the point where there's no time for regret, only for intense emotional and spiritual assessment, and for a hard evaluation of their capacities to love.

The audience watching *On the Beach* is under sentence, too, even though our deaths seem not quite so imminent. And that, perhaps, is why some still reject the film: it's really about the horror of wasting life and about the vain pursuit of power and expediency. It affirms that our worst fear should be that we'll not have time to develop further our own humanity. And having proposed that, the film finally gives us back our hope: there *is* still time.

Spencer Tracy, Harry Morgan, Fredric March.

CHAPTER 22

"Kramer Is the Anti-Christ!"—
Inherit the Wind, 1960

Inherit the Wind, Kramer's production of the successful Broadway play by Jerome Lawrence and Robert E. Lee, dramatizes the internationally famous Scopes trial of 1925. Nathan E. Douglas and Harold Jacob Smith (Oscar winners for the script for *The Defiant Ones*) wrote a scenario faithful to the broad outlines of facts, but which also expands both the play and the historical detail so that larger human issues are considered.

The trial was occasioned by a Tennessee law passed in March 1925, which forbade the teaching of any scientific principles or theories believed inconsistent with the Bible. John T. Scopes, a biology teacher in Dayton, Tennessee, was brought to trial in July of the same year for having taught Darwinian evolutionary theories in the classroom, and the case at once became widely infamous. Civil libertarians flocked to the town court, where Clarence Darrow arrived to defend the accused, and where William Jennings Bryan volunteered for the prosecution. Darrow tried to demonstrate that the law not only limited academic freedom but, in affirming specific guidelines for biblical interpretation, also violated the principle of separation of church and state. Darrow challenged in court the fundamentalist beliefs of Bryan, and showed how the teaching of the Scriptures and of Darwin were not mutually exclusive nor incompatible. Nevertheless, Scopes was convicted—partially because of Darrow's request: he feared that acquittal would be granted on a technical rather than a constitutional basis. (The state supreme court did in fact acquit Scopes later on a technicality.) Bryan died in his sleep five days after the trial concluded, and the furor of the proceedings made it possible for other states to allow more liberal teaching practices. The state of Tennessee, however, still has on its books the law that brought Scopes to trial.

Inherit the Wind is especially remarkable for the performances of Fredric March and Spencer Tracy, and for Kramer's canny capturing of the texture of small-town Southern life and feeling, over a half century ago.

The film opens with the ticking of the clock above the Hillsboro Court House, followed at once by the gradual crescendo of voices raised in triumphant, defensive song—"Gimme that ol' time religion . . ." Soon Henry Drummond (Spencer Tracy; the character is based on Darrow) enters, walking confidently into town, refusing a ride. He has a full head of bushy white hair, he wears a light shirt and matching tie, but underneath his jacket are boldly patterned suspenders, which he thumbs proudly in the courtroom later. His words seem to roll slowly over a hard, purifying gravel pit as they're manufactured. Playing the shrewd, stoic attorney, he has a way of pitching his chin forward when he makes a point, as if to stick the words onto his hearers so firmly that they'd have to work like the devil to peel away the sheer force of them.

March is in every regard the opposite: as Matthew Harrison Brady (modeled on William Jennings Bryan), he rides with proleptic triumph into Hillsboro and is loudly acclaimed by the crowds. He's bald, wears print shirts and bow ties and colorless suspenders. His voice is manufactured from deep within a crackerbarrel chest that he's fond of patting, as if it were a puppy, and his words are wrapped in beguilingly learned and polite tones. The vicious snap of the bigot can be heard overriding his legal sensibilities, however.

These performances always ring true. Tracy and March carved the personalities so finely and measured the cadences of their questions and responses so accurately, that although the men certainly seem colorful characters, they are never sloppy caricatures. Watching his easy confidence, you think March will live forever. But he tries to dispel the heat by cooling himself with a fan "compliments of Mason's Funeral Parlor," and this is a neat touch on Kramer's part, for it anticipates and prefigures March's death at the end of the trial.

Tracy's challenge to March—slyly built up from bits and pieces of homey logic—does not attempt a sophisticated argument from the principles of biblical form criticism, but Tracy's eyes seem filled with so much behind-the-brow meaning that you have little doubt that he's crammed a minicourse on ancient literature and could deflate March's wonderfully calculated pomposity with little effort. Because Kramer has. emphasized the larger issue of the film (the right to think, the necessity always to investigate further), he chose not to emphasize the singular issue of biblical language and meaning. Rather he directed Ernest Laszlo's camera to study the faces of the people in the room as much as those of the main actors, to search the confusion and anger of minor folk, and to stress the human as well as the legal aspects of the Hillsboro drama.

The filming is straightforward, as befits a courtroom drama, but as the jousting heightens in intensity, the camera—which early on had kept its medium shots at eye level—begins to see more and more from a higher angle, and as Bertram Cates (the Scopes character) begins to lose the faith of his fiancée and her preacher father, the whip-panning reinforces the feelings of tension and of a settled madness within the genteel ordinariness.

Kramer had an unerring sense of time and place, and as the drama thickens, so does the courtroom claustrophobia: everyone is oppressed by the Tennessee summer heat; shirt collars wilt, brows are beaded with perspiration. Kramer also filled the room with pea-brained locals who hoot at the young man on trial and hurl bitter insults at his lawyer. There's a substantial dramatic subtheme, too, in the relationship between March and his wife (played by his real-life wife, actress Florence Eldridge). In a brief and tender scene, the elder statesman cries, "Mother, they laughed at me. I can't stand it when they laugh at me." He nearly weeps, his head in her lap, and she strokes him, comforting him as she would an offended child and calling him her "baby." Left to lesser actors, this scene might have been hopelessly overstated; with the Marches, however, the emotional honesty has the dimensions of a small human tragedy, and illuminates the complex corners of what could have been merely a simplistic soul. It's sequences like this that show Stanley Kramer at his directorial best—when he's concerned not only for the ideas at stake, but for what these ideas do to people in private as well as in public.

"The film got extravagant reviews," Kramer told me, "but it died at the box office. United Artists said this was just a silly story about two old men, so they didn't distribute it properly. Then the fundamentalists called me the anti-Christ, so there were some local problems in booking the film, too. It just died. But lately it's gotten some revival on television and on the campuses."

There is a problem, however, with the ending of the picture. Unfortunately, Kramer apparently thought it necessary to counteract the anger of those who might consider the film irreligious. As Tracy leaves the courthouse in the final sequence, therefore, Leslie Uggams' voice on the sound track triumphantly proclaims *The Battle Hymn of the Republic.* She's joined by an invisible chorus, thus making clear that although the film carries no banner for fundamentalism, it is not for all that a nontheistic picture: "Mine eyes have seen the glory of the coming of the Lord" is ringingly repeated. . . .

Old Clarence Darrow might not have liked this, nor would H. L. Mencken, the journalist who covered the trial (here called E. K. Hornbeck, and bouncily played by Gene Kelly, who seems always to be on the verge of breaking into a little gavotte). This ending, of course, tries to broaden the film's appeal, but in so doing it muddies the impact of what has just preceded.

When the picture was released, Stanley Kramer issued an extended personal statement. Because it illuminates his conviction about the work, and its timeliness and timelessness, it is worth citing:

Just before the verdict . . .

Spencer Tracy, Gene Kelly, and a relative.

"It is a misconception to believe that the present atmosphere of freedom from hysteria and constraint is something new. It is also a misconception to believe that only *now* may we make a film like *On the Beach,* which challenges some of our fundamental concepts on national security and international peace, or *Inherit the Wind,* which suggests the conflict between the traditionalists and the modernists. Hollywood in fact has been making pictures with significant themes for many years. One may suppose that in the light of his day D. W. Griffith, who presented the South in a favorable light in *The Birth of a Nation,* attacked a daring and highly incendiary theme, for this was still in a year when many living men held memories of the War Between the States.

"Even during the years of what one historian has euphemistically called the 'Post War Unpleasantness in America' there were producers and writers who were touching on controversial themes, ideas which provoked discussion and, one may assume, not a little misgiving in some quarters.

"No, it would be wrong to say that precisely now we have reached the Day of Enlightenment, and that all that has gone before was a period of Middle Age darkness.

"I would say two things on that score.

"First, from the very first days of American film, pioneers and men of conviction had wedded the movie screen to ideas. The film of social ferment like *Grapes of Wrath* and *Black Fury;* the films of protest like *Fury* and *Black Legion;* the films of antiwar content like *All Quiet on the Western Front* and *Boy with Green Hair* are a few examples. Frank Capra's films were films of protest against corruption and tyranny. In that sense, the American screen has not suddenly 'found its freedom.'

"Second, there must be a continuing presence of ideas in film and on films. Final truths are never those truths which are but once uttered. They must be stated over and over again, not only in films, but in books, in music, in art.

"It was this concern with ideas and truth, as well as its inherent dramatic qualities, that attracted me to *Inherit the Wind,* which was so successful in its Broadway presentation. Inspiration for the play and for the motion picture came from the famed Monkey Trial,' held in Dayton, Tennessee, in the hot summer of 1925, when Clarence Darrow defended John Scopes, a high-school biology teacher who propounded Darwin's theory of evolution to his pupils. It may be thought by some that Darrow's defense of Scopes settled the issues of that trial once and for all. But this is not the case. The spirit of the trial lives on, because the real issues of that trial were man's right to think and man's right to teach. These are issues for which the never-ending struggle continues and they constitute the real theme of *Inherit the Wind.*

"For me, *Inherit the Wind* completes a trilogy of what have been called by some 'controversial pictures,' of which the first two were *The Defiant Ones* and *On the Beach.* I am not sure what is meant by 'controversial'—an often misused word—but in this trilogy I have attempted, and I hope succeeded, in making pictures that command attention. Enjoy them or not—agree with them or not—these are motion pictures that hit people hard, force people to see them, to think and to take a stand. I hope that *Inherit the Wind* will do this too.

"*Inherit the Wind* dramatizes one of the world's oldest themes: knowledge is not enough; freedom of enquiry is a living, dramatic process. Aristotle and Plato said it; so did Francis Bacon. And so must we in 1960."

Spencer Tracy and Marlene Dietrich.

CHAPTER 23

Clift Grieves for Garland, and Tracy for the World—

Judgment at Nuremberg, 1961

"I think there's something seriously wrong with every one of my films, and so it's hard for me to mention a favorite. But I think there are some good things about *Judgment at Nuremberg.* The ideas in it are terribly important to me. The whole theme of the film, the single idea that stands behind it, is stated by Spencer Tracy toward the end of the picture: 'This, then, is what we stand for: truth, justice, and the value of a single human being.' That's sort of a summary of my work, in a way, and I'd like to think the films encourage thought about that."

In the fall of 1961, Kramer's *Judgment at Nuremberg,* based on a shorter television play from 1959 (originally presented on CBS' *Playhouse 90*) opened in America after its world premiere in Germany. It shocked many, angered some, disgusted others. But it bored no one, and it remains today an emotionally exhausting film to watch. It's an intense intellectual drama—not intellectual in the sense that it's philosophical or abstract, for in fact it deals head-on with the hard postwar trial of Nazi war criminals. It's intellectual rather in the sense that watching it you feel that the director, his writer (Abby Mann), and his cast have tried not to rehearse old hatreds and pleas for vengeance, but rather to reflect on and understand one of the most hideous eras in the history of civilization.

The major trials of war criminals on which the film is based were held in 1945 and 1946, immediately after the war. Following these, many smaller trials were held separately by American, British, French and Russian courts, which has shared the judgment at Nuremberg. Additional criminals were then indicted and sentenced. But the film, like the television play, concentrates on the first and most important trial. It is not a documentation of actual facts and names, but a fictional composite. The most important creative contribution involves the quartet of Nazi judges as the sole defendants. Instead of treating the actual historical situation of the twenty-two defendants, therefore, the issue is focused and becomes the judgment of justice, and the theme of the corruptibility of the legal system is thus thrown into greater relief.

Essentially a courtroom drama, the film centers on the presiding judge (Spencer Tracy), who must render a monumental decision, and the principal defendant (Burt Lancaster), an enigmatic, brooding figure who refused to enter a plea because he does not accept the valid authority of the court. The prosecuting attorney is an American colonel (Richard Widmark), the defense attorney a shrewd and complex German (Maximilian Schell). In this trial of four Nazi judges, witnesses are introduced, among whom are a frightened, sad victim of the Nazi's sterilization experiments (Montgomery Clift) and a woman (Judy Garland) victimized by one of the defendants in a notorious miscarriage of justice. The issues of the trial are illuminated and clarified through these testimonies, through the actions and reactions of the three presiding judges and the four defendants, and through the conflicts between prosecution and defense attorneys. A particularly harrowing moment occurs when the prosecution introduces actual footage detailing Nazi atrocities in the concentration camps. This was a bold stroke by Kramer, since this of course tends automatically to reduce to insignificance everything else in the film, and to make this film within a film the most memorable element.

At the end, the four are sentenced to life imprisonment, but

Montgomery Clift.

"This, then, is what we stand for—truth, justice and the value of a single human being."

not before the enigmatic, stoical defendant played by Lancaster rises in an outburst of soul-searching, to pinpoint the real guilt of all who rationalized or ignored the inhumanity of Nazism—a system, he maintains, which demanded the denunciation of all those of extraordinary power and ability, of which he was a prime example. The tension of the courtroom drama has its climax here: it's the moment of surgical lancing of infection, as it were—the moment in which all the disease and horror are located within a nation's spiritual sickness—a condition, he reminds, which can arise anywhere, in any place.

The Nuremberg trials were very different from what is here represented. Judges were not defendants in them—politicians were, as well as government, navy and army officials, Gestapo leaders and SS (elite guard) officials. (Hermann Goering and Albert Speer were among the most infamous defendants.) Also, there were no women witnesses at these trials, and although the real-life basis for the character of the presiding judge portrayed by Tracy was indeed an American (Francis Biddle of Massachusetts), there were also Russian, British and French presiding judges; here, all three are Americans. In addition, the actual trials convicted twenty-two men, of whom twelve were sentenced to hang, three to life imprisonment, two to twenty years, one each to fifteen and ten years, and three acquitted. (Biddle's important book, In Brief Authority, appeared in 1962. The best recent work on the subject is Bradley F. Smith's carefully researched work, Reaching Judgment at Nuremberg: The Untold Story of How the Nazi War Criminals Were Judged, published in 1977.)

Kramer has been careful to stress in his direction of the courtroom drama the respect for order and legality that prevailed at Nuremberg. As Professor Richard Plant, himself a noted authority on the history of the period, told me: "The Nuremberg war trials were a masterpiece of improvisation by the Americans. The court managed to remain surprisingly and wonderfully dignified, and the trials therefore did not look like, nor were they in fact, a prettified vendetta. This, of course, was exceedingly difficult to achieve—there was no precedent in the history of jurisprudence for a trial of mass crimes against humanity!"

The production of the film involved difficulties in America and Germany, as did its eventual release. "Do you think United

Artists wanted to get involved in a film about war trials?" Kramer asked rhetorically. "They weren't interested at all in war guilt, people in ovens, or crooked judges. 'That's a courtroom thing,' they said, 'and besides, no one knows who the protagonists are!' So what I did was something of a compromise: I studded it with stars to get it made as a film that would reach out to a mass audience, made in America at the prices necessary to pay here." Kramer had hoped, when he first went to Nuremberg to prepare the film, to shoot the film in the actual courtroom there: "We couldn't," he said, "because it's still in use today. So we took measurements and carefully recreated it on the soundstage in Hollywood, although we finally had to scale down some of the dimensions for the involved camera movements. A courtroom—like the operating room in *Not as a Stranger*—is a very static set. The attorneys had to be separate and distant from the defendants and witnesses, by law. So the film becomes a ping-pong game unless you try to move the camera, which I tried—not always successfully—to do.

"At the time of the picture's release, it was submerged by many pressures. The film had a world premiere in Berlin and was sponsored by Willy Brandt, whose speech at the opening I shall always remember. All of Berlin came, all those who had been officials in the previous administration, people from Nuremberg and Munich, as well as foreign diplomats. Brandt stood up and warned the audience that they might not find the film pleasant, but that if Berlin was ever to regard itself as a capital city, then this film should be shown there because it was about all of them. 'We may like or dislike or disagree with many things,' he said, 'but here it is.' Well, the film went on, and when it was over there was a deafening silence. I'd like to say it was like the silence that greeted the conclusion of Lincoln's Gettysburg Address, a perfect tribute, but it wasn't so. It was the most frightening evening in my life. The film was totally rejected: it never did three cents' business in Germany. It played so many empty houses it just stopped. People asked how could I, an American, try to rekindle German guilt? Well, I said that it would indeed have been better if the Germans had made it, but the fact is they didn't. So I did."

A negative reaction to the film by Germans is a somewhat

narrow viewing of it, however, for the script is quite clear on the universality of the guilt and the danger of making simplistic judgments. The theme of the film is the conflict of obedience: ought one to obey one's country regardless of the orders given, or can one be counted as a traitor? Perhaps most disturbing of all is the conclusion, in which a politically wary senator who has sponsored the trials reminds the judges that, considering the new Russian trouble (the fictional trial is set in 1948, and the cold war is getting chillier), the United States needs German support: now, therefore, it is unwise to alienate the sympathy of all German people. In fact, things never got this obvious or dramatic: the military commander of American forces in Germany at the time, John J. McCloy, did suggest that harsh verdicts might have new, unforeseen ramifications, but no such political consideration ever weighed in the final sentences, as the record indicates. This point of the script certainly widens the concern to include the notion of depraved politics in peacetime and its relationship to national atrocities, but it does juggle the facts somewhat—even though it adds impact to the ultimate sentence of life imprisonment.

Stylistically, *Judgment at Nuremberg* is very different from most other Kramer films: although it has the most static set, it has more moving camera shots than any other film. "There's too much camera movement, in fact," Kramer said. "This was a very authentic situation, a long courtroom, very wide, and the spacing between the original attorney's box and the witness box was at least forty feet. That's a long distance if you try to photograph it! Also, the attorney was never allowed to depart from the box. Unless you want to play a Ping-Pong game in the cutting room, you have to move the camera. I think I moved it a little bit too much. If I had it to do over, I wouldn't move it quite so much—it might be more effective. But at the time I felt trapped by these positions—the judges, the attorneys and witnesses in that big spread. So the forty feet were compressed to twenty-eight feet. We had to put a lot of light on the far figures to hold the forms in focus, and the actors perspired a lot during these shots." Because of this technique, Ernest Laszlo's camera brings both intimacy and mobility to a drama that needs both values. The frequent glides round the courtroom serve to vary the audience's perspective, and the many sudden zooms into or away from a character heighten dramatic effect. In addition, no dissolves or fancy opticals were added in the lab: the film has straight, uncluttered transitions that underscore its stark, black-and-white austerity.

There's an arresting moment when the camera circles 360 degrees around Richard Widmark, as he delivers a long speech. "Everyone in the crew had to carry the cables and equipment around in a circle for that," Kramer explained. "It's the funniest thing in the world to see happen on the set. Out of the dullness of the situation I circled him in order to pick up Tracy and the judges in the shot without simply cutting. It was just something I worked out—where Widmark's lines would occur in relation to who is seen in the background. We rehearsed a long time for that—to photograph people just at the right Widmark line. But it feels a little indulgent to me now. I can't think of a specific purpose for a shot like this except to avoid repetition and boredom, and since I think there were too many movements in the picture to start with, I'll just have to plead guilty to bad judgment here." But Kramer may be a bit too self-critical: there are only two such moments in the film, and they are entirely justified by the words of the prosecuting attorney as well as by the need to see the effects of these words *on the other hearers in the court* at the very moment he utters them! The cutting would have been too disorienting and would have stressed the face suddenly filling the frame instead of the face in relation to the words that are heard.

The editing emphasizes theme, language and action throughout. Words and gestures, particularly, are often joined by matched cuts: a mention of a cup of coffee precedes a cut to coffee being poured; a gavel is banged on the judge's bench as a recess is declared, and we cut to a beer stein banged on a pub table as a song is sung; a man says he needs help, and there is a cut to a waitress asking if a group wants more strudel. The problem of the language translation is neatly handled, too, moving from German to English and back again by tuning the audience into the bilingual translation device such as that used in the United Nations. Thus subtitles are unnecessary, and the Germans appear to be speaking German, since we "hear" them in English over the translation device (although it is, of course, the actual voices of the actors).

The casting is highly creative. Spencer Tracy gave a performance of considerable intelligence and intuition, a towering but gentle figure, compassionate but realistic, warm but objective, a man of insight and eloquence, but also a plain man who finds himself caught between politics and justice. He's calm, grave, unflappable, but the wheels of his jurist's mind are always sensed working behind that wise, sometimes tired brow, and you never feel that there is any shred of inordinate pride in the man. It's Tracy's point of view through which we see and feel the events of the trial and outside the courtroom. Here (as in *Inherit the Wind* and in *It's a Mad Mad Mad Mad World*), Tracy seems to be Kramer's *alter ego*—he actualizes on the screen Kramer's own bewilderment, his horror, his passion about the primacy of conscience. And there's a mature poignancy to his scenes with Marlene Dietrich, who plays the widow of a German general hanged by the Nazis, and whose house is now taken over for the residence of the American judges. (This is fiction, since the major defendants were actually housed in such a home; the American judges in fact stayed at American army headquarters. But this shift makes possible a new dramatic confrontation.) "I want to understand," Tracy says with humility and a kind of epic bereavement for all the unnamed and unknowable dead who were the victims of Hitler's madness. "I really do want to understand. I have to. I must."

Burt Lancaster was not so felicitously cast, however. "He wasn't my choice for it," Kramer admitted, "but that's no reflection on him. In *Elmer Gantry* he was just magnificent, but I thought he was the least believable person I had in this film. Laurence Olivier was supposed to play the part, because the British have a way of portraying Germans. But he chose to marry Joan Plowright at that moment and he dropped out of the picture. I had to make a quick substituion. I would have liked, alternately, to have a German play the part; I just couldn't get one." Which is too bad, since it certainly is jarring to have the other three German defendants played by German actors with appositely heavy accents!

Richard Widmark and Maximilian Schell, on the other hand, are entirely credible: Schell deepened the role that he created in the television original, and Widmark's icy precision found the right combination of professional acumen and outrage at atrocities.

"Montgomery Clift," said Kramer, "was a really wonderful actor. In his youth he was the most beautiful man on the New York stage. He was a matinée idol, the juvenile of all time. But he had a very bad automobile accident which scarred him, and by the time of our film it had affected him emotionally, he was drinking heavily, and he had severe problems—even a death wish. He needed somebody to be terribly kind, somebody who would say, 'You're wonderful and I know that you're having a little trouble and you don't remember the lines, but what difference? Within the scope of the thing, you just do it as you feel it should be, and we'll manage. But, Monty, you're wonder-ful, and I wanted you for the part,' etc., etc. I had to bolster his confidence all the time.

"Once he watched Judy Garland do a scene and he huddled in a corner like a puppy dog, weeping. When it was over he came up to me and said, 'She didn't do that right!' Well, if you didn't have sympathy for him, you couldn't use him." Kramer appar-ently had that sympathy, for Clift's brief appearance as the exploited, half-witted baker's assistant is perhaps his last memo-rable performance—full of pain, embarrassment and terror. It's quintessentially method acting à la Clift, but it's right in this case: the role and the actor fuse to form a brief, tragic personal moment of screen history.

As for Judy Garland, she's almost unrecognizable as a terrified, dumpy German hausfrau, forced to take the stand and describe the humiliation of the testimony she'd been forced to give to a group of corrupt attorneys and judges. (She had to accuse an elderly Jewish friend of having made advances to her when she was much younger, and thus of sullying the pure Germanic stock). Garland conveys a dry-mouthed fear for herself, a simpering childlike paralysis that betokens the horrors of her memories, and her feeling that life and truth have eluded her. It is a broken woman we see on the stand, and there is just enough of art imitating life at the time to make her performance, like that of Clift's, painfully memorable.

Kramer's film is filled with affecting moments like these. The emotional tone of the film is always muted—perhaps because the trauma was too great. The horrors are terrifying enough in themselves, they need no emphasis in voice or gesture, for in the final analysis *Judgment at Nuremberg* affects the viewer because its

Cast, crew and director.

style, as well as its theme, supports the director's belief in the sanctity of human life.*

"I keep on directing," Kramer told an interviewer, "because I'm arrogant and I enjoy it. Somebody asked me about handling all the problems. But the real reason I keep on directing is the moments of wonder. Because I once heard Spencer Tracy say, 'This, then, is what we stand for: truth, justice and the value of a single human being.' To be able to hear that is worth a lot of other incidents."

* Earlier, in the spring of 1961, the Motion Picture Academy of Arts and Sciences awarded Kramer an Oscar for his contributions to the industry, citing especially his "consistent high quality of production."

Bobby Darin and Sidney Poitier.

CHAPTER 24

Variations on a Theme of Madness—
Pressure Point, 1962

In *Home of the Brave,* Stanley Kramer used psychiatric therapy and narcosynthesis as dramatic devices to reveal the tragic and finally groundless feelings of inferiority inbred into the black man, and to show how deeply and subtly prejudice invades the most innocent white man in America.

In *The Defiant Ones,* the theme of racial prejudice was particularized and made more intimate in the situation of two escaped convicts who, chained together at the wrist, discover their common inhumanities and prejudices and, finally, their mutual need of one another. In this film, Kramer suggested that the road to brotherhood begins with the acknowledgment that all men are imprisoned and chained by hatred and ignorance of one another.

In *Pressure Point,* these two themes—psychological disturbance and enchainment-as-metaphor—are fused, and it's made clear that all racism, whether against color or religion, is psychotic.

Based on a composite of case histories from Dr. Robert Lindner's book *The Fifty-Minute Hour, Pressure Point* had a scenario by Hubert Cornfield and S. Lee Pogostin. Because Kramer was preparing the script for his first comedy, a kind of odd epic called *It's a Mad Mad Mad Mad World*, he turned the property over to Cornfield to direct.

The film begins as a graying psychologist (Sidney Poitier), director of a mental institution, listens to the exasperated account of difficulties being experienced by a younger colleague (Peter Falk). In reply, the older man reveals an experience he had as a young doctor—and thus the real story, told in flashback, begins.

The doctor had known an explosive relationship with a psychotic young American Nazi (Bobby Darin) who, during World War II, was imprisoned for sedition and thus came under his care. The (nameless) young man rejects the (nameless) doctor's help because he cannot accept aid from a black man, and he is pushed further into the horrors of his own crippling fantasy life. Driven to insomnia and the brink of total break-down, he at last admits his need for help, and begrudgingly tells his own life story to the doctor.

The man's father, it seems, was a demanding, hard-drinking butcher who neglected his wife and son. The boy's mother was a neurotic, possessive malingerer who placed demands on the child that only barely stopped short of the sexual. Thus resent-ful, early in life, of authority, he grew up harboring delusions of grandeur and power. When the father of a Jewish girl rejects him as unsuitable, he turns his hatred of parental authority to hatred of Jews, and on the eve of the war identifies with the Nazi movement. This, he felt, would give him a sense of group solidarity, and approval for striking out at authority figures. This group allows him, too, the minority groups as scapegoat, the hate objects of his paranoia turned into bigotry. After many months of therapy in the prison, the young man applies for and is granted parole, although the doctor does not agree and does not believe he has changed his beliefs or his personality.

The flashback dissolves to the present, as Poitier concludes his narration to Falk: ten years later, the American Nazi was hanged, for beating to death a stranger, an old man. Poitier urges the young doctor not to yield to the pressure point, but to stay with his own young patient and to stand by his professional assess-ment, no matter the pain or despair.

In Lindner's book, the psychiatrist was not a black man.

"I was trying to push forward the barriers to the categories of roles for black actors," Kramer told me. But his explanation for the choice of Sidney Poitier does not explain the addition to the production of an entirely new theme which is not in the book either: the fact that antiblack sentiment thus becomes a logical component of an American fascism. Hatred of minorities must include any convenient minority. Thus the film becomes a strong and carefully developed attack on bigotry, and the sickness is shown to have potentially disastrous consequences not only for the individual and the people he hates, but also for a larger society and, by implication, for all civilization. It's only a short step from this man's paranoia, in other words, to his support of a destructive political movement, and the persecution of those seen as threats to his idea of "racial purity."

The theme is introduced early in the film: Darin rejects Poitier's help "because you're a Negro."

"What have you got against us Negroes?" asks Poitier.

"What have you got against us whites?" asks Darin in turn— it's the first sign of his paranoia, and with this the young man sets up an unbridgeable barrier between them. "Now that the Jews got that cripple in the White House," he continues (referring to Franklin Roosevelt), "you think you got it made." The man's anti-Semitism is now indistinguishable from his antiblack sentiment. "You blacks are just like weak men who can't compete in a game, although you keep trying," he says later. "But the Jews are more dangerous because they pass for white and are smug about it."

Later still, justifying his support of Nazism against American ideals and failing to see their fundamental irreconcilability, he says, "It's a cause like any other. The ordinary man needs a leader. He wants things and he needs the excuse to get them. That's where you come in. We need you. Where there is no definite enemy, we make you the enemy. You and the Jews will be responsible for our triumph."

This little speech, of course, is wrongly put on the lips of the prisoner-patient himself. It's too keen an autoanalysis, and would have been better as a report from the doctor. Had the patient in fact delivered such a ringing indictment of himself, and with such psychological acuity, he'd hardly have been as unwell as the rest of his remarks reveal. The plot of *Pressure Point* and the consistency of character development thus get bogged down by the film's own good intentions.

The indication that racism is totally antithetical to everything that America stands for is a noble theme. Oddly, however, the film's impact is occasionally weakened by the very virtuosity of the director, and by the otherwise creative use of the camera to describe the mind of a lunatic, as well as by the shrillness of the dialogue and the illogical ending.

Cornfield's direction is admirable, if a trifle self-conscious; you have the impression that Kramer himself would have directed the picture more matter-of-factly, with less bravura, perhaps with less affectation. In his cell at night, for example, Darin has weird fantasies: he hears sounds, has an anxiety attack, sees

The patient as young terrorist.

himself as a pathetically tiny man trying to crawl grotesquely out of an enormous sink drain. He then turns on the faucet and washes himself down the drain, but suddenly it's the drain's point of view, so the audience is washing itself down the drain, as the water splashes over the camera's lens. Up to this moment in the sequence, the grotesquerie of the hallucination is arresting, but the last shot merely calls attention to the cinematic trick and, by abruptly changing the point of view, shifts the audience's objective observance of the man's sickness to a sudden and unjustified identification *with the hallucination!* This tendency to shift viewpoint abruptly in the film is disorienting and finally confuses what should be a carefully maintained, distanced point of view.

At other times, however, the director's sense of rhythm works successfully. Each psychotic incident is alternated with a blatantly racist remark: "Wise up, black man," he says, "and go back to Africa." Shortly thereafter, he collapses in the doctor's office and is forced to ask for help. Cornfield's direction is best when there is an inventive use of dissolves and transitions to link past and present. As Darin recounts his childhood to Poitier, for example, the camera slowly circles from the doctor's office to the child's bedroom—without a cut—and because the soundstage is half dressed with the props of each, there is a visual uniting of the two settings which reinforces the sense of psychic linkage. Cornfield has also manipulated both sound and images to make the viewer feel the state of the patient's mind. As Darin recounts a childhood incident, his voice suddenly takes on the timbre of the boy soprano; when he repeats his mother's words to the doctor, then, it is not her voice but the boy's that we hear as we see her lips move.

Cornfield also insists on the swift cut from past to present, so that eventually there is a subjective-hallucinatory quality to each. We move from a daydream fantasy to the reality of past or present, and in the many flashbacks within flashbacks (to the boy's home life) there are sudden omissions of background and setting which place the family in general, and the boy especially, in a bleak nonworld, where the absence of specificity gives the boy the effect of being lost, unrooted. It is just this sense of nonbelonging which will find its horrible response in the Nazi party's exploitation of his sickness years later.

The two major performances are impressive. Poitier's portrayal of the doctor is always credible: he projects just the right balance between quiet confidence in his own abilities and the sudden rush of bewilderment at this young man that gives the character

Bobby Darin, Mary Munday, before the rape scene.

of the doctor a real humanity. He is no idealized black professional, any more than Darin's intelligently limned portrait of the psychotic is a stock picture of a social misfit. "This is a very special movie," observed a major film critic, "obviously not to everyone's taste, but surely no one can mistake the directorial stature that it reveals in Cornfield."

That was typical of the critical response to the film, which drew modest audiences at theatres in the northern half of the country. It is difficult to judge how the film was received in the South, where it ran for a very short time, and where distributors and bookers reported sketchy returns.

What remains one of the curious things about American film audience and critical response, however, is that no one thought to see just how *Pressure Point* is the logical sequel to Kramer's previous film, *Judgment at Nuremberg*. Shifting the center of interest from a German court to an American prison enables him to play variations on the same theme, and to suggest the endurance of the danger of fascism at home, regardless of the decisions of juries, lawyers and judges.

Pressure Point, in other words, became Stanley Kramer's more personal involvement in the issue of racial hatred. Ironically, however, it was necessary that it be directed by another. With all due honor to Hubert Cornfield, I can't help thinking the lower Kramer key would have been more apt.

Judy Garland and Burt Lancaster.

CHAPTER 25

Variations on a Theme of Kindness— *A Child Is Waiting*, 1963

Pressure Point was the story of a sick young man and a stern but patient doctor. Stanley Kramer's next film, *A Child Is Waiting*, transferred the setting from prison hospital to school, but kept, with some variation, the theme of mental disturbance.

Perhaps the most emotionally exhausting film he produced— for him and for his audiences—*A Child Is Waiting* was in many ways a disappointment for Kramer. Because he was still working on preproduction for *It's a Mad Mad Mad Mad World*, he had, once again, to entrust the shooting to another director—in this case John Cassavetes. It remained a very special interest for Kramer, however, and the project involved him as often as his schedule allowed.

The original story and screenplay by Abby Mann documents, with telling simplicity, the problems faced by those who care for the retarded and for children afflicted with brain damage either from birth, injury or disease. Dr. Matthew Clark (Burt Lancaster) is an earnest, wise and competent man in his field, and he must battle the indifference of bureaucracies and the neuroses of staff, grief-stricken parents and well-meaning outsiders. To his school

for special children comes a woman seeking meaning in her
restless and rootless life: she is Jean Hansen (Judy Garland), and
she soon becomes emotionally involved in her work—too involved, indeed, and unhealthily attached to one particularly sad
and lovable little boy, Reuben Widdicombe (Bruce Ritchey).
Since the script avoids an easy romanticism, however, we sense
early on that the story won't go very far: the children cannot
experience any fundamental improvement, nor can their parents
hope the children will be cured. The futures of the youngsters,
in fact, depend on just how much the adults change *their*
attitude: teaching, encouraging and loving the children, but not
smothering them into inactivity, nor providing for their needs so
completely that all vestiges of elemental human dignity are
withdrawn, and even their willingness to execute simple tasks
and chores. The film ends on a minor note, as the woman learns
the necessity of tempering her attachment with more professional standards.

"John Cassavetes belongs to the 'let it happen' school of
directing," Kramer recalled. "He didn't understand the nature of
the story—especially the unique fact that we had, for the most
part, retarded children who were actual patients from the Pacific
State Hospital in Pomona. It was a very delicate film to make,
and he didn't seem to sympathize, nor to have the patience. It
made me very unhappy, to tell the truth." At the time of the
film's release, Cassavetes simply said that Kramer interfered too
much. He has not said much more about it since that time, and
in fact there were six years before Cassavetes' next directorial
effort. He is highly regarded by some for his improvisational,
quasi-documentary style of filmmaking, and his most admired
films—*Shadows, Faces, Husbands, A Woman Under the Influence*—have
earned him considerable critical acclaim.

Whatever the personal differences between producer and
director, the film has an emotional impact that is uncontrived,
honest and forceful, and Joseph LaShelle's camera is an agile,
alert and always inquisitive observer. But it is the omnipresence
of the exceptional children that provides an emotional texture
that is never exploitive, never gratuitous.

The film opens with a precredit sequence: there's a slow dolly shot to the open door of a parked auto, through which we see a child waiting inside. He gets out and goes to a small toy car on the path, on which he pedals away contentedly. His parents take advantage of his momentary distraction to depart: we learn later that they have gone through considerable anguish to arrive at the realization that the boy needed a special school. Noticing their departure, the child becomes hysterical. Only then do the credits roll—and we are thus put on notice that this film is not an evening's light entertainment.

A Child Is Waiting is indeed draining to watch: it tugs at every human emotion relentlessly. But it's a necessary and beneficial experience if an audience is to understand the special problems confronted by people who work with children such as these.

Judy Garland was not in fact well cast as the teacher whose

Producer confers with director.

obsession is more unhealthy for the child than it is for herself. But there is a special, sad intensity in watching the scenes with Bruce Ritchey, one of the very few child actors in the picture. He slurred his speech, blanked out his vision, affected that curious gray glance and attitude that are the mark of the child who lives in his own restricted, innocent world. There was an almost tangible chemistry about his scenes with Garland. Oddly, she is not entirely credible when she appears without him: her scenes with Lancaster seem underrehearsed and awkward, but this may have been due to the unfortunate circumstances of her own life at the time.

"She was the greatest single person to captivate an audience since Al Jolson," Kramer said. "But in my second picture with her she was awfully difficult. She would be terribly wearisome to those around her. She would keep people up all night, calling on the phone at three in the morning and never hanging up. I was only making a film with her, but she'd call me in the middle of the night about the damnedest succession of things. She'd have her agent there, and her business manager, and a publicity man, and she'd keep them up all night, too. And then of course everybody would be sick the next day and couldn't work very well, while she would go on like firecrackers as though nothing had happened at all.

"What's the story of Judy? I guess the story of Judy Garland is the story of an innocent eleven-year-old named Frances Gumm, and the villain is Louis B. Mayer. He put her in four pictures a year—dieting, singing, dancing, personal appearances, every-thing—and she had her first nervous breakdown when she was only fifteen years old. I suppose you can't blame any one person for what happens to a life, but Mayer didn't do well by her. I was at MGM during some of those years, and I know it."

Probably Garland and the film's most poignant moment, and the one which allows us to see the mutual needs of the exceptional child and of the emotionally vulnerable, exceptional adult, is the scene in which the child looks up at her with his great saucer eyes and asks, "Do you like me, Miss Hansen? Do you like me?" The camera remains a quiet observer, and you can catch the reflected grief and perhaps even the memories on Judy

Garland's own face at that moment, as her reservoir of pain turns slowly to a river of warmth and acceptance.

Burt Lancaster is asked to do little more than be a sort of *père manqué* in all this, but he does represent a Platonic form of moral earnestness, and his height and his square-jawed confidence provide the needed manly strengths of the film. Lancaster had been a problem in *Judgment at Nuremberg*, according to a number of gossips; here, however, he seemed to believe in the character and the story, and also to accept direction somewhat less chafingly.

The critics were embarrassed by and angered at the film. Peter Morris, editor of the revised edition of Georges Sadoul's important book *Dictionary of Filmmakers*, spoke for many when he said it was "a disaster in every way," and the public, when they *could*

Burt Lancaster, with boys from the Pacific State Hospital.

see it (it was neither widely nor well distributed in 1963), seemed unwilling, in those Camelot days, to sustain somber social statement. In a few short years, the country would be surfeited with all sorts of "relevant" films that turned out to be instant antiques, and meanwhile, modest films like this were virtually ignored.

A Child Is Waiting is most remarkable, in the final analysis, because of the children, who walk off with the film and with the hearts of the viewers, too. They are shown in all their primal innocence and simplicity, and they are quite unforgettable. This quiet black-and-white picture argues for our understanding, our acknowledgment of their plight, and our support of proper homes for them, educational programs and teacher-training institutes to serve them, and public attitudes toward them. And this it does with candor and uncondescending compassion.

CHAPTER 26

Mad Money, Without Economy— *It's a Mad Mad Mad Mad World, 1963*

It was Stanley Kramer's first comedy in fifteen years—since *So This Is New York*—and it seems he felt compelled to answer for the years' lack of lightness. *It's a Mad Mad Mad Mad World* is so self-consciously funny and so overloaded with homage to classic comedy that it finally overstates everything; it's as redundant as its title. But it's also, in the edited two-and-a-half hour version (instead of the original three-hour, twelve-minute print) raucously, modishly funny, and evidently was made in a great spirit of fun by its gifted, wacky crew of comedians.

After superb cartoon credit designs, and the first hearing of Ernest Gold's bouncily recurrent theme music, the film opens on a broad aerial view of a car chase. Virtually everything that follows consists of variations of the theme of chase, in fact.

Immediately, a car driven by Jimmy Durante crashes through a guard rail and into a ravine in the California desert. Just before he literally kicks the bucket moments later, the nicely unbloodily dying Durante gives five anxious Good Samaritans a clue to the whereabouts of buried loot totaling $350,000. The eager recipients of this news are Milton Berle, a hypochondriac traveling

The opening sequence: Jonathan Winters, Milton Berle, Mickey Rooney, Sid Caesar, Buddy Hackett—and Jimmy Durante, just before he (literally) kicks the bucket.

The Three Stooges.

with his shrieking, shrewish mother-in-law, Ethel Merman, and his pretty, demure young wife, Dorothy Provine; Sid Caesar, a twitchy, moon-eyed dentist on holiday with wife Edie Adams; Mickey Rooney and Buddy Hackett, writers of comedy; and that boyish teddy bear, Jonathan Winters, here cast as the archetype of the brainless truck driver. They all pile into their respective vehicles and begin the chase to find the cache of cash. A knowledgeable sheriff, Spencer Tracy, ostensibly the guardian of a sane morality amid all this scrambling for money, knows about the stolen money, however, and foils their plans.

Along the way to their goal, these four little groups representing various American types run, walk, slip, fly and smash into

Beginning the search: Edie Adams, Sid Caesar, Jonathan Winters, Dorothy Provine, Ethel Merman, Milton Berle, Mickey Rooney, Buddy Hackett.

Phil Silvers, a free-lance swindler; Terry-Thomas, a British botanist; Dick Shawn, Merman's muscular grownup baby; and, in roles ranging from small to microscopic, all the comic actors able to walk in 1963: Jim Backus, Eddie ("Rochester") Anderson, Ben Blue, Buster Keaton, Paul Ford, Edward Everett Horton,

Spencer Tracy, with his friend and director.

Peter Falk, William Demarest, Don Knotts, Carl Reiner, The Three Stooges, Joe E. Brown, Andy Devine, Sterling Holloway, Arnold Stang, Marvin Kaplan, Bobo Lewis, Mike Mazurki, Jerry Lewis, ZaSu Pitts and Jack Benny. Crowded with cameos it surely is, but not annoyingly so, like Mike Todd's *Around the World in Eighty Days,* or George Stevens' overstudded epic *The Greatest Story Ever Told,* which seemed rather like the longest movie ever made. The latter film's superficial solemnity upset itself by the interruptions of John Wayne, as the centurion at the foot of the cross; Ed Wynn, as a man cured of blindness; Dorothy McGuire, as the Virgin Mary; and, most piously, Sidney Poitier as Simon of Cyrene. And so on and on and on.

Kramer's madcap comedy doesn't parade its stars merely to add prestige to the picture: they're in fact part of his aim in making the film. "I wanted to make a comedy to end all comedies," Kramer said at the world premiere screening. Well, he didn't do that, of course, and his enthusiastic overstatement tells us a good deal about his energy, zeal and earnestness, as well as about the manic energy that went into this production. The album of comic players helps make the film a homage to classic American comedy.

There are two ways of making a film like this, and Kramer pursued both ways at once: he peppered it with people associated with classic comedy, and he accumulated episodes and gestures which have become typical (sometimes even stereotypical) of the genre. The various incidents, too, are usually accidents: his film collects all the slapstick tricks and chase routines that were established as pure cinema in the style of Keaton, Chaplin and Lloyd. At the very end of the film, when Ethel Merman slips on a banana peel, we're reminded (with perhaps unnecessary reinforcement by this time) that the picture we've been watching is in fact a résumé of references to the comic tradition—partially inspired by the traditions of burlesque, partially drawing on the history of vaudeville, but most of all developed according to the wonderful, breathless illogic of filmed comedy.

In spite of excesses, *Mad World* has some gloriously amusing moments. Airplane pilot Jim Backus passes out in midflight and, from the ground, Paul Ford bumblingly talks down the plane, in which Hackett and Rooney are now frozen at the controls. Sid Caesar and Edie Adams resort to dynamite to escape from a hardware store's basement. Jonathan Winters literally tears apart

Kramer's homage to the cinema of Harold Lloyd.

a garage. Ben Blue maneuvers a prewar biplane that gradually comes apart at its antique seams. Kramer has an obvious fondness for the cinema of Harold Lloyd in all this, and the Lloydian references pile up toward the end of the picture—the dangerous dangling over the city, for example, in which an expert crew of stuntmen cling precariously to a collapsing fire escape, as errant currency whirls about them like inappropriate snowflakes in the hot climate.

Underneath all the madness, however, it's easy to discern Kramer's ubiquitous concern for an issue, for the film is nothing so much as a satire on money madness and on the avarice which we frequently pursue in our ever quicker modes of transportation. The zany trip thus becomes, in William and Tania Rose's script, a metaphor for the commercial scramble that has invaded every aspect of modern American life. "It's a comedy about greed," Kramer told me, and, like the classics it mimics, there's much the movie owes to conventions of Restoration farces, which were also frequently comedies about greed, though they had more leering and bloodletting. The violence here is highly stylized and never repellent.

There are, however, two big problems with *Mad World:* one is that there are so many characters crowding the frame in increasingly frantic sequences that none of them has much depth. Spencer Tracy, in his four films for Stanley Kramer, increasingly serves as the director's *alter ego*—expressing Kramer's beliefs, issuing his warnings and toying with his placebos. But here even Tracy gets lost in the shifts and shuffles of the film's sacrifice to speed.

The second flaw is the film's excess: there is simply too much of its muchness. Filming in Technicolor and Ultra Panavision (actually, single lens Cinerama) Kramer could not resist the extra car crash, the additional race, the next breakaway building, the repeated gag. He gave us a comic morality tract about money, but without economy.

George Segal and Pat Hingle.

CHAPTER 27

Gunfighting at the *Psycho* House— *Invitation to a Gunfighter*, 1964

It's hard, years later, to find anyone who was involved in *Invitation to a Gunfighter* who will discuss it. Kramer, who gave the property to Richard Wilson to direct in 1964, says only, "Oh, that. Well, there's not much to say about it, is there?" He was himself in preproduction for *Ship of Fools*, which was having problems of its own, and *Gunfighter*, a small and complicated story, had gone through several revisions: the screenplay was finally hammered out by Richard and Elizabeth Wilson, from an adaptation by Alvin Sapinsley, based on a story by Hal Goodman and Larry Klein. It's a confused psychological Western, inconsistent in tone and marred by awkwardly patched editing. But it's also one of the most intriguing failures to come from Hollywood in the sixties, and it has a haunting plot quality. Because the major characters are not carefully drawn, there's more mystery than usual in the story, but the theme of social discretion is so unusually handled that it's hard to shake off a certain wonder about what the picture *might* have been.

The story seems to be about the return of a Confederate soldier (George Segal) to his home in the New Mexico Territory in 1865. A rebel, he lost his wife and farm in the Civil War, and now finds that his homestead has been swindled away from him by the town's pompous boss (Pat Hingle). A fight follows, and soon Hingle is accusing Segal of murdering the man who now inhabits Segal's former home. Segal barricades himself in the house, although seriously wounded. To smoke him out, the townspeople hire a deadly dandy of a gunfighter (Yul Brynner). But it turns out that Brynner, half-black son of a slave mother and Creole father, was himself mistreated by the hypocritical town leader in the past, and so he is out to avenge himself rather than kill Segal. At the end, Brynner and Hingle lie dead, and Segal wins both the town and the now conveniently widowed Janice Rule, Segal's former mistress and the woman to whom Brynner was attracted during his stay in the town.

This brief outline does not describe the many twists and turns in the plot, and they were the critics' main objections. The story, whose psychological configurations are fascinating, simply cannot justify the arbitrary shifts of character and the sudden changes in emotional temperature.

There's a key moment toward the end of the story which gives a fair example of this muddy motivation. After trying to bribe Janice Rule to come away with him in exchange for Segal's life, Brynner goes (or pretends to go) quite mad: he lurches down Main Street, smashing store windows and wrecking businesses while the helpless townspeople follow in dismay. Then, in a draw, he kills the drunken, arrogant one-armed husband of Rule (lumpily played by Clifford David) and allows himself to be shot by Hingle, who also dies in the shootout. This unexpected sequence—designed perhaps to add to the mysterious nobility of the Brynner character—disorients the film's attention and reduces the Segal/Hingle conflict to virtual insignificance. It also suggests rather extreme measures for Brynner to salve the wounds of Rule's rejection.

The film was shot, obviously, on the Universal Studios' back lot. Rather than attempt to avoid photographing the famous Gothic house that appears in Alfred Hitchcock's classic *Psycho*, this film uses it for Hingle's house, and scenes are shot quite close to it—even on its steps! Since the house was, by 1964, part of the national iconography, it's hard to imagine any structural or narrative or thematic reason for the director's perverse insistence on it here.

Curiously, however, even though the plot is as clear as pea soup, the atmosphere of the film and the attitudes of the major characters remain somehow fascinating. Brynner, smoothly enigmatic, tries valiantly to fulfill the odd requirements: as Jules Gaspard D'Estaing, he plays the spinet, quotes French poetry, sings early Creole chansons, speaks several languages, plucks the guitar admirably, manages a mean game of poker and charms everyone from the doe-eyed Rule to a poor old widow, to whom he displays a characteristic generosity. Few strong actors in leather and shiny vest could make this kind of mysterious gunfighter credible, and when Brynner dismisses a rival with a mere flick of his finger and a slow blink, everyone onscreen and in the audience probably smiles at the bravado. The sheer exoticism of such a character has long been linked to Brynner, ever since the stony sexiness in his portrayal of the King of Siam for Rodgers and Hammerstein. Brynner has a steel-voiced, self-confident machismo—not the sort that blazes forth or is defined in harsh tones by much physical violence, but the sort that prevails by the simple means of his hard presence, with his eagle eyes piercing through subterfuge like a laser beam. This is what he brought to films like *Anastasia* and *The Brothers Karamazov*, and what presumably made him such a desirable commodity in lesser Westerns after *The Magnificent Seven*, John Sturges' lively American version of Kurosawa's *Seven Samurai*.

There's a nice contrast between Brynner's smoothly unsmiling ambiguity and Janice Rule's slightly sad, pensive and attractive (but too neatly coiffed) heroine. At first drawn to his low mumbling, which promises both protection and unguessed sexual energies, she suggests rather than defines the character: her inability later to trust Segal is conveyed in a quietly tender scene in which her eyes, shining with desire, glance back toward her home, to her forlorn and sour husband; to the wounds of her former lover, helplessly before her now, and to the empty street along which comes the gunfighter to throw into disarray all her previously arranged emotions. Segal himself is occasionally a

Janice Rule observes Yul Brynner's kindness.

The happy ending, sort of . . .

little too intense, but his naturally quizzical expression and his inference that pain is not felt only by children or cowards, have an affecting quality that were used even to better effect by Kramer in *Ship of Fools*.

Wilson's otherwise unremarkable direction catches fire only once during the picture, during the sequence in which Brynner is boarding with Rule and her ornery husband. The strife is generated in the house as he plays harpsichord with style and sensitivity for Rule and her husband and then, as if it were the most consistent action in the world, sits down to dinner wearing gun and holster. The dialogue here is filled with subtle asides and half-expressed fears, and the banality of the situation lightly veils simmering tension among the three. There is the husband's neurotic jealousy and frustration over his loss of an arm; the wife's frightened glances at the odd stranger; and Brynner's easy omniscience about the two of them, in spite of her diminishing patience at the state of things in the corrupt town.

The film places the audience's sympathies now with Segal, now with Brynner—and always with the darkly silent Rule. When Hingle says that the modification of law is justified because Segal is a killer and it's still wartime, the film recalls the spirit of *High Noon*. It has, too, the subtheme of waiting women, and the principle of law overcoming ignorance and injustice. Hingle, apparently the repository of civilization and order, is actually the most corrupt of all, and the strange and curious Brynner, a sort of unmasked Lone Ranger, in fact invites his own death rather than an avenging gunfight.

Few of the psychological complexities of the story have been adequately discerned by the script, and therefore the film remains something of a disappointment. Its failure is particularly sorry (and therefore the film retains a measure of perverse attraction) because there are, just beneath the surface, indications of a much better movie, and especially of real people who, if probed more deeply, might reveal sharper characters.

Michael Dunn and George Segal.

CHAPTER 28

Grand Hotel Afloat, or a Steamboat Named Desire—

Ship of Fools, 1965

The first *Ship of Fools* wasn't Katherine Anne Porter's novel, which was published in 1962; it was a long poem by Sebastian Brant called *Das Narrenschiff*, which appeared in 1494. In rhyming couplets, the work assembled representatives of every age, class and quality on a ship bound for Narragonia, the land of fools. The poem helped prepare for the Reformation, since it especially exposed evils within the Church. Written in Alsatian dialect, *Das Narrenschiff* was adapted and translated throughout Europe; and English versions included Alexander Barclay's *The Ship of Fools* (1509) and *Cock Lovell's Bote,* which was published anonymously soon after.

Porter collected a group of fools aboard her fictional ship *Vera,* bound for Bremerhaven from Veracruz, Mexico, in 1931. For the author, as for her forebears in the nautical allegories, the boat trip is an archetype of the journey of the human family at a time of crisis. Stanley Kramer's two-and-a-half-hour rendering of the Porter novel, with script by Abby Mann, is more concerned with relationships than with plot, and more with character than with drama. Little, in fact, happens aboard the *Vera,* other than the meeting, loving and sparring among the passengers. The film advances the trip to 1933, thus to make more acute the advancing tide of Nazism. Aboard the ship are David (George Segal), a struggling young painter who's being kept by his rich girlfriend Jenny (Elizabeth Ashley); Mary Treadwell (Vivien Leigh), a middle-aged, tippling Southern belle who would like nothing so much as to believe in her own cosmetic elegance, and whose simmering passion is ultimately ignited by the meeting with Tenny (Lee Marvin), a rich and vulgar Texan; Rieber (José Ferrer), a fussy, loud-mouthed Nazi; La Condesa (Simone Signoret), en route to exile in Tenerife for conspiring with the peasants against the Cuban government—a woman whose last desperate loving is experienced in her shipboard affair with the doctor (Oskar Werner), who dies of a heart attack after her departure; Lowenthal (Heinz Ruehmann), a merry Jewish fellow who's convinced that patience, understanding and compassion will solve all these nasty world problems; Freytag (Alf Kjellin), a Gentile divorced from a Jewish wife, who makes a passionate speech against anti-Semitism; Pepe (José Greco), leader of a troop of Spanish dancers; Captain Thiele (Charles Korvin), in command of the ship but perhaps not of his own thoughts about the passengers (about the ship's doctor especially, for whom his friendship seems tinged with eroticism); Glocken (Michael Dunn), a philosophizing dwarf who acts as a sort of Greek chorus, offering sage comments to the audience and being a link to all these other "small" people. There are other passengers aboard who float in and out of the dialogue in minor roles, offering emotional counterpoint to the larger figures in the rather static album.

Ship of Fools is, as you can see, a floating Grand Hotel. Full of Germans and Jews, and plowing the deep in 1933, it is laced with conscious social and psychological significance. At the beginning of the film, Dunn informs us that we might even find ourselves aboard this ship of fools—and at the end he asks, "What has all this to do with us today? Why, nothing at all!" But he speaks with a knowing, ironic smile, so . . .

It's this sort of elementary school exposition that critics and audiences found annoying. (One particularly dyspeptic critic,

Simone Signoret and Oskar Werner.

George Segal and Elizabeth Ashley.

whose lengthy article got more and more vicious, began with the observation that the film was "the shoddiest example of fakery since the days of Ann Corio's Monogram epics.") The major problem with Mann's script, so gravid with clichés that it nearly sinks the *Vera*, is that the ironies are quaintly based on a knowing hindsight. As the Nazi barks inanities, an innocent German says, "Every time I listen to him I know no one will support his party." And a particularly loyal and homeland-loving Jew remarks with confidence, "There are nearly a million Jews in Germany. What are they going to do—kill us all?" (This kind of remark is supposed to be especially ironic—and ends up especially infelicitous—since it's made by the noted German actor Heinz Ruehmann. "He was a big star in pre-Hitler Germany," Kramer told me. "I wasn't too popular there after the showing of *Judgment at Nuremberg*, and I got a very stony reception when I arrived later to cast the Germans for this picture. I met Ruehmann, who himself was not Jewish but felt a great burden of guilt for the whole nation. When I told him I was looking for someone to play a Jew, he said 'I'm your man!' ")

The banality of these several characters and the monumentally unimaginative script are compensated by Kramer's smoothly controlled direction. The situation of La Condesa and the ship's doctor, for example, which very nearly tilts into soap opera, is brilliantly handled. Kramer drew from Signoret and Werner such sharply drawn portraits of pain and withdrawal, and of a momentary human communication, that their scenes make the rest of the film look like a Little Lulu cartoon. They're both characters who have ceased to believe in their own futures and have forgotten their own hopes. Signoret is an expert at those dark, withdrawn glances, the traits of a woman whose death has already begun in her drug addiction. She hears her heartbeats like knocking on the tomb, and so her brief affair with Werner does not revive hope; it only reminds her of the exile to which she's doomed, which will put the final touch to an emotional exile she's inhabited for years. Werner plays a man with a sick heart, whose last opening to feeling is so distressing that once she leaves the ship there's nothing left for him but to die, on deck, from a heart seizure. With a saber scar slashed across the

George Segal, Michael Dunn, Lee Marvin.

Werner Klemperer and Vivien Leigh.

cheek, and his icy reserve, Werner, too, is a man long exiled from communion with others.

They are the most recognizably human pair in the lot, the most mature, the least self-indulgent in their unself-pitying pain. (Werner, however, made heavy demands on his director in exchange for such an extraordinary performance. "In the scene with the captain," Kramer recalled, "the bar was built stage left. But Werner wouldn't work stage left, and so I had to have the whole set rebuilt just for him!")

La Condesa's haze of addiction has its foolish counterpart in Vivien Leigh's blowsy drinker, a widow whose diplomat-husband has beaten her so frequently that she thought life could hold no more love for her again. Cherishing the dreams of her own false glamour, the character becomes, as Judith Crist remarked, a presence in something like "A Steamboat Named Desire." Her Mary Treadwell is fascinating, but perhaps not fragile enough, so that when she runs head-on into that rhinestone in the rough, Lee Marvin, we wait with perverse glee until the veneer is stripped away. But she has a wonderfully Sternbergian scene before a mirror, in which she pencils her eyebrows and seems to glance even further than her own reflection, into the depths of her own empty image. Her silence, the slow upturn of one brow and the drooping corners of her mouth, are worth more than all of Ferrer's strident bellowing.

Kramer has paced the film so well that it's easy to see how he understood the various pairs of characters: "They're all aspects of Katherine Anne Porter herself," he said, "and of what she feels and responds to." More than that perhaps, his method of building the sequences suggests that all the couples are a single *couple*, seen at various stages of life and in various countries. He cuts from Signoret/Werner to Ashley/Segal to Leigh/Marvin at just the right moments in order to indicate the reactions of an older couple that are being nurtured now in a younger set; and just when their essential shallowness begins to wear thin, he moves on to an analogous situation with another pair. Kramer was greatly helped in this by the unifying cinematography of

Ernest Laszlo, which won the Academy Award in the black-and-white category, and by Robert Clatworthy's art direction and Joseph Kish's set decoration (similarly rewarded), which made almost dreamlike the rooms of a ship that was really all sound-stage plasterboard.

Sidney Poitier, Spencer Tracy, Katharine Hepburn.

CHAPTER 29

An Epitaph for a Taboo and for Spencer Tracy—

Guess Who's Coming to Dinner, 1967

For the critics, virtually unanimously, it was loathsome. For the public, who in great crowds everywhere made it one of the great box-office successes of all time, it was delicious entertainment of a very special kind. For the people involved in the production, it was one of the most important events of their various lives.

The picture was the last of Stanley Kramer's tetralogy on the black man in white America, a series which began with *Home of the Brave*, which examined the black man and his white buddies in a rarefied, wartime setting. The theme was picked up again in *The Defiant Ones*, which particularized the struggle in terms of two prisoners chained at the wrist, trying to flee their prison and one another. In *Pressure Point*, the themes of mental illness and imprisonment were fused, and racism was equated with Nazism. Thus far in his career Kramer had treated friendship between men of different races, and professional and social equality based on an understanding of common humanity. All that remained was the most difficult and delicate issue of all—interracial marriage. One of Hollywood's strictest taboos kept this theme out of the movies for over forty years, since the implementation of the Production Code. No one would touch this most explosive of social issues.

Not, at least, until Kramer proposed *Guess Who's Coming to Dinner* to Columbia Pictures. The very mention of the film still raises looks of benign repugnance from those sophisticates who have no sense of American cinema or social history. . . .

It's the story of Joey Drayton (Katharine Houghton, actually the niece of Katharine Hepburn), who brings her fiancé, Dr. John Prentice (Sidney Poitier) home to sunny San Francisco to meet her affluent parents (Hepburn and Spencer Tracy). Their liberal persuasions are now put to the test, for although the young man is an ideal choice (he's highly and internationally respected in the medical field, and he's impeccably mannered, handsome, well dressed and of a respectable California family), he's black. The film, which covers one busy day in the Drayton home, is essentially a drawing-room comedy, a series of cross-conversations between the young doctor and the girl's parents, and then between the girl and his parents, and finally between all sets of parents and offspring. A simple dinner is extended to include the doctor's parents, who fly up from Los Angeles for the evening, and the crusty but benevolent old Irish priest, friend of the family (Cecil Kellaway). Thus the title of the film . . .

Although the young couple's future problems are acknowledged, it's ultimately the expression of the meaning of love by the two mothers, and a quietly eloquent speech made by Tracy, that win the blessing of all upon the marriage. The film ends as the dinner finally begins.

William Rose won the Academy Award for best original story and screenplay for 1967 (as did Katharine Hepburn, for acting). The film had actually begun, however, shortly after he and Kramer had collaborated on *It's a Mad Mad Mad Mad World*. "Bill Rose and I were walking in my driveway," Kramer recalled, "and he was telling me a story about intermarriage in South Africa. It was then the idea hit me. We changed the time and place, and even before Bill had worked out a treatment—much less a script—I talked to Hepburn, Tracy and Poitier about it. They were all excited, and agreed to do it before a word of script was written. From the start, it was a very special project for all of us." As the script progressed, almost every familiar racial prejudice was brought up in discussions, found its way into the script and was eventually treated and illuminated, if not actually demolished. Throughout the writing and shooting, *Guess Who's Coming to Dinner* was conceived as having a consistently light tone: fundamentally a salon comedy, not above using sight gags and double takes, weak jokes, visual ironies and snappish, cynical humor.

Nor is it without flaws: the genial Irish priest is a refugee from *Going My Way*, and although his presence and manner are designed to apply the approving unction of organized religion to this marriage, the character seems a deliberate, intrusive afterthought. There's the problem, too, of the painted sunsets, indoor gardens and muddy process photography—although these may have been necessitated by Tracy's terminal illness, which demanded special attention to scheduling and the simplification of all shooting problems, since his energies were fast dwindling.

But the critical outcry goes deeper than minor characters or hasty technique: the objection remains that the race issue is prettified and preguaranteed a happy resolution here because of the extraordinary character of this black man, and the built-in liberal stance of the parents, especially since Poitier represents the quintessentially respectable and unthreatening black, and Tracy and Hepburn represent the settled, establishmentarian liberals who can win over any case and make the nastiest world safe for love and ideals. This view, which didn't keep millions of delighted moviegoers away, fails to consider either the unprecedented aspect of the picture or the fundamental aim, which was to entertain while suggesting gently a new way of regarding people in a delicate situation. Many critics, too, considered the race issue "no longer relevant in 1967." They were tragically disproved in the months to come, when rioting broke out from coast to coast. . . .

"We took special pains to make Poitier a very special character in this story," Kramer said, "and to make both families, in

Kramer on the set of *Guess Who's Coming to Dinner.*

fact, very special. Respectable, yes. And intelligent. And attractive. We did this so that if the young couple didn't marry because of their parents' disapproval, the *only* reason would be that he was black and she was white. They had everything else in their favor, and we wanted the audience to feel that the relationship was so right, and the compatibility between the families was so possible apart from this one aspect, that the audience could only think, 'Hell! The racial difference just isn't enough to prevent those other things from saving their relationship!' The critics simply missed the point." In another way, of course, the film is about a larger social reality—the so-called generation gap. "Who says it's a story only about the black man?" Kramer asked rhetorically. "It's about young and old viewpoints, and in this case the bone of contention happens to be the acceptance of interracial marriage. But this film says that the new generation won't live like the last generation simply because that's the way it's supposed to be. Life has moved on."

Sidney Poitier feels even more strongly:

"People said I was cast as the stereotype of the intellectual black man with no flaws. And the critics refused to see beyond the images of Stanley Kramer and of me that they'd held for a long time. There was a great hue and cry at the time of the film's release, and it had to do, mostly, with the respectability and success of my character in the film. They said I should have played a garage mechanic, or someone like that, brought home to this wealthy San Francisco family by the daughter and presented as a candidate for marriage.

"Well, this objection has absolutely no historical sense. In 1967 it was utterly impossible to do an in-depth interracial love story, to treat the issue in dead earnestness, head on. No producer, no director could get the money, nor would theatres in America book it. But Kramer made people look at the issue for the first time, and he prepared such a fine production that Columbia agreed to back it. He treated the theme with humor, but so delicately, so humanly, so lovingly that he made everyone look at the question for the very first time in film history! *Guess Who's Coming to Dinner* is a totally revolutionary movie, and this is what so many critics failed to see. For the very first time, the characters in a story about racism are people with minds of their own, who after deliberations in a civilized manner, and after their own private reflections, come to a conclusion—the only sensible conclusion that people could come to in a situation like this!

"What the critics didn't know," Poitier concluded, "and what blinded them to the great merit of the film, was that Hollywood was incapable of anything more drastic in 1967. It just couldn't have been made, it couldn't have been distributed. So Kramer created an idea and molded it so lovingly, while retaining just enough of objective truth and allowing his cast just enough latitude of creative input, that a totally unheard-of theme opened in theatres everywhere around the country without incident."

This was also an important film for Poitier himself. In many of his earlier films, as *Variety* observed, "he seemed to come from nowhere; he was a symbol. But here he has a family, a professional background, likes, dislikes, humor, temper. In other words, he is a whole human being. This alone is a major achievement in screenwriting, and, for Poitier himself, his already recognized abilities now have expanded casting horizons." For Kramer, "Sidney Poitier is one of the greatest men in the world. He has always been very close to me, and the three roles he's played in my films have been psychologically and emotionally important for both of us."

But for many viewers the film is not primarily about race or racism, or young love trying to conquer all: it's about Spencer Tracy, who was dying during the filming and who passed away just after the completion of the principal photography. Tracy plays a fighting newspaper publisher (complete with photo of Franklin Roosevelt on his desk), an aging liberal who's not quite ready to turn over all the reins to the younger tribe. There's a glorious scene (some saw it, wrongly, as a needless digression) in which he and Hepburn stop at an ice-cream stand and he tries to recall an exotic flavor he recently enjoyed. As an unreasonable substitute, he accepts boysenberry sherbet. "This isn't the stuff," he says with disappointment, after a tiny taste. Then his face lights up: "But I like it!" It's a lovely gesture, a perfect momentary metaphor for the changes an older generation must learn to accept, and even for the sudden appearance of a man who may not be *his* choice for son-in-law, but who, after he thinks about it, he can really like.

The climax of the film occurs after all possible combinations of characters have had their separate discussions and are waiting in a tension-filled living room for Tracy to give his own decision about the issue. Kramer cuts from the families to Tracy, pacing on the terrace alone. After several cuts, the camera stays with him. He thinks and thinks and thinks. The lines of his face seem to grow deeper by the minute. He gazes out over San Francisco Bay, then glances straight out at us and murmurs, "Well, I'll be a son of a bitch!"

He then returns to the waiting group, where earlier Mrs. Prentice had asked, "What happens to men when they get old? ... When sexual things no longer matter, they forget what real passion means." This is one of the items denied by Tracy in his final speech, a gently carved epitaph not only for an antique racism, but also for Tracy himself. Andrew Sarris, writing in *The*

The happy couple.

Village Voice, described the final moving scene: "As Tracy repeats the charge to himself, Kramer shifts deliberately to a profile shot of Tracy on the left foreground of the screen and Hepburn, her eyes brimming with tears, on the right background looking at Tracy, and Tracy says no I have not forgotten, and he says it very slowly, and the two-shot is sustained in its ghostly immortality, recording the rapturous rapport between a being now dead and a being still alive, but a moment of life and love passing into the darkness of death everlasting, and anyone in the audience remaining dry-eyed through this evocation of gallantry and emotional loyalty has my deepest sympathy."

Tracy and Hepburn were appearing together before the cameras for the last of nine times. They and everyone else knew it. His last role was exactly what it should have been: an honest portrayal of a large-souled man whom Kramer himself always wanted to play his other self on the screen, for Tracy is everywhere the mouthpiece for the struggles, hopes and beliefs of Stanley Kramer. The deep friendship between these two men supported and confirmed their ideological unity.

"Spencer Tracy is the greatest actor I ever worked with. He had no physical energy for the shooting of this film, and so we had to film it only in the morning. Columbia doesn't know to this day that we shot only half days. They didn't believe the film would be a commercial success anyway, and if they'd known our schedule they would have been doubly furious.

"For *Guess Who's Coming to Dinner,* Hepburn was paid something in excess of $250,000 and I was to be paid about twice that, plus a generous percentage of the profits. Now of course it's prescribed that each major performer has to be insured for the length of the film's production. But no company would insure Tracy, it was so clear that he was living on borrowed time; so it looked as if we couldn't make the film. So Kate and I put our salaries in escrow and we agreed not to take a penny of it, so that if anything should happen to Tracy, our combined monies could be used to remake the film with another actor. Well, of course, we did finish the picture. And the day before his last scene was to be shot, Tracy came to me and said, 'I've been looking over the script. You really don't need me after tomorrow. If I die on the way home, you and Katie are in the clear.' Well, we finished next day, and ten days later he was dead. I'll never forget how much he meant to me, and to everyone who loved good men in the movies, or anywhere else, for that matter."

Anthony Quinn as Italo Bombolini.

CHAPTER 30

Magnani Breaks Her Foot on Zorba the Italian—
The Secret of Santa Vittoria, 1969

It wasn't long after World War II that writers and filmmakers discovered the enormous comic potential in stories involving a battle of wits between German occupying forces, notorious for their sense of discipline and organization, and Italian villagers, known for a life of sweet leisure—*dolce far niente,* as it's called by the natives. Those who had lived through the period might not agree that the people were a constant embodiment of mirth, but Robert Crichton's best-selling novel *The Secret of Santa Vittoria* attracted Stanley Kramer's attention with its skillful blend of suspense and humor. It was written in the tradition of John Hersey's *A Bell for Adano* and the "Don Camillo" stories. William Rose and Ben Maddow retained that spirit in their faithful screenplay from Crichton's novel.

The story concerns Italo Bombolini (Anthony Quinn), his wife, Rosa (Anna Magnani) and the people of Santa Vittoria. Bombolini is a clownish semisouse who suddenly finds himself mayor of the small town that's known far and wide for its excellent and abundant wine. As the German forces are retreating to the north at the end of the war, Bombolini has the task of seeing to it that more than one million bottles of wine are kept safe. The Germans arrive, led by Captain Von Prumm (Hardy Kruger), but because the villagers have quickly hidden all but 300,000 bottles of wine in ancient underground caves (they realized they'd better have some on hand to turn over), and because they would rather give up their lives than the rest of the wine, the Germans finally leave without discovering the secret of Santa Vittoria. The film ends when the Germans depart, and the whole village breaks out in a merry dance. Italo and Rosa seem to have patched up a stormy marriage, too, and thus life, love and wine are safe in this sleepy old town.

"The Secret of Santa Vittoria was for me a sort of vacation film which I did in a little town on a hilltop in Italy," Kramer said. "When I brought the film back and showed it to the United Artists hierarchy at the Screen Directors Guild, there were eighteen men there, and at the end of the screening they got up and applauded: they thought they had the biggest box-office sensation in the world. Well, they had nothing. Oh, I thought it was kind of entertaining, but I didn't really think too much of it. I would have liked to have made a dollar and been successful with it. But I really didn't look forward to revolutionizing the form with it. They thought they had a real winner, but they had nothing."

Well, that's a somewhat harsher judgment than even the critical consensus. This was Kramer's only film made in Italy and, just as with The Pride and the Passion, which he'd made in Spain ten years earlier, some of the production details are more interesting than the film. But Kramer ignores the picture's virtues because he's disappointed in its failures. It does, after all, have Anna Magnani—although we see far too little of her—and she gives grit to an otherwise affable, lazy comedy, and trenchancy to the stereotypical moments in the awkward screenplay. There's also stunning cinematography by Giuseppe Rotunno, who shot the film as if it could be a new national treasure, it's that much of a celebration of Italian rural beauty.

"It's an endearing folk legend," proclaimed the bulletin for the 1969 San Francisco Film Festival, "spiced with truth and the delicious aftertaste of forbidden brew." The metaphor seems forced: it's wine that's at stake, after all, not holiday rum punch. But the film does indeed combine folk legend and history. Crichton's novel is based on fact. There *is* a Santa Vittoria: far north of Rome, in a place that has uncertain weather, is the headquarters of Cinzano International, makers of wine and vermouth. During the Germans' retreat at the end of the war, that town was faced with exactly this dilemma. But Kramer was looking for the sleepy, medieval town Crichton had described in his novel, and the real Santa Vittoria had become quite modernized—warehouses, a small electric power plant, packing sheds and an abundance of television antennae. The author had described colorful old stone buildings, a charming piazza, an ancient fountain, crooked cobblestone streets running to the edges of the mountains, and a panorama of hills, terraces and

Anticoli Corrado, the key location in Italy for *The Secret of Santa Vittoria*.

vines. Production designer Robert Clatworthy and manager Ivan Volkman joined Giuseppe Rotunno on a search throughout central Italy for this sort of town. They kept their journey below the weather line of the north, where capricious summer rains could ruin their shooting schedule, and finally scoured 168 towns looking for the piazza, the fountain, the old houses. On the 169th try they found it—Anticoli Corrado—and after Kramer arrived from California to confirm the aptness of the setting, hasty meetings were called with the town council for the virtual takeover of the place during four summer months in 1968. It was agreed that the inhabitants would remain in their homes, and some of them would even be hired to work in the film. A small number agreed to take paid vacations elsewhere, at Kramer's expense, so their homes could be used for key company personnel.

Lying about forty miles southeast of Rome, Anticoli Corrado has long been known to Romans as a culturally stimulating place in which they can escape the city's summer heat. The town is also a haven for European artists, who find it an inspirational place for their work: Kokoschka, Bonnet, Rodin and Corot worked there, as do several major European and American artists today. The place is remarkable not only for its natural beauty and almost palpable sense of medieval history (it's a thirteenth-century Norman village), but also because the natives are reputed to be among the most beautiful people in Italy and are usually ready to serve as models.

"Architecturally," Kramer said, "the contours and dimensions of the square and the adjoining streets, made me settle on this town. The art department added a bell tower, one single façade and a water tower for one particularly funny (and, it turned out, dangerous) scene."

In an interview with Hank Werba published in *Variety* when shooting began, Kramer spoke of working in Italy. "One thing I learned is that we cannot expect Italy to adapt to Hollywood ways. The only logical approach is to learn all you can about filmmaking Italian style, and then adapt to it. Some of our attitudes are pretty different from theirs, but we are guests here, at full liberty to take over an entire Italian town for many weeks.

It would be hopeless to impose our methods, pace and tensions on them." A major difference between American and European filmmaking is the method of sound recording: here, sound is recorded simultaneously with the action; almost everywhere else in the world, however, sound is added later. "I will not yield on the question of direct sound," Kramer said at the time. "Except for Anthony Quinn and Hardy Kruger, all cast principles are Italian. They have been going to school with our dialogue coaches for months to learn to speak their lines in English."

When he arrived in the town, Kramer outlined the project for his crew: "Every inhabitant of the town will be engaged in one way or another in this film, and it will take full cooperation to

The water tower sequence.

get it done. For almost two months, the inhabitants of Anticoli Corrado will have to be on tap as extras when we want them and kept awake during our six calls for night shooting; they will be stumbling over our cable lines, find familiar streets and alleys blocked, listen to our noisy generators and suffer many inconveniences. If a single member of the community objects to our night work, he can by law have our whole operation shut down after 11 P.M.

"But this is only one example of the human- and community-relations aspects of this project. Money and good will often go together in our industry. But money alone will not get the kind of community adherence we must have for filming. We have to establish their confidence in us as serious filmmakers who will turn out a film about a tiny moment of recent history—and one they will themselves accept when the picture is released."

Although some filming was also done in Capranica and the natural Roman caves near Tivoli, the bulk of the shooting during eighty-nine days was done in this town, whose normal population is something around fifteen hundred. It was augmented, for this period, by five hundred additional outsiders, plus the summer-vacation crowd from Rome. The citizens benefiting most from the Hollywood invasion were those employed on camera as extras, background people or participants in the scene where wine is passed down the hill to be concealed in Roman caves. Of the money paid to five hundred villagers for their parts in the film, it was decided by all of them, in common council, to withhold a significant part of their wages for the restoration of the Renaissance frescoes adorning the Romanesque church of San Pietro, which is a national monument. The church was built in the eleventh century, and the frescoes (of Sts. Ambrose, Augustine, Gregory and Jerome) are probably the work of Antoniazzo of Rome and his group of artisans, and date from the end of the fifteenth century.

The extra inhabitants naturally put a strain on the town's resources. No guarantees could be made for the utilities: electric lines there are strained even under normal conditions, and candles always enjoy a brisk sale at the local store. The gas is bottled butane, and water pressure suffers when a matron faints

on a hot day and needs more than a single glass of water!
Accordingly, engineers employed by the Kramer company arranged for rewiring the entire town—offices, houses, wardrobe
headquarters and commissary included—and small water pumps
were installed in the homes of cast and company department
heads. It was hoped this would provide electric power, but
candles were always on hand, just in case, and they were often
needed. Faced by a meager supply of telephones and operating
on the limited lines of the Italian countryside, Kramer's aides
made arrangements for couriers to dash back and forth to Rome,
to keep the company in touch with the rest of the world.

One day the couriers brought the tragic news of the assassina-

Anna Magnani and Anthony Quinn.

tion of Robert Kennedy. Very soon, Kramer received a message: "The Italian union has asked that the workers should interrupt their job today for five minutes to honor the memory of Robert Kennedy. The particular conditions of our work at this moment do not give us the possibility to honor him in a more fitting way. However, we have decided in full agreement that the best way to honor the memory of a man of action is by action. Therefore, the Italian crew will dedicate one extra hour of work, tomorrow, Saturday, June 8th, to the memory of Robert Kennedy. We should like you, Mr. Kramer, and the American members of the crew, to accept our deepest sympathy."

Kramer replied to this touching letter in an announcement read the next morning: "The decision of the Italian crew of *The Secret of Santa Vittoria* to dedicate one extra hour of work to the memory of Robert Kennedy has no parallel in motion-picture history. The American group in Anticoli Corrado is deeply honored to know you and privileged to be your coworkers."

So much for *dolce far niente.*

Ten days later, an important scene was scheduled—the relaying by hand of tens of thousands of wine bottles from the town's cellars to the hidden caves just outside the walls. The problem was more than a fictional one for Kramer and his staff, and at this point the Cinzano Company came to the rescue. They supplied teams of technical experts, bottles and even vine-growing specialists for the film's needs. The bottles were quickly supplied, labels from the 1940s were found and reprinted, studio personnel were trained in bottle stacking, and hillsides soon blossomed—literally overnight!—with thousands of grapevines of the quick-growing variety, to be ready in time for the shooting of the scene on June 17, 1968.

The scene is handled brilliantly, as the camera follows a line from the center of town all the way out to the caves, and, in extraordinary crane and helicopter shots we see men and women passing bottles from hand to hand. At the right moment, there are cuts to close-ups of the natives: lined, weathered faces, old and shining with pride and joy, the faces of men confused by all this artificial activity, the faces of women with their toothy grins and natural, rustic moustaches, the faces of giggling children and the faces of lovers jostling for position on line so they can stay together. It's a beautiful sequence, and more amusing and convincing than any travelogue designed to show native solidarity in a common task.

Alternating with the faces of the locals are those of the principals, and never have they, too, looked more natural. Anthony Quinn sometimes plays the role of Bombolini too much like Zorba the Italian, but his speech rightly resembles a cross between a bark and a belch, and he conveys the strutting, the flashes of cunning and the egregious stupidity for which he has been justly famous since his performance as Zampano in Fellini's *La Strada*. In one very fine scene, he feigns hysteria when told by the Germans that they want all the wine of the village—a fact he and his *paesanos* have already provided for—and he sobs, rolls on the floor, begs the German captain not to do this. Quinn straddles the delicate line between comic bravado and, in his scenes with Anna Magnani, a sort of adolescent cowering before this image of Mother Earth.

"He and Magnani didn't get along at all," Kramer recalled. "It's a wonder their scenes ever got finished. She didn't like him one bit, and in their big fight scene, when she was supposed to literally kick him out of the house, she did it so hard during the shooting that she broke her foot!" Magnani, of course, is no one so much as she's herself in this film: the beauty of the fiery Italian is tempered with a depth of passion and a unique kind of Continental world-weariness. ("Oh, God," cried one noted woman critic when she saw the film, "why can't bags under the eyes do for us what they do for her?") Magnani first met Kramer at the Cinecittà Studios at Rome, when he offered her the part. "She was a perfect lady. She greeted me in a formal gown, used a cigarette holder and spoke perfect English. She told me all about the studio there, where we would be doing some important interior sequences, and she described the business and artistic aspects of moviemaking in Rome with a great deal of insight and intelligence and class. I thought wow, what a lady she is! And then she gave me a warning: 'Don't eat at the commissary here—the food is shit.' It was then I knew she had another side to her. She could be difficult, too: she refused to

The grand finale.

have her right side photographed, because she thought it unattractive!"

There was one particularly amusing and momentarily dangerous moment during the shooting of the water-tower sequence. Quinn was to climb the tower to erase a slogan he himself had painted ("Mussolini is always right!") in order to pacify the Fascist government. After treating his buddies to a day of wine bibbing, he volunteers to whitewash the sign, now that Il Duce is dead and the Fascists are out of power. But by this time he's quite drunk, and he has to be hauled down by Fabbio (Giancarlo Giannini), his daughter's boyfriend. The crowd below breaks into wild cheers and the Fascist politicians, hiding in the city hall, completely misunderstand: they think Bombolini has become a national hero, so they hand over the office of mayor to him! More cheers, more celebration . . . and more wine.

While shooting the water tower-sequence, Quinn was several hundred feet in the air on a platform. With Giannini he had to pretend to resist being helped down. The most dangerous part of the scene had to be shot on the ground, but several key gestures were actually done on the tower in order to provide the comic suspense for long shots. And at one nerve-racking moment, both actors nearly became casualties.

Perhaps the flaw of *The Secret of Santa Vittoria* is a shifting and inconsistent tone, and a patchy script. The first several reels are an unexceptional rustic comedy, with some flashes of brilliant acting that keep it going. Then (and only in reel eight!) the Germans enter; and even though Hardy Kruger is benevolent, handsome and not especially interested in living up to the German army's reputation for exploitation, the tone changes. There's a nasty scene in which Quinn is pistol-whipped for not cooperating with the Germans, and there are several scenes in which the town fathers are heard shrieking from more cruel torture. These moments are rudely intercut with the rich comic bumbling of Magnani and Quinn, and with gratuitous subplots of unconvincing love relationships (Virna Lisi as a bored countess bedding down with Sergio Franchi or with Kruger, and Patrizia Valturri as Bombolini's daughter, passionate for young Giannini). These shifts in tone give the impression of a kind of emotional elevator: we're moved from comedy to romance to melodrama to suspense somewhat too arbitrarily, and several sequences do not arise organically from the central situation of the concealment of the wine.

But this lapse in continuity certainly does not make the film a "nothing," as Kramer put it. *The Secret of Santa Vittoria* is a pleasant enough diversion, and a beautifully photographed comedy of bad manners.

CHAPTER 31

Kramer on Campus, Disastrously—
RPM, 1970

During the late 1960s, just after the rush of enthusiasm and hope that accompanied the blooming of flower children across the country, many universities endured upheavals unprecedented in history. Driven by anger over the war in Vietnam, and over vaguer matters of political and intellectual irrelevance, students staged protests, called strikes against classes and engaged in acts of violence which, sadly and ironically, reproduced the situations they deplored.

Eager to cash in on the youth market's support for films about such a social phenomenon, a number of filmmakers produced pictures about student protest. These films seem like amusing antiques today: their instant topicality has made them instant period pieces, and it's hard not to regard them like ancient advertising for Wendell Willkie for President, or Ban the Bomb buttons. Films like *Flick, The Strawberry Statement, Getting Straight* and *The Revolutionary* came and went, never to return—for which all may be thankful. At the very end of this series, as a sort of unintentional epitaph to a sorry lineage, came Stanley Kramer's *RPM* (subtitled, in case anyone should have lived on Saturn during the last quarter century, *Revolutions Per Minute)*, and although it was a very personal work for him, it is perhaps the nadir of Kramer's directorial career.

RPM unimaginatively unwinds the story of Paco Perez (Anthony Quinn), a fifty-three year-old university professor of sociology, well liked by his students and highly respected in his field, who is chosen to guide the academic community through a period of student violence. Having made his way up through Spanish Harlem and through a doctorate degree in sociology to what appears to be a California state college, he's caught between opposing forces—student demands and the intransigence of the old-guard board of trustees. Because the students

Anthony Quinn as Paco Perez, university president.

clamor for confrontation, because their demands cannot be met, and because they start to destroy the campus computer (after taking over the administration building), the inevitable clash with police occurs. Perez has by this time also had a crisis with his twenty-five-year-old mistress, Rhoda (Ann-Margret), who is herself studying for a graduate degree in sociology when she's not inviting her professor/lover to dinner or bed. He, like the whole campus, is the loser at the end.

But the real loser is the audience who has sat through the film, and Kramer is the first to admit this.

"It's about the most unsuccessful film I ever made—unsuccessful by any standards. You make a film in relation to the times in which you live. By the time you make it and get it edited, is it out of date? Well, this one sure was! The times and events have a way of moving so fast these days, they zip past the back of your head before you can turn around. That usually doesn't trap me, but in *RPM* I sought more than anywhere else to reflect the times in which I lived, and I got caught very badly. The reason I was trapped was because I was looking for myself. I was looking for something to believe in, too, just like the professor *and* the students, and I wasn't sure. I feel confident enough of myself to say that I was and am unsure. I just don't know. . . .

"I don't know about the issues. I was trying to say *I* couldn't burn the library or the computer—and that's why I sympathize with Perez, who couldn't countenance the students doing that. But *RPM* didn't come off and it didn't ring true, and it didn't because it was attempting to join into the confusion of the times, rather than to take a step ahead and speculate on the reason for that confusion. That would have been more interesting."

Erich Segal's screenplay might have been expected to catch the tang of campus speech patterns and issues more acutely, since he was at the time a professor of classics at Yale, and a recent social *arrivé* by virtue of his fame from having written *Love Story*. But any expectations of accuracy or depth were too great: the film is merely a chain of clichés, insufficient character development and misreading of the very movement it so disinterestedly documents. "Oh, that's my book on sociology that just came out in paperback," says Quinn—it's the sort of talk you'd expect from a student trying to write expository dialogue. And not doing very well at it. The language of the students as they press for their demands had become stereotyped even in 1970: "Hey, man, we thought your head was on straight. But you don't know where it's at." This kind of talk seeps through the film like a bad smell, the kind of patter that Cyra McFadden calls "semantic spinach," or that Richard Rosen terms "psychobabble."

In this regard, the students ask to have "a say" in hiring and firing faculty members, in granting degrees and determining curriculum. The vagueness is never seized for discussion by teachers or board, which says something about *their* intelligence (or their hearing). And, worst of all, we're never told exactly

Ann-Margret and Anthony Quinn.

what the students at *this* university are rebelling against, nor just what makes their university so intolerable for them. We never see the academic conditions at the school which gave rise to this particular crisis, so it's hard to judge the validity of the protests or the demands.

The clichés extend to the visuals, too. Everyone chews gum for the final confrontation between the students and the police who've come to oust them when they've started to dismantle the campus computer (presumably in protest against impersonal technology, although it's never clear). The cops chew gum as a sign of bourgeois machismo; and the students blow bubble gum, as if the chewing and snapping and being studiously childish would taunt adult tempers to explode.

Apparently the story was structured and edited with a fine-tooth sledgehammer. It opens and closes to the strains of *Gaudeamus Igitur* (in English, yet), and the Quinn character is at once introduced, so broadly drawn that he's emotionally smaller than a cartoon. It's hard enough to imagine him as lover to Ann-Margret (who, as Vincent Canby so nicely put it, has the only lines in the film that sound as if they hadn't been written after someone had taken a public opinion poll), but when the two of them start racing around campus on a motorcycle, the stomach turns. Ann-Margret in perforated peek-a-boo nightshirt is one thing. But Quinn in toupée, dark glasses, jeans and sandals (and, once, in only jockey shorts) is almost a self-contained parody of the tenacity of his image: he was Zorba the Italian in *The Secret of Santa Vittoria*, here he's Zorba the Teacher. He'd be more convincing as the Archbishop of Canterbury.

What is quite significant about the film, however, is the clear identification Kramer has made with the character of Paco Perez. "I was looking for something to believe in, too," Kramer has admitted, and it's easy to pick out those lines of dialogue where you can hear Kramer's collaborative touch. "I've written four books on sociology and the social order and I'd like to see one of them work," says Perez/Quinn, and, later, "I've been fighting the establishment for thirty years and I still don't know what it means." One of his students (Gary Lockwood) has a suggestion: "Maybe it's you!"

This exchange is a precise repetition of something Stanley

Preparing for the stadium sequence.

Kramer repeats in interviews: "In my films about values, I've been trying to determine my own sense of values, and I'm still confused. . . . I've aspired to so much in my films; the canvas is so big that there has to be something wrong with each of them. The dream was fantastic, but the realization is less than the dream. Once I told a group of students at Stanford, 'I've been fighting the establishment for thirty years, and I still don't know what it is,' and a kid in the back of the room called out, 'Maybe it's you!' He was absolutely right!"

RPM is a good example of Stanley Kramer so close to the material and to one of the characters that he can't function successfully on the level of craftsman or filmmaker. His passion gets in the way of his patience, his confusion results in a confounded work. He makes no justification for this picture, and neither should I. What is keenly interesting, however, is the way in which the cartoon-like film reveals the man's deeper concerns. The picture is like a telephone doodle—negligible in just about every way except what it reveals about the psychological and emotional state of the doodler.

Bill Mumy and Stanley Kramer.

CHAPTER 32

A Response to *Lord of the Flies*— *Bless the Beasts and Children,* 1971

Spencer Tracy and Katharine Hepburn, Marlene Dietrich, Gregory Peck, Cary Grant, Frank Sinatra, Anna Magnani, Montgomery Clift, Judy Garland—Kramer's films boasted the biggest movie stars of our time. Everyone was surprised, therefore, when his film *Bless the Beasts and Children* appeared without a single billable or bankable name. A handful of unknown teenagers and adults in a small, television-style movie wasn't expected from him, especially at the beginning of the uncertain 1970s. He certainly seemed up to something strange. But the adjectives trotted out by big-city critics when the film opened ran along the lines of "superficial . . . pompous . . . unbearable . . . uninspired." Hardly a lukewarm reception. But seen almost a decade later, *Bless the Beasts and Children* seems not quite as bad— in fact it's a rather engaging little piece, ill-received because ill-timed: at the height of the Vietnam war, few people were much interested in a movie about middle-class boys at camp who get excited over an endangered species. After all, there were people burning in the streets of Asian cities, and men dying in foreign jungles.

Kramer's film is a modest, funny and finally sad little piece, full of passion for life and compassion for children with mature hopes and for the adults more childish than their kids. Mac Benoff's screenplay, based on a novel by Glendon Swarthout, concerns a group of boys at summer camp who, after being taken to a ranch and shown the shooting of buffalo for sport, are so horrified that they set out—on horseback, on foot and by stolen truck—to free the captive animals before the next massacre. When they finally accomplish their purpose, the animals rush out of the compound, but only to graze nearby, not knowing where else to head. As a particularly emotional youngster commandeers a truck to disperse the herd, a corps of sportsmen, rifles drawn, shoot the boy dead.

"When I finished the film, I found out that it really was a film about gun control in America, which I never intended it to be. But it was picked up by the National Rifle Association as an antihandgun film, and then I joined in discussions because they provoked me so much I had to get into the arena. I found myself on the David Frost show one night with a fellow from a sports magazine, and I just let go at him. In one fell swoop, I seemed to destroy my own film by making it into an antigun picture. In fact it goes far beyond that." (Kramer didn't win any points that night by revealing that the film, made at Arizona's Hidden Valley Ranch, used actual shots of the killing of buffalo for sport—footage supplied by an association there.)

But as the title of the film suggests, there's an immediate identification between the animals and the leading children. In a series of flashbacks, early on, we learn that each of the half-dozen boys comes from a problem-ridden family: one is ignored by his parents; another is suffocated with counterfeit affection; a third is overwhelmed by his father, a television stand-up comedian who sees all of life as a show ("You could have ad libbed it," he says when his son forgets the assigned words of the Bar Mitzvah service. "Six months of rehearsals gone for nothing!"). But the picture is as pointed, as timely as any antiwar film then or now: it's concerned (simply and sometimes simplistically) with the sanctity of all living beings—not just humans—in a disintegrating environment. "What concerns me in the 1970s," Kramer said, "is the disintegration of values in society." And in this gentle movie he addressed himself to that disintegration.

The film has a bold precredit sequence: children are rounded up, fenced in and, as adults take careful aim, are rifled down—but the scenes are intercut with quick shots of falling beasts. Then the

Barry Robins as Cotton.

scene is revealed as a nightmare suffered by one of the boys at Box Canyon Boys' Camp. The six who later assign themselves the task of freeing the buffalo represent a cross section of American youth and backgrounds; each has a different look and personality, each wears a different style of hat: soldier cap, painter's cap, cowboy hat, Indian headband, tennis cap, plain beanie.

As the adventure progresses, cruelty toward children is equated with the grand tradition of adult supremacy in machismo. Sport is the link that the picture uses to make this equation between the cruel and thoughtless treatment of children with the slaying of an endangered species, and sport is seen not as a way to health and the experience of camaraderie, but as part of a cult of violence. "Send us a boy, we'll send you a cowboy" is the camp's motto, and the counselors are above all concerned for the development of typical (even stereotypical) aspects of American manhood: the prizes at camp are animals' severed heads, stuffed and mounted: the campmaster recites what might (with great license) be called a poem, about "State of Mind," which is really about winning, whatever the competition. And in addition to the development of machismo and a deadly serious sense of competition (which none of the sensitive youngsters shows much interest in cultivating), there is also the poisonous effect of American momism and popism. Although the abundant flashbacks suggest rather facile roots for each boy's psychological disturbance and confusion, they serve further to connect the human, ancestral, ecological and genetic aspects of the story. The kids are disoriented, ill-prepared, helpless and hopeless when they're with their parents—and are at ease, free and relaxed when they're in the open country, heading toward their mission of mercy.

(In the opening nightmare, the militaristic sergeant and coleader of the group, Barry Robins, sees himself shot. Since he then becomes the target of the adults' gunfire at the end, there may be a reference to the student killings at Kent State University a couple of years before—a comparison which gave the film added timeliness.)

Right from the start, the children's crusade to freedom (of themselves as well as of the animals) is a sort of group picaresque tragicomedy, and one which, oddly, occurs largely at night. This gives the whole picture the quality of a filmed dream as the band of six treks toward adulthood in a world notable for its lack of adult moral maturity. The boys have within themselves the potential for real growth, based partly on their premature suffering. On their T-shirts are pictures of the American Indian; they will be treated with the same sort of contempt, and one of them is even exterminated like an Indian: the cowboys, it seems, regard a buffalo and a boy as fair game to be picked off. (The final sequence, moving as it is, may stretch credibility somewhat, but so does the belief in the possibility of such mob violence as erupted during the late 1960s on the American campuses, and which was met with such deadly force by some police and government troops.)

Bless the Beasts and Children is really, in the final analysis, a

The adults take aim . . .

counterstatement to *Lord of the Flies*, a work whose vision it seems (at times almost consciously) to invert and correct. The same theme is really at the heart of each—the examination of the basic nature of man. William Golding's novel (and Peter Brook's film of it) represents what has been called in literature "the excremental vision"—i.e., human experience and nature thus become a negative reality, and man is literally dung, the "lord of the flies." Here, as in Golding's work, the children are isolated in a primeval forest where they have the opportunity to trade on their knowledge of one another and of the adult world. They also develop jealousies and some even absorb power plays into a

. . . and the buffalo scatter.

more or less mature sense of ethics and conscience, and learn of their mutual interdependence. The leader of the group (Bill Mumy) is a lanky, laconic, long-haired boy whose eyes are filled with craftiness and even, on occasion, with precocious wisdom. He's the opposite of the dark, volatile Cotton (Barry Robins), whose death is at once the necessary sacrifice to an odious adult supremacy and the tragic inevitability in a world quickly growing stale on its insistent indifference that masks a searing hatred.

In addition, there are several boys in *Bless the Beasts and Children* who seem like American versions of those in *Lord of the*

Kramer, at play with some of his cast . . .

Flies: there's an American "Piggy" (Miles Chapin) and a younger, blond, quiet-eyed youth with a vaguely mystical look (called, appropriately, "Simon" in Lord of the Flies; here, he's called, with equal aptness, "Goodenow," and is played by Darel Glaser). At the conclusion of the Golding book and its film version the children, having reverted to total savagery on the island, are rescued by the arrival of sailors—but they come from a battle-ship, which suggests no real alternative. But in Bless the Beasts and Children, it is the adults who actually deliver the final deadly gun blast at those who are still innocent, and the cold, staring looks of the survivors is finally a strong indictment.

The picture is sometimes naïve, sometimes technically crude, and the dialogue frequently lacks the spontaneity that children's talk should have. But the youngsters in this picture are so thoroughly winning that they could have come from a Truffaut film—in fact, there are few American directors who have had success with teenagers as has Stanley Kramer here. He recalls that the production of the film was one of the most enjoyable experiences of his career. His enthusiasm for the project remains undimmed by the film's undeserved and premature death at the box office, and to watch the film with Stanley Kramer is to see the delight and satisfaction of a craftsman in his own work, regardless of its reception. It has a questioning spirit and a fundamentally compassionate and kind view of human possibility that are part of Kramer's own character, and those who know him know how much of him is in Bless the Beasts and Children.

CHAPTER 33

Scuba Diving Suits and Ice Cubes in Their Mouths—
Oklahoma Crude, 1973

"We wanted it authentic. The film's title was *Oklahoma Crude*, a story of the wildcatters in the oil industry in Oklahoma, 1913. It was a rough place at a rough time, and if it was rough for men, it was even rougher for women. In recreating that gritty, inhospitable time and place, *Oklahoma Crude* put our representatives of what we used to condescendingly describe in prewomen's lib days as the 'weaker sex' through an endurance test of sorts. But the women of our cast and crew made it almost seem like a woman's picture—in more ways than one!"

If his last several films had startled audiences by their widely variant tones and topics, *Oklahoma Crude* virtually shocked people who thought Stanley Kramer was locked into a small range of genres. In it he not only took advantage of the new freedom in American film to describe graphically physical and emotional torment with realistically crude speech patterns and a generous lacing of scatological humor. He also saw the striking contrast of a dark and complex psychological study of personalities in a simple and beautiful landscape.

Marc Norman's screenplay is fresh, alive and very much of

our own time. It's about headstrong, asexual Lena (Faye Dunaway). She's spent most of her adult years trying to keep her
wildcat oilwells from the big business interests who, by fair
means or foul, want to take them away from her. Aided by her
weak but well-meaning father, Cleon (John Mills), and an
opportunistic but finally loyal bum turned hired hand named
Mase (George C. Scott), she endures threats and violence from
the Pan-Oklahoma Oil Company, headed by the villainous and
aptly named Hellman (Jack Palance). Her father is killed defend-
ing the property, but finally Lena and Mase let their humanity
overcome their posturing: they temper business with pleasure,
and at the last moment it looks like their relationship will be as
personal as it's been professional.

George C. Scott and Faye Dunaway.

Although the film is rigorously faithful to place and period, *Oklahoma Crude* really seems to be about the unfreezing of a woman's soul, not primarily about oilmen and women. And although this idea could be as condescending and chauvinistic in 1973 as it was in some of the worst melodramas of the 1940s and 1950s, it is supported and given grit and substance by the character of Lena, who is brightly played by Dunaway. Since Arthur Penn's *Bonnie and Clyde*, Dunaway has been associated with a kind of quiet, angular glamour, with a glistening intelligence and a carefully controlled sensuality combined. Here, as the London *Observer* remarked, she manages to wear grubby long johns and make them looks as sexy as a baby-doll nightie.

The character of Lena is rich and complex: she deeply resents her father for his weakness and just as deeply needs him. The opening scene shows her chasing him from the property with a rifle, but when she's delirious from a vicious beating by her enemies, she cries for him, and at his death she breaks down in anguish and loss. Lena is a woman whose strengths don't often play her false: you have the impression of so much manufactured courage that the accidental solitude of her life as a wildcatter has spiritually hardened her, made her impenetrable to any kind of warmth. But any character that obdurate is a cliché with a foregone conclusion, so the script suggests from the start that behind her thin female Buddha exterior is a Vesuvius of unacknowledged, unspent passion. "Most women would like to be men, but haven't got the guts," she says in one of the film's many enigmatic lines. "If I had the choice I'd like to be a third sex, in between the two." Unfortunately, the psychomystical implications soon get washed away in more explicit, funny-serious talk about their respective sex organs, but Dunaway and Scott spar so well together that they surmount the material. This is one of the moments in the film when modern frankness goes against the period atmosphere and the somewhat more subtle psychology: men and women of crude times in crude places may have had crude mouths, but it's hard to imagine that they offered Freudian psychojargon.

If Dunaway is comparable to Barbara Stanwyck in *Forty Guns,* or to Marlene Dietrich in *Rancho Notorious,* or to Joan Crawford in the more consciously psychological *Johnny Guitar*, she's more modern and therefore perhaps less easy for some to accept in this period piece. But her beauty, her almost glassy cheeks and intelligent, high forehead suggest a woman with more aspects to her personality than a kaleidoscope's patterns. *Oklahoma Crude* may lack some of the entertaining polish of a picture like *Boom Town*, which had Claudette Colbert, Spencer Tracy and Clark Gable in interestingly analogous roles. But it has all the energy and a lot more wonderful photography, which seems to be nature's corrective, here, to their seamy life. *Newsweek* saw a similarity to the classic Western *Shane*, and this may not be farfetched: Scott, an enigmatic drifter, is hired by Cleon to be a

John Mills and Faye Dunaway.

kind of down-at-the-heels Shane, in order to rid them all of the fear of Palance (who in fact played the villain in *Shane!*). Here, he's grimmer and slicker and viler than ever. *Shane* has more provocative mystery, but *Oklahoma Crude* is more adventurous.

Scott, of course, is just the right foil for this too-confident woman. In his early scenes, as a railroad bum, he gives the impression of a man whose options are as dry as the local wells: all he knows is the value of a dollar, and he seems as excited about a tough job as he would be about a ticket to the opera. When approached with an offer, he has to be cajoled, like a schoolboy urged to a chore. But when he's at the wells, in the bunkhouse, sidling up to the slithery menace of Palance, you get the idea that here's a complicated character, full of self-contradiction. The neat twist in these character studies is that Scott's moral torpor and Dunaway's emotional stasis are complementary—and soon they realize, in a memorable eating scene, that they're doomed apart, even if they haven't all that much together.

"I never thought I would have the opportunity to work again with as great an actor as Spencer Tracy," said Kramer. "But then I met George C. Scott, who is certainly one of the two or three great actors of our time. He has the same skills and genius Spence had: an ability to say more with an expression than with a page-long speech. They're the kind of actors who react better than most actors act. Whether in cowboy hat, leather cap or derby, dressed cleanly or in his long johns, George, with his droopy nose, slightly excessive girth and ambling gait is the perfect drifter and bum he plays in the film."

The perfect balance is achieved by John Mills. He plays Dunaway's desperate, disillusioned and cowardly papa as a man who discovers he can at last defend his daughter's wells as if they were the crown jewels. His portrayal is of a man who's spent most of his life missing life: everywhere are people and situations that frighten him, everywhere people who know even less about his emotional needs than he. There's a dampness in his eyes, and his moustache looks too much chewed, as if late at night, out of boredom. His rootlessness has given him nervous habits.

If the script isn't always consistent with theme, the visuals of the film certainly are. And because the preparation and production were so demanding (and so painful), Kramer issued details in a press release at the time the film premiered.

There was, first of all, location scouting, in 1972, throughout the South, where Kramer visited Oklahoma, Louisiana, Texas, New Mexico and Arizona. Frustration followed along: "The wooden derricks are gone, replaced by steel and concrete and underground pipe lines. Also, we needed a low flat hill, under which gas or oil pockets could be found, a legitimate rise of ground in the center of open country, upon which would sit a wooden derrick to be built by our carpenters." Finally, production manager Ralph Black remembered a ranch in northern California, thirty miles from Stockton. Inhabited now by a Basque sheep farmer whose father purchased five thousand acres from the railroad before 1900, its terrain closely resembles turn-of-the-century Tulsa, where the story is set. Kramer approved the spot at once.

Although the actual shooting took ten weeks in the fall of 1972, the crew spent almost thirty weeks there. Twenty-five life-size wooden derricks were built on the property, in addition to the principal derrick located on the top of the rise. That one also demanded an enormous special effects construction: underground tanks were built which held 50,000 gallons of a special solution resembling oil (but not dangerous when running into the eyes and ears of the actors), and twenty tanks of compressed air under more than 400,000 pounds of pressure—to set the special solution skyrocketing at the right moment. Roads had to be built, fences torn down and relocated, houses built, and any resemblance to a sheep ranch obliterated. (When principal photography was completed, it took a large crew more than a month to restore the place to its pristine condition.)

No compromises were made on the script's demands, as the requisition sheets show: a 1903 steam train, twenty-five horses, freight wagons, three Model T Fords, a 1906 Cadillac, a 1904 Winton, a 1907 Mack Truck, a 1907 Reo Truck and a 1910 Chevrolet.

Kramer was assured by the good citizens of Stockton that autumn was the ideal time for filming, but when the first takes were done on September 18, 1972, the temperature reached one hundred and ten degrees. The danger of flash fire was so great that the government Forest Service demanded the set be closed to visitors, to reduce the chance of accidental fire. Within two weeks, the daytime temperature had plunged to the fifties, with considerable wind, and the quality of the daylight changed several times within a single setup, making photography and lighting extremely difficult for Robert Surtees. Almost miraculously, he produced stunning color photography. One day during November, thick fog blanketed the entire area, and the company lost two and a half days of shooting time. When the fog lifted, the rain began, so Kramer took his people to Sonora for the train sequence, hoping to find more clement conditions there. Instead, their nighttime shooting was accompanied by a temperature of fifteen degrees. (There was one happy accident during this time, however; the same train that was used for *High Noon* was brought back for use here in the railroad sequence.)

Back near Stockton, seven nights of photography were set for the rain sequences at night. It actually rained at that time, but this was no blessing: rain does not photograph well, and special effects men had to produce an artificial rain, too. When filming was resumed during the day, the weather had gotten so cold that exterior scenes with dialogue required the actors to put ice cubes in their mouths just before speaking a line, so their breaths would not mist in the "warm summer air of Oklahoma." ("The cast really suffered," Kramer recalled, "and they were all splendid about it.") Scott, Dunaway, Mills and Palance wore scuba divers' suits under their costumes, to keep warm and dry.

The action sequences were just as difficult. Sixteen special effects men, under the direction of Alex Weldon, and after counsel with photographic adviser Albert Whitlock set off charges to resemble the explosions of hand grenades, while twenty-six stunt men raced up a hill. This sequence alone took nine days because of dozens of camera setups required, some for a shot that lasted less than a second on the screen.

British, French and Russian cinéastes seemed more enthusiastic about the final result than critics at home, and the Eighth Moscow Film Festival gave it first prize in 1973. Stanley Kramer was cited "for his humanist contribution to the development of the world cinema, and for his new film, which shows how two persons win a moral victory over the despotism of business and force."

This does not at all seem to me an inflated judgment, although it must be admitted that the film promises in its first half more than it later delivers. But the characters, their hauntingly antique setting and the natural splendor of the terrain for their violence and perfidy encourage the mind to wander off in all sorts of reflective directions once the movie is over. No more could be asked of any film maker.

George C. Scott and Stanley Kramer.

CHAPTER 34

Falling with the Pieces—
The Domino Principle, 1976

In recent years, after the disclosure of various assassination plots involving government agencies, Hollywood has sent forth into the land a series of films about what might be called the New Paranoia. Easy chatter about the unknown, unidentified "they" has now become an ominous, deadly topic of conversation. It's no longer *"They* are building a new highway" or *"They* say it's going to be a hard winter," but rather *"They* tried to kill Castro," or *"They* are trying to fool the public." Films like *Executive Action, Three Days of the Condor, Twilight's Last Gleaming* and *The Parallax View* have come and, mercifully, gone. They traded heavily on this new, amorphous fear. Better examples within this subgenre combine a strong plot with an equally strong psychosocial or moral issue behind it (as do all good espionage thrillers). Francis Ford Coppola's film *The Conversation* did that, and critics were comparing that picture to the espionage stories of Graham Greene. The star, Gene Hackman, was in 1973 regarded as a screen actor of considerable quiet depths, a man we should watch.

Well, we watched and waited. Hackman appeared in a series

of interesting films which finally disappointed due to their inadequate scripts. Arthur Penn's *Night Moves* was perhaps the most disappointing until Stanley Kramer's film of Adam Kennedy's novel *The Domino Principle*. Hackman will need a real winner to salvage his screen image after this film: his performance was as monotonous and automated as the script, and he very nearly sank in its quicksand of meaninglessness and improbability.

Kennedy's novel, from which he did the screenplay, sold briskly when it was published in 1975. When Kramer negotiated the screen rights, he said the story dealt with "a man serving a life term in prison, who is secretively released by shadowy but powerful types and is forced into becoming the assassin of an

Gene Hackman and Richard Widmark.

important governmental figure in a national conspiracy." That sounded intriguing, and it seemed reasonable to expect that the film would clarify, particularize and locate within recognizable reality the details of that outline. Alas, it was not to be. The problem with *The Domino Principle* is that it's a suspense movie, a murder mystery, an espionage thriller, a modern funky love story—but it's all of these *without a coherent plot!* For a hundred minutes, Gene Hackman grits his teeth and forces beads of sweat on his brow, as an unwitting pawn in the machinations of a nameless secret intelligence organization. His problem (it's ours, too, but it apparently wasn't Kennedy's or Kramer's) is that he doesn't know what the conspiracy is about, why he is involved, or why anyone should care. All that's clear is that Hackman, sentenced to life at San Quentin on a murder charge, is suddenly freed by Richard Widmark and Edward Albert, who represent some organization (government intelligence agency? political party? Sears Roebuck?). They offer him freedom, a load of cash and a house in Spain (which turns out to be in Costa Rica) if he will put his widely admired marksmanship to use. For what? Against whom? Well, we don't know that, either.

Hackman is reunited with his wife (Candice Bergen, in beehive 1940 wig, frumpy clothes and soft focus photography) and then taken on a helicopter ride, where he's shown the "target," which appears to be some compound in southern California. "I done some lousy things in my time," objects Hackman, "but I ain't going to do this!" What? Assassinate the President of the United States? The governor of California? For Vincent Canby, writing in *The New York Times,* the target suggested "someone who might be the membership officer of a private country club." That's as plausible as any other explanation, if you just watch the film and impose nothing on it.

Hackman's refusal to cooperate leads to an escalation, as it's called, of violence and death, in which people fall over even more swiftly than they hitherto have—thus, I presume, the title's significance, which derives from the theory of collapsing countries under Communist influence in Southeast Asia.

"We are all used to hearing about 'they,'" Kramer said. "'They' push the stock market up or down. 'They' made Joe

Doe President. 'They' arrange for the assassinations of John and Robert Kennedy and Dr. Martin Luther King. 'They.' I didn't explain in the film why these people want a public figure assassinated. That isn't the point. The point is the powerful unknown force which affects our destiny without our knowing it. We suspect the existence of 'they' without having the faintest idea of who or what 'they' is or are."

Those who appreciate such explanation as defense for an unsatisfactory plot might say that precisely because we don't know its details, or who's involved, the "broader issues" are raised. By "broader issues" is presumably meant some comfortable moral truism: People lie and kill; the government teaches men to kill, and they kill; the organization, the bureaucracy, is

Gene Hackman and cell-mate Mickey Rooney.

murderous; the intelligence system is no better than the family of organized crime. These ideas remain unmoving and ineffectual dramatically unless they're incarnated in a hefty plot, and unless there's an inner logic between story and the characterizations and themes that emerge organically from that story.

The mutual inherence of these ingredients is responsible for the success of an earlier film which also had at its center the plotted assassination of an unknown figure, Alfred Hitchcock's remake of *The Man Who Knew Too Much* (1956 version). In that film, too, we know not for whom the assassin is working, nor why, nor who is the target, nor why the plot has been activated, nor what is, internationally, at stake. And yet Hitchcock's film succeeds in every way where Kramer's does not, because the characters are fully realized human beings, and because the psychological dimension of fear is specified in the issue of the kidnapped child. (The son of James Stewart and Doris Day is held as ransom for their silence about the planned assassination.)

In the climactic scene of *The Man Who Knew Too Much*—the concert at Albert Hall—the moral issue is as clear as the suspense. Will Doris Day cry out, thus risking her son's life, to save a politician she doesn't know? Or will she remain silent, witnessing the man's death but perhaps saving her son? This is where the suspense lies, not first in the external order, but in the order of mind and will. Flannery O'Connor, in the preface to the second edition of her novel *Wise Blood* (1962), wrote of the dilemma of the internal order: "Free will does not mean one will, but many wills conflicting in one man. Freedom cannot be conceived simply. It is a mystery, and one which a novel, even a comic novel, can only be asked to deepen." That is exactly the scope of the moral tension in *The Man Who Knew Too Much:* many wills conflict in one person. And Doris Day's scream, which interrupts the harmony and order of the concert, is the inevitable result of the conflict of external and internal forces.

We need not know too much about the politics of the Hitchcock film because the characters are so alive and important to us. The theme of singing in that film finds its significance in the scream at the concert. Doris Day plays a woman forced to give up her career as singer for her husband's life as doctor in

Indiana; thus her scream becomes a song—the cry of anguish, the cry to be saved, to be reborn; a concert becomes a struggle to decide in favor of life; a man's height (that of James Stewart, whose gangly, awkward verticality is everywhere comically emphasized in the film) becomes an image not only of his domi-

Candice Bergen, off-camera.

nance (of his family, by his insistence on more perfect knowledge) but also of his vulnerability. And the journey from Morocco to London becomes the family's journey to discovery of their mutual interdependence.

In *The Domino Principle* there is no suspense in the external order simply because we don't know who anyone is, or why they're doing whatever it is they're doing. They have no individuality against which their fate is enacted. Worse, there is no suspense in the order of mind and will, either. There is a notable absence of any moral or psychological tension in *The Domino Principle*—necessary ingredients for a film in this style—and this reduces it even beneath the level of a compelling character study. Vagueness is justified in a mystery thriller only if a carefully gauged suspense is generated *with a film idea or a universal theme behind it.*

The absence of any of the elements of success is pinpointed in the penny-dreadful script, which is loaded with high-sounding references to Kafka, and with truisms—"If we can't tell each other the truth, we don't have anything," the kind of empty aphorism one expects from weekend seminars on "interpersonal relationships," but not from professional writers.

Elsewhere in the dialogue, however, lurk lines which, in fact, reveal more than the writer was aware.

"None of us knows the whole thing—we just know the pieces," says an unctuous Richard Widmark.

He was speaking for the audience, too.

FILMOGRAPHY

I: *Produced by Stanley Kramer*

SO THIS IS NEW YORK (1948)

Credits:

Direction	Richard Fleischer
Screenplay	Carl Foreman and Herbert Baker

Based on the novel *The Big Town* by Ring Lardner

Music	Dimitri Tiomkin
Editor	Walter Thompson
Cinematography	Jack Russell, ASC
Art direction	Frank Sylos
Wardrobe	Elois Jenssen

An Enterprise Studios Production, released through United Artists

Cast:

Ernie Finch	Henry Morgan
Herbert Daley	Rudy Vallee
Jimmy Ralston	Bill Goodwin
Mr. Trumbull	Hugh Herbert
Ella Finch	Virginia Grey
Kate Goff	Dona Drake
Sid Mercer	Leo Gorcey
Francis Griffin	Jerome Cowan
Willis Gilbey	Dave Willock
Western Union Clerk	Arnold Stang
A. J. Gluskoter	Frank Orth
Hotel Clerk	William Bakewell

CHAMPION (1949)

Credits:

Direction	Mark Robson
Screenplay	Carl Foreman

Based on Ring Lardner's story "Champion"

Music	Dimitri Tiomkin
Editor	Harry Gerstad
Cinematography	Franz Planer, ASC
Production design	Rudolph Sternad
Wardrobe	Joe King and Adele Parmenter

Released through United Artists

Cast:

Midge Kelly	Kirk Douglas
Grace Diamond	Marilyn Maxwell
Connie Kelly	Arthur Kennedy
Tommy Haley	Paul Stewart
Emma Bryce	Ruth Roman
Mrs. Harris ("Palmer")	Lola Albright
Jerome Harris	Luis Van Rooten
Johnny Dunne	John Day
Lew Bryce	Harry Shannon

HOME OF THE BRAVE (1949)

Credits:

Direction   Mark Robson
Screenplay   Carl Foreman

Based on the play by Arthur Laurents

Production design   Rudolph Sternad
Music   Dimitri Tiomkin
Cinematography   Robert De Grasse, ASC
Editor   Harry Gerstad
Wardrobe   Joe King
Poem   Eve Merriam

Released through United Artists

Cast:

Major Robinson   Douglas Dick
T.J.   Steve Brodie
Doctor   Jeff Corey
Finch   Lloyd Bridges
Mingo   Frank Lovejoy
Moss   James Edwards
Colonel   Cliff Clark

THE MEN (1950)

Credits:

Direction	Fred Zinnemann
Story and screenplay	Carl Foreman
Music	Dimitri Tiomkin
Cinematography	Robert De Grasse, ASC
Production design	Rudolph Sternad
Editor	Harry Gerstad
Wardrobe	Joe King and Ann Peck

Released through United Artists

Cast:

Ken	Marlon Brando
Ellen	Teresa Wright
Dr. Brock	Everett Sloane
Norm	Jack Webb
Leo	Richard Erdman
Angel	Arthur Jurado
Nurse Robbins	Virginia Farmer
Ellen's mother	Dorothy Tree
Ellen's father	Howard St. John
Dolores	Nita Hunter
Laverne	Patricia Joiner

CYRANO DE BERGERAC (1950)

Credits:

Direction	Michael Gordon
Screenplay	Carl Foreman

Based on Brian Hooker's translation of Edmond Rostand's play

Music	Dimitri Tiomkin
Editor	Harry Gerstad
Production design	Rudolph Sternad
Cinematography	Franz Planer, ASC
Wardrobe	Joe King, Dorothy Jeakins and Ann Peck
Fencing master	Fred Cavens

Released through United Artists

Cast:

Cyrano	José Ferrer
Roxane	Mala Powers
Christian	William Prince
Le Bret	Morris Carnovsky
De Guiche	Ralph Clanton
Ragueneau	Lloyd Corrigan
Duenna	Virginia Farmer
Orange girl	Elena Verdugo
Sister Marthe	Virginia Christine

DEATH OF A SALESMAN (1951)

Credits:

Direction	Laslo Benedek
Screenplay	Stanley Roberts

Based on the play by Arthur Miller

Production design	Rudolph Sternad
Musical direction	Morris Stoloff
Music	Alex North
Cinematography	Franz Planer, ASC
Editor	William A. Lyon, ACE

Released through Columbia Pictures

Cast:

Willy Loman	Fredric March
Linda Loman	Mildred Dunnock
Biff	Kevin McCarthy
Happy	Cameron Mitchell
Charley	Howard Smith
Ben	Royal Beal
Bernard	Don Keefer
Stanley	Jesse White
Miss Francis	Claire Carleton
Howard Wagner	David Alpert
Miss Forsythe	Elizabeth Fraser
Letta	Patricia Walker

MY SIX CONVICTS (1952)

Credits:

Direction	Hugo Fregonese
Production design	Rudolph Sternad
Cinematography	Guy Roe, ASC
Editor	Gene Havlick, ACE
Screenplay	Michael Blankfort

Based on the book by Donald Powell Wilson

Music	Dimitri Tiomkin
Associate producers	Edna and Edward Anhalt

Released by Columbia Pictures

Cast:

James Connie	Millard Mitchell
Punch Pinero	Gilbert Roland
Doc	John Beal
Blivens Scott	Marshall Thompson
Clem Randall	Alf Kjellin
Dawson	Harry Morgan
Dr. Gordon	Regis Toomey
Steve Kopac	Jay Adler
Warden Potter	Fay Roope
Knotty Johnson	John Marley
Convict	Charles Buchinsky (later Charles Bronson)

THE SNIPER (1952)

Credits:

Direction	Edward Dmytryk
Screenplay	Harry Brown
Story	Edna and Edward Anhalt
Music	George Antheil
Production design	Rudolph Sternad
Cinematography	Burnett Guffey, ASC
Editor	Aaron Stell, ACE

Released by Columbia Pictures

Cast:

Lieutenant Kafka	Adolphe Menjou
Eddie Miller	Arthur Franz
Sergeant Ferris	Gerald Mohr
Jean Darr	Marie Windsor
Inspector Anderson	Frank Faylen
Dr. Kent	Richard Kiley
Landlady	Mabel Paige
Pete	Jay Novello

HIGH NOON (1952)

Credits:

Direction	Fred Zinnemann
Screenplay/associate producer	Carl Foreman
Cinematography	Floyd Crosby, ASC
Editor	Elmo Williams
Music	Dimitri Tiomkin

Released through United Artists

Cast:

Will Kane	Gary Cooper
Jonas Henderson	Thomas Mitchell
Harvey Pell	Lloyd Bridges
Helen Ramirez	Katy Jurado
Amy Kane	Grace Kelly
Percy Mettrick	Otto Kruger
Martin Howe	Lon Chaney
William Fuller	Harry Morgan
Frank Miller	Ian MacDonald
Ben Miller	Sheb Wooley
Mrs. Simpson	Virginia Christine
Mrs. Fletcher	Virginia Farmer

THE HAPPY TIME (1952)

Credits:

Direction   Richard Fleischer
Production design   Rudolph Sternad
Music   Dimitri Tiomkin
Screenplay   Earl Felton

Based on the play by Samuel Taylor and the book by Robert
Fontaine

Produced on the stage by Richard Rodgers and Oscar
Hammerstein II

Cinematography   Charles Lawton, Jr., ASC
Editor   William A. Lyon, ACE

Released through Columbia Pictures

Cast:

Jacques Bonnard   Charles Boyer
Uncle Desmonde   Louis Jourdan
Susan Bonnard   Marsha Hunt
Uncle Louis   Kurt Kasznar
Mignonette Chappuis   Linda Christian
Bibi   Bobby Driscoll
Grandpère Bonnard   Marcel Dalio
Felice   Jeanette Nolan
Peggy O'Hare   Marlene Cameron

THE FOUR POSTER (1952)

Credits:

Direction   Irving Reis
Screenplay   Allan Scott

Based on the play by Jan de Hartog

Cinematography   Hal Mohr, ASC
Editor   Henry Batista, ACE

Interscenes created by U.P.A., directed by John Hubley

Animation artists   Paul Julian, Art Babbitt, Lon
Keller
Gowns   Jean Louis
Production design   Rudolph Sternad

Released by Columbia Pictures

Cast:
Abby   Lilli Palmer
John   Rex Harrison

EIGHT IRON MEN (1952)

Credits:

Direction	Edward Dmytryk
Associate producers	Edna and Edward Anhalt
Screenplay	Harry Brown

From his play, *A Sound of Hunting*

Music	Leith Stevens
Production design	Rudolph Sternad
Cinematography	Roy Hunt
Editor	Aaron Stell, ACE

Released through Columbia Pictures

Cast:

Collucci	Bonar Colleano
Carter	Arthur Franz
Mooney	Lee Marvin
Coke	Richard Kiley
Sapiros	Nick Dennis
Ferguson	James Griffith
Muller	Dick Moore
Small	George Cooper
Captain Trelawny	Barney Phillips
Walsh	Robert Nichols
Lieutenant Crane	Richard Grayson
Hunter	Douglas Henderson
Girl in the dream	Mary Castle
Cafferty	David McMahon

THE MEMBER OF THE WEDDING (1952)

Credits:

Direction   Fred Zinnemann

Screenplay by Edna and Edward Anhalt, based on the book
and play by Carson McCullers

Cinematography	Hal Mohr, ASC
Music	Alex North
Production design	Rudolph Sternad
Editor	William A. Lyon, ACE
Associate producers	Edna and Edward Anhalt

Released through Columbia Pictures

Cast:

Berenice Sadie Brown	Ethel Waters
Frankie Addams	Julie Harris
John Henry	Brandon de Wilde
Jarvis	Arthur Franz
Janice	Nancy Gates
Mr. Addams	William Hansen
Honey Camden Brown	James Edwards
T. T. Williams	Harry Bolden
Soldier	Dick Moore
Barney MacKean	Danny Mummert
Helen	June Hedin
Doris	Ann Carter

THE JUGGLER (1953)

Credits:

Direction	Edward Dmytryk
Screenplay	Michael Blankfort

Based on the novel

Music	George Antheil
Associate producer	Michael Blankfort
Production design	Rudolph Sternad
Cinematography	Roy Hunt
Editor	Aaron Stell, ACE

Released through Columbia Pictures

Cast:

Hans Muller	Kirk Douglas
Ya'El	Milly Vitale
Detective Karni	Paul Stewart
Yehoshua Bresler	Joey Walsh
Daniel	Alf Kjellin
Susy	Beverly Washburn
Rosenberg	Charles Lane
Emile Halevy	John Banner
Kogan	Richard Benedict

THE 5,000 FINGERS OF DR. T. (1953)

Credits:

Direction	Roy Rowland
Screenplay	Dr. Seuss and Allan Scott

Story and conception by Dr. Seuss

Production design	Rudolph Sternad
Cinematography	Franz Planer, ASC
Color by Technicolor; consultant	Francis Cugat
Music	Frederick Hollander
Lyrics	Dr. Seuss
Choreography	Eugene Loring
Gowns	Jean Louis
Editor	Al Clark, ACE

Cast:

Zabladowski	Peter Lind Hayes
Mrs. Collins	Mary Healy
Dr. Terwilliker	Hans Conreid
Bart	Tommy Rettig
Uncle Whitney	John Heasley
Uncle Judson	Robert Heasley
Sergeant Lunk	Noel Cravat
Stroogo	Henry Kulky

THE WILD ONE (1954)

Credits:

Direction	Laslo Benedek
Screenplay	John Paxton

Based on a story by Frank Rooney

Cinematography	Hal Mohr, ASC
Editor	Al Clark, ACE
Music	Leith Stevens

Released through Columbia Pictures

Cast:

Johnny	Marlon Brando
Kathie	Mary Murphy
Harry Bleeker	Robert Keith
Chino	Lee Marvin
Sheriff Singer	Jay C. Flippen
Mildred	Peggy Maley

THE CAINE MUTINY (1954)

Credits:

Direction   Edward Dmytryk
Screenplay   Stanley Roberts

Based on the novel by Herman Wouk

Additional dialogue   Michael Blankfort
Cinematography   Franz Planer, ASC
Production design   Rudolph Sternad
Music   Max Steiner, ACE
Editors   William A. Lyon, ACE, Henry
                        Batista, ACE

Released through Columbia Pictures

Cast:

Captain Queeg	Humphrey Bogart
Lieutenant Barney Greenwald	José Ferrer
Lieutenant Steve Maryk	Van Johnson
Lieutenant Tom Keefer	Fred MacMurray
Ensign Willis Keith	Robert Francis
May Wynn	May Wynn
Captain DeVries	Tom Tully
Lieutenant Commander Challee	E. G. Marshall
Lieutenant Paynter	Arthur Franz
Meatball	Lee Marvin
Captain Blakely	Warner Anderson
Mrs. Keith	Katharine Warren

PRESSURE POINT (1962)

Credits:

Direction	Hubert Cornfield
Screenplay	Hubert Cornfield and S. Lee Pogostin

Based on Robert Lindner's book *The Fifty-Minute Hour*

Cinematography	Ernest Haller
Music	Ernest Gold
Production design	Rudolph Sternad

Released through United Artists

Cast:

Doctor	Sidney Poitier
Patient	Bobby Darin
Young psychiatrist	Peter Falk
Chief medical officer	Carl Benton Reid
Bar hostess	Mary Munday
Mother	Anne Barton
Father	James Anderson

A CHILD IS WAITING (1963)

Credits:

Direction	John Cassavetes
Screenplay	Abby Mann

Based on a story by Abby Mann

Cinematography	Joseph LaShelle
Editor	Gene Fowler, Jr.
Music	Ernest Gold

Released through United Artists

Cast:

Dr. Matthew Clark	Burt Lancaster
Jean Hansen	Judy Garland
Sophie Widdicombe	Gena Rowlands
Ted Widdicombe	Steven Hill
Reuben Widdicombe	Bruce Ritchey
Miss Fogarty	Elizabeth Wilson

and the children from the Pacific State Hospital, Pomona, California

INVITATION TO A GUNFIGHTER (1964)

Credits:

Direction	Richard Wilson
Screenplay	Richard and Elizabeth Wilson
Adaptation	Alvin Sapinsley

Based on a story by Hal Goodman and Larry Klein

Cinematography	Joe McDonald
Music	David Raksin
Editor	Bob Jones

Released through United Artists

Cast:

Jules Gaspard D'Estaing	Yul Brynner
Ruth Adams	Janice Rule
Matt Weaver	George Segal
Sam Brewster	Pat Hingle
Fiddler	Strother Martin
Crane Adams	Clifford David

II: *Produced and Directed by Stanley Kramer*

NOT AS A STRANGER (1955)

Credits:
Screenplay   Edna and Edward Anhalt

Based on the novel by Morton Thompson

Cinematography   Franz Planer, ASC
Music   George Antheil
Production design   Rudolph Sternad
Editor   Fred Knudtson, ACE
Wardrobe   Joe King
Technical advisors   Morton Maxwell, MD
Josh Fields, MD
Marjorie Lefevre, RN

Released through United Artists

Cast:
Kristina Hedvigson   Olivia de Havilland
Lucas Marsh   Robert Mitchum
Alfred Boone   Frank Sinatra
Harriet Lang   Gloria Grahame
Dr. Aarons   Broderick Crawford
Dr. Runkleman   Charles Bickford
Dr. Snider   Myron McCormick
Job Marsh   Lon Chaney
Ben Cosgrove   Jesse White
Oley   Harry Morgan
Brundage   Lee Marvin
Bruni   Virginia Christine
Dr. Dietrich   Whit Bissell

THE PRIDE AND THE PASSION (1957)

Credits:

Story and screenplay   Edna and Edward Anhalt

Based on the novel *The Gun* by C. S. Forester

Music	George Antheil
Cinematography	Franz Planer, ASC
Production design	Rudolph Sternad
Editors	Frederic Knudtson, ACE
	Ellsworth Hoagland, ACE
Wardrobe	Joe King
Choreography	Paco Reyes
Title song sung by	Peggy Lee

Location work in Spain

Released through United Artists

Cast:

Captain Anthony Trumbull	Cary Grant
Miguel	Frank Sinatra
Juana	Sophia Loren
General Jouvet	Theodore Bikel
Bellinger	Jay Novello

THE DEFIANT ONES (1958)

Credits:

Screenplay	Nathan E. Douglas and Harold Jacob Smith
Production design	Rudolph Sternad
Cinematography	Sam Leavitt, ASC
Editor	Frederic Knudtson, ACE
Wardrobe	Joe King
Music	Ernest Gold
Song "Long Gone"	William C. Handy and Chris Smith

Released through United Artists

Cast:

John "Joker" Jackson	Tony Curtis
Noah Cullen	Sidney Poitier
Sheriff Max Muller	Theodore Bikel
Captain Frank Gibbons	Charles McGraw
Big Sam	Lon Chaney
Angus	Carl ("Alfalfa") Switzer
The Woman	Cara Williams

ON THE BEACH (1959)

Credits:

Screenplay	John Paxton and James Lee Barrett

From the novel by Nevil Shute

Cinematography	Giuseppe Rotunno
Production design	Rudolph Sternad
Editor	Frederic Knudtson, ACE
Special effects	Lee Zavitz
Music	Ernest Gold
Song "Waltzing Matilda"	Marie Cowan and A. B. Patterson
Technical adviser	Admiral Charles A. Lockwood
Royal Australian Navy Liaison	Lieutenant Commander A. A. Norris-Smith

Released through United Artists

Cast:

Dwight Towers	Gregory Peck
Moira Davidson	Ava Gardner
Julian Osborn	Fred Astaire
Peter Holmes	Anthony Perkins
Mary Holmes	Donna Anderson
Admiral Bridie	John Tate
Lieutenant Hosgood	Lola Brooks

INHERIT THE WIND (1960)

Credits:
Screenplay   Nathan E. Douglas and Harold
Jacob Smith

Based on the play by Jerome Lawrence and Robert E. Lee

Cinematography   Ernest Laszlo
Music   Ernest Gold
Wardrobe   Joe King
Editor   Frederic Knudtson, ACE

Released through United Artists

Cast:
Henry Drummond   Spencer Tracy
Matthew Harrison Brady   Fredric March
E. K. Hornbeck   Gene Kelly
Mrs. Brady   Florence Eldridge
Bertram T. Cates   Dick York
Rachel Brown   Donna Anderson
Judge   Harry Morgan
Davenport   Elliot Reid
Mayor   Philip Coolidge
Rev. Brown   Claude Akins
Meeker   Paul Hartman
Stebbins   Noah Beery, Jr.

JUDGMENT AT NUREMBERG (1961)

Credits:

Screenplay	Abby Mann
Cinematography	Ernest Laszlo
Associate Producer	Philip Langner
Music	Ernest Gold
Production designer	Rudolph Sternad
Editor	Frederic Knudtson, ACE

Released through United Artists

Cast:

Judge Dan Haywood	Spencer Tracy
Ernst Janning	Burt Lancaster
Colonel Ted Lawson	Richard Widmark
Mme. Bertholt	Marlene Dietrich
Hans Rolfe	Maximilian Schell
Irene Hoffman	Judy Garland
Rudolph Petersen	Montgomery Clift
Captain Byers	William Shatner
Senator Burkette	Edward Binns
Judge Kenneth Norris	Kenneth MacKenna
Emil Hahn	Werner Klemperer
Werner Lamppe	Torben Meyer
Friedrich Hofstetter	Martin Brandt
Mrs. Halbestadt	Virginia Christine

IT'S A MAD MAD MAD MAD WORLD (1963)

Credits:

Screenplay	William and Tania Rose
Cinematography	Ernest Laszlo
Editors	Frederick Knudtson, Robert C. Jones and Gene Fowler, Jr.
Music	Ernest Gold
Stunt supervisor	Carey Loftin

Dance sequence played by The Shirelles, sung by The Four Mads

Filmed at Santa Rosita Beach State Park

Cast:

Captain C. G. Culpepper	Spencer Tracy
J. Russell Finch	Milton Berle
Melville Crump	Sid Caesar
Benjy Benjamin	Buddy Hackett
Mrs. Marcus	Ethel Merman
Ding Bell	Mickey Rooney
Sylvester Marcus	Dick Shawn
Otto Meyer	Phil Silvers
Lieutenant Colonel Hawthorne	Terry-Thomas
Lennie Pike	Jonathan Winters
Monica Crump	Edie Adams
Emmeline Finch	Dorothy Provine
First Cab Driver	Eddie "Rochester" Anderson
Tyler Fitzgerald	Jim Backus
Airplane Pilot	Ben Blue
Colonel Wilberforce	Paul Ford

And: Alan Carney, Barrie Chase, William Demarest, Edward Everett Horton, Buster Keaton, Peter Falk, Leo Gorcey, Don Knotts, Carl Reiner, The Three Stooges (Moe Howard, Larry Fine, Joe DeRita), Joe E. Brown, Andy Devine, Sterling Holloway, Marvin Kaplan, Charles Lane, Charles McGraw, ZaSu

Pitts, Madlyn Rhue, Arnold Stang, Jesse White, Lloyd Corrigan, Stan Freberg, Ben Lessy, Bobo Lewis, Mike Mazurki, Doodles Weaver, Jerry Lewis and Jack Benny.

SHIP OF FOOLS (1965)

Credits:
Screenplay   Abby Mann

Based on the novel by Katherine Anne Porter

Art director   Robert Clatworthy
Cinematography   Ernest Laszlo
Music   Ernest Gold
Editor   Robert C. Jones
Special photographic effects   Albert Whitlock

Released through Columbia Pictures

Cast:
Mary Treadwell   Vivien Leigh
La Condesa   Simone Signoret
Rieber   José Ferrer
Tenny   Lee Marvin
Dr. Schumann   Oskar Werner
Jenny   Elizabeth Ashley
David   George Segal
Pepe   José Greco
Glocken   Michael Dunn
Captain Thiele   Charles Korvin
Lowenthal   Heinz Ruehmann
Frau Hutten   Lilia Skala
Freytag   Alf Kjellin
Lieutenant Huebner   Werner Klemperer

GUESS WHO'S COMING TO DINNER (1967)

Credits:

Story and screenplay	William Rose
Cinematography	Sam Leavitt, ASC
Editor	Robert C. Jones
Music	Frank DeVol
Production design	Robert Clatworthy

Released through Columbia Pictures

Cast:

Matt Drayton	Spencer Tracy
John Prentice	Sidney Poitier
Christina Drayton	Katharine Hepburn
Joey Drayton	Katharine Houghton
Monsignor Ryan	Cecil Kellaway
Mrs. Prentice	Beah Richards
Mr. Prentice	Roy E. Glenn, Sr.
Tillie	Isabell Sanford
Hilary St. George	Virginia Christine

THE SECRET OF SANTA VITTORIA (1969)

Credits:

Associate producer	George Glass
Screenplay	William Rose and Ben Maddow

Based on the novel by Robert Crichton

Cinematography	Giuseppe Rotunno
Production design	Robert Clatworthy
Editor	William A. Lyon, ACE

Location work in Anticoli Corrado, Italy

Released through Columbia Pictures

Cast:

Italo Bombolini	Anthony Quinn
Rosa Bombolini	Anna Magnani
Caterina Malatesta	Virna Lisi
Tufa	Sergio Franchi
Sepp Von Prum	Hardy Kruger
Fabio	Giancarlo Giannini

RPM (1970)

Credits:

Screenplay	Erich Segal
Cinematography	Michel Hugo
Editor	William A. Lyon, ACE
Music	Barry De Vorzon and Perry Botkin, Jr.
Production design	Robert Clatworthy

Released through Columbia Pictures

Cast:

Paco Perez	Anthony Quinn
Rhoda	Ann-Margret
Rissoiter	Gary Lockwood
Dempsey	Paul Winfield
Thatcher	Graham Jarvis
Hewlett	Alan Hewitt
Reverend Blauvelt	John McLiam

BLESS THE BEASTS AND CHILDREN (1971)

Credits:
Screenplay   Mac Benoff

Based on the novel by Glendon Swarthout

Cinematography   Michel Hugo
Music   Barry De Vorzon and Perry
Botkin, Jr.
Title song sung by   The Carpenters
Editor   William A. Lyon, ACE

Location work in Arizona

Released through Columbia Pictures

Cast:
Teft   Bill Mumy
Cotton   Barry Robins
Shecker   Miles Chapin
Goodenow   Darel Glaser
Sid Shecker   Jesse White
Camp Director   Dave Ketchum
Wheaties   Ken Swofford

OKLAHOMA CRUDE (1973)

Credits:

Screenplay	Marc Norman
Cinematography	Robert Surtees, ASC
Production design	Alfred Sweeney
Music	Henry Mancini
"Send a Little Love My Way"	Henry Mancini and Hal David
Sung by	Anne Murray
Editor	Folmar Blangsted, ACE
Special photographic consultant	Albert Whitlock
Wardrobe	Bill Thomas

Released through Columbia Pictures

Cast:

Mase	George C. Scott
Lena	Faye Dunaway
Cleon	John Mills
Hellman	Jack Palance
Marion	William Lucking
Wilcox	Harvey Jason
Jimmy	Rafael Campos

THE DOMINO PRINCIPLE (1976)

Credits:

Screenplay	Adam Kennedy

Based on the novel by Adam Kennedy

Cinematography	Fred Koenekamp and Ernest Laszlo
Editor	John Burnett
Music	Billy Goldenberg
Production design	William Greber
Wardrobe	Rita Riggs and Laurie Riley
Stunt coordinator	Bear Hudkins

Released through Avco Embassy

Cast:

Roy Tucker	Gene Hackman
Ellie Tucker	Candice Bergen
Tagge	Richard Widmark
Spiventa	Mickey Rooney
Ross Pine	Edward Albert
General Reser	Eli Wallach
Warden	Ken Swofford
Gaddis	Neva Patterson
Captain Ruiz	Jay Novello

Index